The Divorce Book

By Matthew McKay, Ph.D.

Peter D. Rogers, Ph.D.

Joan Blades, J.D.

Richard Gosse, M.A.

Edited By
Kirk and Susan Johnson

Copyright © 1984 by New Harbinger Publications
2200 Adeline St., Suite 305
Oakland, CA 94607
All rights reserved
Printed in the United States of America
ISBN 0-934986-06-1

First Printing January, 1984, 5,000 copies
Second Printinng February, 1985, 5,000 copies
Third Printing March, 1989, 3,000 copies
Fourth Printing November, 1991, 3,000 copies

To Louise Long LaBrash
Gretel and Heinz Rosenbaum
Charles and Virginia Blades
Ana Teresa and Andrew Gosse

Table of Contents

Introduction

The average marriage in the United States now lasts 6.8 years, and the divorce rate has soared to 50 percent. Twelve million American children have experienced a family breakup.

The rising divorce rate is suggestive of a basic change in the ways Americans see their lives. Fear of social disapproval has declined. While past generations of women were deterred by the stigma and financial hardships of divorce, women today live in a climate of increased personal freedom and economic independence. The guiding ethic of this age is choice, autonomy, and the freedom to change one's life. People no longer feel compelled to wither in a marriage because they once vowed "till death do us part." Fewer are willing to endure the heavy, unremitting weight of bitter years.

"I have a right to do something about this pain," one man said. "I made a commitment, but must I destroy my life to keep it?" Or as a mother of three put it, "There comes a time when you've had enough of the nonsense. Enough loneliness, enough holding in, enough hunger."

Yet for everyone who decides to leave, there is someone who is left. This is perhaps the greatest tragedy of divorce: that the decision is frequently not mutual, that there is often someone not ready, someone still hopeful, still in love, still holding on. Then the pain can be terrifying in its intensity. It slams one back and forth and sideways: anger, hurt, loss, yearning, guilt, fear—back and forth until the mourning abates and a new life begins to form.

Divorce is hard for everyone: the leaver, the left, the children. Yet despite the trauma, divorce is also an opportunity for growth, a time for beginning as well as ending. In the process of adapting to a new life, many people discover strengths and emotional resources they never knew they possessed. They find they can survive loneliness and loss. They use the new freedom to learn about themselves, seek new interests, change life styles, pursue other careers, and find more fulfilling relationships. They enter a period of "tasting and testing," discovering what feels good and what doesn't, and seeking a life that genuinely nourishes them.

This book is a survival guide. It is written for those who are going through a divorce and for professionals who want the tools to help them. The book begins with a section on emotional survival, including the stages of recovery and an exploration of the mourning process. Also covered are the changing relationships with friends and family and healthy ways of resolving conflict with an ex-spouse.

Section two is a legal primer. The last ten years have ushered in an era of increased legal flexibility for divorcing couples. "No fault" divorce has made possible the do-it-yourself settlement as well as the mediated agreement, and fewer couples are becoming adversaries in court. The legal section presents basic information about your options in a divorce (do-it-yourself, lawyer-assisted, or mediated) and how to determine which option is right for you. Also covered is a review of the major legal issues of divorce and suggestions for selecting your attorney.

Section three reviews research on the effects of divorce on children. It includes chapters on how to tell the children and how to meet the challenge of divorced parenthood. A recent trend toward shared parenting is fully explored, with a detailed "how-to" approach to this increasingly popular custody option.

Section four is about surviving as a single: dealing with the economics of divorce, problems of isolation, issues of sexuality and remarriage.

The Divorce Book is both descriptive and prescriptive. It is designed to provide knowledge as well as a guide for action. An effort has been made to accurately describe what to expect, to prepare you for the emotional and interpersonal changes. The book also focuses on prescription: how to cope with your feelings, your children, your lawyer, your finances, and your future.

1

The Emotional Stages
of Divorce

Despite unhappy marriages, partners often remain very much attached. Although love erodes and the dream of a shared and happy life comes apart, each one still needs the other for a sense of safety and belonging. In many ways attachment is more robust and powerful than love. It survives deceit, betrayal, rage, and bitter disappointment. Attachment persists because inadequate and even hurtful relationships are better than none at all. A little nurture, interspersed with emptiness and disappointment, is often enough to keep a marriage going well past the days of intimacy and passion.

The Threat of Separation

The weeks and months leading to a separation are often characterized by denial. Some deny to themselves that the relationship could ever end. Despite the bitter feuds, the deadness, and all the pointing fingers of blame, a feeling continues that the marriage is solid. It doesn't seem possible that such a strong attachment could be broken. A second kind of denial is the pseudo-indifference that partners use to mask their feelings of hurt and fear. The indifference says, "I don't need you, I have my own life." But denying attachment can make it all the more painful when a separation actually occurs. The feelings all flood in without warning when an awareness of the enormity of the loss finally dawns.

As a marriage becomes more painful, one partner or both begin to lose the faculty for denial. The process of evaluation starts. You begin to question, perhaps for the first time, how much pain you can tolerate, how realistic your hopes are that your partner will change, how well you would be able to cope on your own, and what effect separation would have on your family. The answers may be clear immediately, or it may take months to sort out how you feel. Sometimes this evaluation process takes place on the very simple level of noticing how you feel eating dinner with your spouse or being aware of the emotional atmosphere during such shared activities as watching TV, preparing food, or dealing with the kids.

The evaluation process moves in fits and starts. Episodes of deep dissatisfaction may be followed by weeks of denial. Declarations that you are ready to leave may end in a tearful apology. The path you take toward decision is an individual one, but the oscillation between denial, fear of change, and profound dissatisfaction is almost always part of the process.

The Decision to Divorce

When the decision to separate is finally made, each partner will be profoundly affected. While leavers experience different emotions from the left (guilt and self-blame versus anger and hurt), studies show that both groups undergo roughly equal amounts of emotional turmoil. The shortness or length of the marriage doesn't appear to make much difference either. Therapists who work with divorcing individuals have found that the mourning process can be just as profound for a three-year marriage as for a thirty-year one. It usually takes two or three years to make a strong attachment to a spouse, and once that attachment exists there will inevitably be separation shock.

No two people experience separation and divorce in the same way. Nevertheless, social scientists have discovered that there are clearly definable stages in the recovery process. The four major emotional stages of divorce are:

1. Separation shock
2. The rollercoaster
3. Identity work
4. The recentered self

These stages of recovery are remarkably similar to the grief work done by widows and widowers. It's a process of mourning, acknowledging loss, and letting go. Just as it takes time to mourn a death, it takes time to mourn the loss of a divorcing spouse.

The most important thing to recognize about the emotional stages of divorce is that everyone goes through them. Following divorce, there will be times when you feel very much alone. You may think something must be terribly wrong with you to feel such pain. The truth is that many others have felt what you feel—and survived. A surgeon in her forties described her fear of insanity during separation. "I thought I was crazy. I was in turmoil for months and I thought I was completely losing it. It never occurred to me that other people had the same sleeplessness, the same inability to concentrate, the same loss of control over their emotions."

Separation Shock

When separation finally occurs, the first reaction can be either relief, numbness, or panic. Relief is most often felt when the separation has been a long, drawn-out process. For many people, however, the shock of physical separation begins several weeks of numbness and denial. Numbness can be good for you. It's a way of putting on the emotional brakes or of muting feelings that are still too overwhelming.

A very common reaction to separation is the sudden panic of abandonment. It's the same feeling you had as a child when you got separated from your mother in the supermarket. Although separation panic comes in many forms, most people experience it as apprehensiveness or anxiety. They feel physically and psychologically shaky, and have great difficulty concentrating on any complex task. As a 35-year-old insurance agent described it, "I felt an alertness and constant vigilance. I had to be busy all the time but I couldn't concentrate on anything. I'd start to make a sandwich, only to forget it halfway as I began pacing through the house. I felt that something awful would happen, that I'd get sick or get too nervous to work."

For many, a side effect of the anxiety is a disturbance in sleep patterns. "At night I'd lie awake thinking of what I did wrong. Even when I emptied my mind, I still had a sense of being in danger. I couldn't relax, and then I'd start thinking about handling work and the kids on only a few hours sleep. It was the same thing every night." *(28-year-old secretary)*

A change in appetite is also a common symptom of separation shock. Whether appetite increases or decreases depends on the individual's constitutional tendencies. Some people find that food relieves anxiety and protects them from the worst of the panic. Others feel repelled by food and become nauseated when they force themselves to eat. "I'm falling away to a ton. On top of everything else I'm making myself ugly. But if I stuff myself, it seems to stop that butterfly feeling." *(Operating room nurse)* "Food? Don't mention it. Since Don left, I live on cigarettes and coffee." *(Pediatric nurse)*

Some people are disturbed to find that their anger slips out of control during separation shock. Tension and heightened vulnerability lead to sudden flashes of rage—particularly toward innocent people. You find yourself bawling out the meter maid, the waitress, your tax consultant. You act in ways that seem totally out of character. Yet your anger, as it erupts, is functioning as a safety valve. It's giving you a needed moment of relief.

Separation shock can last anywhere from a few days to several months. Mercifully, the anxiety isn't continuous. The numbness provides intermittent periods of relief. Sometimes a sense of optimism and excitement about your new life will suddenly wash you with a feeling of gaiety. And with equal suddenness your optimism passes as the familiar restlessness and tensions return. The anxiety, numbness, and sudden gaiety are all natural, all part of the process of recovery. Trying to prematurely force yourself past the anxiety will only prolong it.

Dangers of separation shock. The greatest danger of this stage is getting stuck in numbness and denial. It's tempting to retreat into numbness as a refuge because it feels a lot better than scalding bouts of panic. But staying numb is like forgetting to pay your bills. Everything's fine until the car gets repossessed and the landlord politely asks you to move. Numbness can be a healthy way of slowing down and making separation shock livable. But sooner or later you have to mourn, you have to feel what you feel.

The Rollercoaster

During the rollercoaster phase you shoot from one emotion to another at breakneck speed. Your ex-mate calls and you're reduced to tears. Then you suddenly remember all the times that he accused you of emotional coldness, and you feel consuming rage. Five minutes later you're full of shame that you could have felt such hatred. "I actually wanted him dead," one woman said, "and then I despised myself for feeling such a thing."

A 50-year-old stockbroker, who had left his wife after 23 years of marriage, described how episodes of paralyzing guilt were followed by nights of feeling utterly unlovable. "I was never home with her, and when I was home I was angry. I keep thinking, what could anyone see in an asshole like me?"

One of the characteristics of the rollercoaster is that you can fall apart in a matter of seconds. All it takes is a poignant memory, a lonely face, or a remark from one of your kids to punch your emotional buttons.

Stress puts you on the rollercoaster. Homes's Schedule of Recent Experience, a scale designed to measure stress, rates divorce at 73 points, second only to the death of a spouse. Stress is produced by change, and many things change for the divorcing person. Money is tighter, some friendships fade, and you now have to face life without the support of a husband or wife. Often the hardest changes to cope with are the changes in identity.

The divorcing person often faces a major change in self-perception. Instead of being a homeowner and a father, a man may find himself in a dinky apartment where his children come to visit twice a month. Instead of enjoying the status of a married homemaker, a woman may find herself labeled a "divorcee," a term that some unenlightened circles still take to mean a woman who is sexually promiscuous and somehow marred.

The divorcing person, who was once part of a network of friendly couples and who had a clear, socially accepted role in the world, may feel cut adrift. A 38-year-old bank teller explained, "All my friends are married and do things as couples. I just don't fit in anymore. When I took off my rings, I somehow felt defenseless. I kept thinking, 'Now I'm just another woman looking for a man.'" A recently divorced carpenter put it like this: "For ten years I think I'm building something. I get a house, I have two little girls in Catholic school, I'm on a committee to get a playground in our neighborhood. Now it's gone. I don't live there anymore. I live in an apartment that looks out on some clotheslines."

Review work. Review work is a major part of the grieving process. It involves looking back on your marriage to see who was to blame and what you could have done differently. It also means reliving the good times and mourning the loss of intimacy. A social worker described it as "One long replay. All I could think about was what I *should* have done. I'd go to bed thinking about how we met and I'd wake up full of shame remembering the years when I was in school and didn't pay much attention to the marriage."

The review process usually goes on for months. It's a major contributor to the emotional rollercoaster because each memory and each awareness pulls your emotional strings. But the review work also helps you to release pent-up feelings that otherwise would stay locked up in an emotional time bomb. Feelings of guilt and failure, anger, loss, and the sense of being unloved are all a part of the mourning process and are as natural as snow in winter.

People often expect to come to some final conclusion from their review work. The usual result, however, is just a letting go of the past. A few insights may emerge, but the review process functions mostly as a way of putting things to rest, rather than as a method for coming to some deep understanding.

Review work may stir up strong feelings of self-blame, which is not necessarily bad. Blaming yourself functions partly as a protection from the criticism of others. If you kick yourself first, others may be easier on you. Self-blame can also help you take a realistic look at your part in the breakup. It becomes unhealthy when the blame shatters your self-esteem and deepens your depression.

Loneliness. The rollercoaster phase usually includes periods of loneliness. Sometimes a loneliness spiral develops: you feel too depressed to keep up social contacts, the isolation makes you more depressed, and the depression leads to more isolation. This common problem usually passes as your social needs resurface.

Many recently separated people spend a great deal of time thinking about the ex-spouse and regretting the lost chances for happiness. Compared to their old world, the new one seems barren and empty. They see loneliness and distress on every face. The days are hollow, as if all meaning and pleasure had been drained away. Familiar activities bring a sense of just repeating lines and going through the motions. This condition is likely to fade as the review work draws to a close.

Some people have a passive sort of loneliness. They sit at home and listen to the refrigerator turn on and off. They try to read, but their thoughts keep wandering. They walk aimlessly through the house. Nothing seems interesting, nothing holds their attention. Other people are actively lonely. They take long drives which always seem to pass their ex-spouse's home. They go to the old restaurants, shop in the old neighborhood, remember the days of courtship at a sunny beach.

Loneliness can often be heightened by your first experience with the singles scene. A trip to a singles bar or an evening with a singles group can create the impression of a world full of strangers. The sense of loneliness is reinforced by awkward, unsatisfying conversations. As one lawyer put it, "They all looked as depressed as I felt. I felt like a loser. The world was a dismal place. Whenever I went up to a woman, I was thinking, 'She can see how much pain I'm in.' It was humiliating."

Old skeletons. A period of stress sometimes allows old skeletons to re-emerge. Early feelings of worthlessness may come to the surface. The helplessness you felt as a child, when powerful adults seemed to rule your fate, can once again show up with all the accompanying feelings of anger and frustration. You may feel overcontrolled and have urges to rebel against family and friends who try to help.

Some people feel a profound sense of insecurity, a fear that they cannot really take care of themselves. A panic seizes them that is reminiscent of the first days away from home, or even further back, their first morning in kindergarten.

It's natural for old skeletons to show up when you're under stress. They take their moment on the stage, but gradually disappear as you adjust to your new life. The important thing is not to believe everything you feel. If you suddenly begin feeling worthless or terribly insecure, the feeling is probably an old skeleton. Recognize it as such, a symptom of all the changes you are going through, and wait for it to pass. As you get stronger, old skeletons will slip back into your childhood, where they belong.

A fragile euphoria. Periods of relief and euphoria will occur, just as they did during separation shock. You'll suddenly feel on top of the world. The rest of your life awaits you; you're free to do anything and be anything. The euphoria lasts for hours or days, and you may take hope that the worst is over. But when the rollercoaster takes another plunge, when the loneliness or rage returns, those moments of happiness seem in retrospect as fragile as teacups.

Even though the euphoria is temporary, you should enjoy it while it lasts. It's a needed rest from the work of recovery. If you relate to the euphoria as something you must hold on to at all costs, you will be bitterly disappointed when it passes. You'll feel banished from the oasis back to the desert. Accept the euphoria as one of many strong feelings that you have on the rollercoaster.

Dangers of the rollercoaster. The rollercoaster means high stress, and people who ride it often become prone to accident and illness. It's easy to rear-end someone with your car, when you're concentrating on playing tapes of old fights. Illness is more likely because your body has to provide the extra energy for worry, sadness, and anger. Stress depletes your body's reserves and makes you more susceptible to infection.

One 30-year-old psychologist described how his emotional reaction to a separation led to a serious back injury. "I was angry and frightened. And at the same time I was exhausted from months of being angry and frightened. I'd throw myself around the tennis court like a madman, trying to get it all out. I'd run for balls I had no chance of getting. Finally I did it, I twisted my back and injured a disk. From then on most of my anxiety and anger were focused on the injury, not on my wife."

It's an additional hardship that so many important decisions have to be made when you are least equipped to make them. While you're on the rollercoaster you tend to have extremely poor judgment. Yet this is exactly the time when you are trying to deal with lawyers, establish co-parenting agreements, make a new budget, find a new place to live, and support your children through the crisis. Many critical decisions get made while you are heavily influenced by anger, guilt, and other strong emotions.

The best antidote for poor judgment is to consult with trusted family members and friends. Try to make decisions during periods when you are relatively calm and clearheaded. Don't do anything rashly. Only act after you've thought something through for several days and your point of view remains consistent. If confusion persists, seek professional help.

Emotional addictions. The greatest danger of the rollercoaster phase is the possibility of becoming addicted to the strong feelings that wash through you. Many people experience a deep emptiness during this time. The one thing they can count on to fill the emptiness is their anger or grief or blame. Emotion addicts spend most of their waking hours stuck on one theme. A middle-aged real estate salesman described it like this: "All day long I think about how I got the royal screw. She has the kids, the house, everything. I think about how she ruined our marriage with her cold-fish number."

There is a difference between emotional addiction and the mourning you must do as review work in order to put the past to rest. You can tell an addict because he or she sounds like a broken record: the same bitter denunciations, the same obsessive guilt, the same memories dredged up time and time again. Friends are just used as sounding boards and gradually become exhausted.

Identity Work

The rollercoaster stage lasts between a few months and a year. As it draws to an end, emotions become more stable. A sudden sweet memory may bring a few tears, but recovery comes quickly. You no longer have to cancel engagements because you feel too awful to go. Your anger is less intense, your guilt is more bearable.

One consequence of decreasing pain is that you can now pay more attention to your new life. There is a sense of future, of potential and possibility. The identity work is characterized by a kind of second adolescence. It's almost like being fourteen again. You have periods of great exuberance, you feel flirtatious and adventurous. You discover a need for friends, for a support network.

There are other symptoms of adolescence. You may become painfully shy and awkward in social situations. You are more preoccupied with yourself, how you look, how you sound. You suddenly want a better wardrobe, a nicer car.

This new narcissism is a healthy and necessary step for recovery from the rollercoaster. During identity work, as they begin to taste life again, many people experiment with new interests. One woman, who had always had a yen to do weight lifting, described her experience when she joined a gym: "I showed up on the first day and I thought, 'I'm nuts.' There were about fifteen men and only one other woman. I felt really weird until I got on a Nautilus machine and started working out. Then I started to enjoy it. I thought, 'This is what I always wanted to do, and there's the dividend of some pretty nice-looking guys around.'"

A 40-year-old bartender who'd always wanted to play tennis felt embarrassed: "I've seen people move faster in a wheelchair. I lumbered, but I loved it anyway. I found a partner who was on the same level as I was, and I had him out there every night at 5:30. The other thing was the little group that hung around the courts. I made some new friends."

As you stop seeing yourself as a person in crisis and take on the identity of a person who's growing, you feel a new sense of power. You begin to see yourself creating your life. You can pursue the things that interest and pleasure you, while you let go of some old burdens and obligations.

Identity work often includes sexual experimentation. This means a return to dating. Many of the same kind of struggles you had around sexuality as a teenager will reemerge now. You may feel threatened for a time by the opposite sex. You may be confused about how to handle sexual advances, or how to make them. Susan, a 42-year-old public relations consultant, reported feeling so anxious that she became nauseated. "I wasn't prepared for the passes. When we finished dinner he was all over me, and I got so scared I felt like I was going to throw up. I didn't know how to ask him to go slow."

During this period of experimentation, many people try to make up for lost time. "I felt like I'd been trapped for years, like I'd been an indentured servant or something. I had to use my freedom. I slept with anyone who'd go to bed with me. I felt almost compelled to sleep with different women." *(43-year-old store manager)*

Sexual experimentation can serve the same function now as dating did when you were in high school. The object is to find out which people you enjoy and which people you should stay away from. The more you date, the clearer you are about who's out there and what your needs are.

Dangers of identity work. The greatest problem with identity work is the danger of getting stuck in a second adolescence. Some people get so hooked on the wide world of possibilities that they never make a strong commitment to any one activity or person. They stay eternal juveniles who see commitment as a form of bondage. Jill, who worked in a ceramics factory, was afraid to date a man more than twice. "I didn't want him to get any ideas. I was deathly afraid somebody would get attached to me, particularly guys I worked with and had to see all the time. I'd make it clear that a date was just a date and no big thing to me."

The Recentered Self

As you finish your identity work, you may experience a sense of strength and accomplishment. You've endured an enormous test. Now is the time to integrate what's happened to you. It's natural to still have feelings about an ex-spouse, but most of the grief work is over by the recentering stage. The past has largely been put to rest. You may wallow in grief occasionally, but now because you choose to go with your feelings, rather than because you're helpless to do otherwise. Regret is there, but mostly without the rancor of blame. The present is what matters now.

Recentering means sculpting your life to fit the person you are. The divorce has provided an opportunity to experiment, to try new things, to see yourself reflected in new relationships. You may have found that you prefer people who are kind rather than strong, that you like folk dancing better than jogging, or that you prefer having the kids for two days every other week to seeing them every Saturday. New choices come from a new awareness of yourself and your needs.

The recentered self is different from the married person you once were. You've endured separation, ridden the rollercoaster, and survived.

2

The Psychological Traps of Divorce

Much of the emotional pain of divorce is inevitable. But some of it is totally unnecessary. Many divorcing people increase their pain by falling into cognitive and behavioral traps. *Cognitive traps* are habitual thoughts that raise your anxiety, depression, and anger like a thermometer in summer. *Behavioral traps* include a number of classic ways of coping with separation and shock that often do more harm than good.

COGNITIVE TRAPS

Ann, a recently separated mother of three, told the following story in her divorce support group. "I only seem to be in four states: angry, scared, depressed, and asleep. A lot of the time I'm cataloging all the things Jim pulled on me. I go over these scenes in my mind, and I can see him pouting and then making his remarks. I'm completely enraged when I think about it. Then the baby cries, and I go off on a tangent. I start wondering how I'm going to support these kids, whether he'll keep up the payments, and whether I can stand the loneliness much longer. That's when I get scared. Then when I go to bed the blues hit me. I keep thinking that my very Catholic family is disgusted with me. I keep thinking what an awful mess my life is and that the kids have been irreparably scarred."

Ann was in a lot of pain. But her pain was significantly increased by four cognitive traps: blaming, catastrophizing, mind reading, and filtering. Some of Ann's anger, anxiety, and sadness is appropriate and healthy. There is a mourning process to be gotten through. There's real hurt and real anger. But some of her painful feelings are created by cognitive traps that distort what is real.

Notice how Ann's anger is directly related to her ruminations about Jim's failings. The more she thinks about the ugly scenes, the angrier she gets. Blaming Jim may or may not help Ann feel better about her part in the divorce, but it will keep her seething. When Ann catastrophizes she gets frightened. Each scary scenario, each "What if . . ." or "Can I stand it?" scares Ann a little more. Mind reading and filtering lead to depression. Ann imagines what her family thinks of her and imagines that she will lose their support. She filters out anything that's promising or hopeful and focuses instead on her "awful mess."

Aaron Beck, the father of Cognitive Behavioral Therapy, has long argued that emotion is created entirely by thought. It is man's nature to constantly describe the world to himself, giving each event or experience a label. You interpret what you observe. You judge events as good or bad, painful or pleasurable, and predict whether they will bring danger or relative safety. These labels and judgments are fashioned from the unending dialogue you have with yourself and color all your experiences with private meanings. This dialogue, which Beck calls "automatic thoughts," is rarely noticed, but has the power to create your most intense emotions."

If your thoughts form accurate and realistic interpretations of experience, you can expect to have a healthy emotional life. But if you continually dwell on loss, danger, or injustice, you will be plagued by depression, anxiety, or rage. *What you think becomes what you feel.*

DIVORCE AWARENESS SCALE

To help you assess whether you are experiencing some of these cognitive traps of divorce, fill in the following checklist. Put an X in the box by any items which reflect how you think or feel.

- ☐ A1. A lot of people will be upset that I'm divorcing.
- ☐ A2. S/he was a loser.
- ☐ A3. I'll always be alone and lonely.
- ☐ A4. I've wasted my life.
- ☐ A5. I didn't love enough.
- ☐ A6. I should be turned on to this new freedom more than I am.
- ☐ A7. I was too good for him/her.
- ☐ A8. I'll no longer fit into my circle of friends.

- ☐ B1. His/her relatives will hate me. They'll blame me for hurting him/her.
- ☐ B2. S/he is a bitch, jerk, or ____hole.
- ☐ B3. I'll never find anyone else.
- ☐ B4. I can't stand this loneliness.
- ☐ B5. If I'd only worked harder at it, I could have keep the marriage together.

- ☐ B6. I should be going out with a lot of people.
- ☐ B7. If s/he would have done a little changing, improved and compromised, or been more accepting, things would have turned out differently.
- ☐ B8. I'm not going to survive financially.

- ☐ C1. Secretly, people will look down on me now.
- ☐ C2. S/he was basically selfish.
- ☐ C3. My relationships will always fail.
- ☐ C4. I'm overwhelmed by unbearable pain.
- ☐ C5. I wasn't a good husband/wife.
- ☐ C6. Even though I don't feel like it, I should be initiating contact. I should be asking people (of the opposite sex) out.
- ☐ C7. S/he made me miserable and ruined our marriage.
- ☐ C8. My ex-spouse will fall apart without me.

- ☐ D1. My friends won't want to see me.
- ☐ D2. S/he was stupid, insensitive, and/or inconsiderate.
- ☐ D3. Nobody will be attracted enough to me to want a relationship.
- ☐ D4. The hurt is too great.
- ☐ D5. If only I hadn't *(whatever you think you did)*, everything would have been all right.
- ☐ D6. I shouldn't go out at night and abandon my kids.
- ☐ D7. His/her lack of communication had a lot to do with our divorce.
- ☐ D8. I'm not going to be able to stand this; I'll fall apart.

- ☐ E1. People blame me for the breakup.
- ☐ E2. S/he was mean, hostile, and/or sadistic.
- ☐ E3. I'll probably always feel depressed.
- ☐ E4. I spent my youth on him/her.
- ☐ E5. I messed up what could have been a good marriage.
- ☐ E6. I should have stayed married for the kids.
- ☐ E7. His/her hostility ruined things.
- ☐ E8. My children may be permanently harmed by the divorce.

- ☐ F1. People think I'm a failure.
- ☐ F2. S/he is a liar.
- ☐ F3. I'll never feel really close to anyone again.
- ☐ F4. I'm trapped and powerless.
- ☐ F5. I keep regretting the way I was and the mistakes I made in the marriage.
- ☐ F6. I shouldn't have hurt him/her. I should have worked harder to keep us together.
- ☐ F7. If s/he had worked harder, we could have saved the marriage.
- ☐ F8. I'm not going to be able to get back into dating or fit into modern single life.

- ☐ G1. My married friends don't understand. They feel uncomfortable around me.

☐ G2.   S/he was withdrawn, uninvolved, and/or uncaring.
☐ G3.   I'll never succeed in a marriage.
☐ G4.   I feel like a failure.
☐ G5.   I keep thinking that I'm responsible for the pain s/he is suffering.
☐ G6.   I should be closer to people, more outgoing.
☐ G7.   S/he never had enough time or paid enough attention to me. S/he didn't really care.
☐ G8.   I'll have to live the rest of my life alone.

☐ H1.   His/her friends secretly don't like me.
☐ H2.   S/he was lousy at communicating.
☐ H3.   I'll never feel really secure again.
☐ H4.   The anxiety and fear is overwhelming. I feel like I'm falling apart.
☐ H5.   I wasn't flexible enough. I could have saved the marriage.
☐ H6.   I should be independent and comfortable being alone.
☐ H7.   I wasn't treated fairly. I was basically "screwed over."
☐ H8.   New relationships will fail and I'll be hurt again.

Instructions for scoring the Divorce Awareness Scale. This test has eight subscales. Follow the directions for scoring each one.

SUBSCALE 1. Count the marked boxes for all number one questions (A1, B1, C1, etc.).

    Total _____

SUBSCALE 2. Count the marked boxes for all number two questions (A2, B2, C2, etc.).

    Total _____

SUBSCALE 3. Count the marked boxes for all number three questions (A3, B3, C3, etc.).

    Total _____

SUBSCALE 4. Count the marked boxes for all number four questions (A4, B4, C4, etc.).

    Total _____

SUBSCALE 5. Count the marked boxes for all number five questions (A5, B5, C5, etc.).

    Total _____

SUBSCALE 6. Count the marked boxes for all number six questions (A6, B6, C6, etc.).

    Total _____

SUBSCALE 7. Count the marked boxes for all number two and number seven questions (A2, A7, B2, B7, C2, C7, etc.).

Total _____

SUBSCALE 8. Count the marked boxes for all number three and number eight questions (A3, A8, B3, B8, C3, C8, etc.).

Total _____

Scores for subscales 1 through 6 range between zero and eight. Scores for subscales 7 and 8 range between zero and sixteen. Elevated scores on a subscale suggest a tendency toward the cognitive trap tested by the subscale.

Subscale 1: Mind Reading

Higher scores on this scale indicate a tendency to make assumptions about the feelings, attitudes, and motivations of others—all without any direct confirmation. The divorcing person will often use mind reading to guess the reactions of relatives and friends. This becomes a special problem when you're afraid to hear the truth, one way or the other. You assume the worst, anticipating disapproval and rejection. You expect to be hurt, so you pull away or become defensive. This is the beginning of a self-fulfilling prophecy. Your expectations may soon become reality.

In a survey of divorced people (Gosse and McKay, 1981*), one-fourth agreed with the statement, "Secretly people will look down on me now." This is a dangerous thought that can lead to significant anxiety and depression. You feel a loss of self-worth and expect to be shunned.

The best way to deal with mind reading is to commit yourself to making no inferences about people whatsoever. Either accept what they tell you or assume nothing at all until there is some conclusive evidence. Treat all your assumptions about people as hypotheses to be tested by asking them. Sit down with family and friends and find out, individually, how they are reacting to your divorce.

Subscale 2: Global Labeling

Higher scores on this scale indicate your tendency to generalize one or two negative qualities into a global judgment. The label ignores all contrary evidence in favor of a stereotyped, one-dimensional viewpoint. The

*Richard Gosse and Mathew McKay. "Asserting and Treating Cognitive Distortions in the Divorcing Client." Paper presented at the American Psychological Association National Convention, 1981.

trouble with labels is that they turn people into things. Instead of a complex, many-sided person, you see the personification of a single negative quality. Global labels fuel your rage. It's much easier to reject someone when he or she is "selfish" or "a loser" than it is when you see the whole person.

This divorce subscale focuses on labels that attack others. You can also do tremendous damage to your own self-esteem by applying global labels to yourself. In the Gosse-McKay study, one-third of the respondents agreed with the statement, "I'm a loser because I got a divorce." Labeling yourself as a loser, a failure, or a jerk is the kind of self-rejection that can only deepen your depression.

The result of labeling is very simple: negative labels attached to others make you angry and disgusted. The same labels attached to yourself cause guilt and a sense of worthlessness.

The antidote for global labeling is limiting your descriptions of others (and yourself) to specific behaviors. Your ex-wife is not a bitch. She just tends to become angry when negotiating child support. You are not a loser. You are a person who has gone through a divorce and feels the effects of emotional trauma. If you ban global labeling from your vocabulary, you'll find yourself less angry at others and less disgusted with yourself.

Subscale 3: Overgeneralizing

Higher scores indicate a tendency to make broad, generalized conclusions based on a single case or very little evidence. When you overgeneralize, you make absolute statements that imply immutable laws limiting your chances for happiness. The key words are: *all, every, never, always, everybody, none, nobody, totally, continually.*

Overgeneralizations tend to defeat and frighten you. When you say to yourself, "I'll *always* feel depressed," you're depressing yourself even more. When you say, "I'll *never* feel secure again," you're increasing your fear. Notice how the words *always* and *never* add so much more negativity to the statement. Saying "I feel insecure" is one thing, but saying "I'll *never* feel secure" is condemning yourself to a lifetime of pain.

One-quarter of the divorced people in the Gosse-McKay study agreed with the statements, "I'll *always* be alone" and "I'll *never* find anyone else." These statements tend to paralyze and defeat their victims. And they can become self-fulfilling prophecies. Since you don't expect to meet anyone, you may not bother to look.

Some generalizations undermine your relationships. Statements such as "No man can be trusted," "All women are possessive," "Men only want sex," or "Women are out for the bucks," close you off to the opposite sex.

You can fight the tendency to overgeneralize by banishing the key words from your vocabulary. You can also fight this tendency by examining how much evidence you really have for your conclusions. If the conclusion is based on one or two cases, or merely on the feeling that it must be true, then throw it out until you have more convincing proof. Avoid absolutes. Admit the exceptions and the shades of grey; use words such as "sometimes," "may," or "often."

Subscale 4: Filtering

Higher scores indicate a tendency to focus on the worst possible aspects of a situation and ignore everything else. Because filtering creates a kind of negative tunnel vision, the divorcing person will often magnify and "awfulize" his or her fears and losses. When you filter, you ignore the sunshine and look at the clouds. You magnify your fears and losses until they fill your awareness to the exclusion of everything else. Key words for filterers are "terrible," "awful," and "horrible." Key phrases are "can't stand it," "falling apart," and "completely overwhelmed." When you magnify in this way, your anxiety or depression will tend to skyrocket.

One-quarter of the respondents in the Gosse-McKay survey agreed with the statement, "I've wasted my life." This is a perfect example of filtering. From a lifetime of ups and downs only the downs are remembered. The pain of divorce erases every happy memory.

To stop filtering, you have to stop thoughts such as "I can't stand it" and "This is terrible, horrible." The truth is you *can* stand it. History shows that human beings can endure almost any psychological blow. You can survive and cope with almost anything. Instead of saying, "I can't stand it," use phrases such as "There's no need to magnify" and "I can cope." Filterers also need to shift their focus. You can do this in two ways. First, you can put your attention on coping strategies that deal with the problem, rather than obsessing about the problem itself. Second, you can change your mental theme. If your theme is danger, you need to refocus on the things in your life that represent comfort and safety. If your theme is loss, concentrate on what you do have that you value. If your theme is injustice ("I've been screwed"), shift your attention to the ways you have been treated fairly.

Subscale 5: Self-Blame

Higher scores indicate a tendency to exaggerate responsibility for a spouse's pain and the breakup of the marriage. You perceive whatever happened as largely your fault. There is an inclination toward self-attack for mistakes, insensitivity, failing to work harder, love more, and so on. People who experience this cognitive trap feel the weight of the world on their shoulders. They have to right all wrongs, fill every need, and salve each hurt. If they don't, they feel guilty.

In the Gosse-McKay study, one-third of divorced people agreed with the statement, "I didn't love enough." One-fifth believed "If only I hadn't _____, everything would have been all right." These statements are ideal for generating guilt. They leave you with all the responsibility for the breakup and ignore the interactive nature of every relationship.

Blaming yourself for your ex-spouse's problems is a form of self-aggrandizement. Basically you are saying, "I'm more responsible for your life than you are...I have more control of your happiness than you have...You're helpless without me." The truth is that your ex-spouse bears equal responsibility for the outcome of your marriage. Each of you must accept the consequences of your own choices. By taking all the blame, you're turning your spouse into a child who depends on you for everything. You are denying his or her adulthood.

Subscale 6: Shoulds

Higher scores indicate a tendency to have strict rules governing what are acceptable thoughts, feelings, and actions. These rules often contradict what is healthy, natural, and needed at a particular stage in the divorcing process. Cue words indicating the presence of this cognitive trap are *should, ought,* or *must.*

The problem with "should" is that you often feel compelled to do or not do things despite your genuine needs to the contrary. One-third of the people surveyed reported, "Even though I don't feel like it, I *should* be asking people out." Another third agreed with the statement, "I *should* be turned on to this new freedom more than I am." These "shoulds" may force you into doing something that could be inappropriate at your point in the divorcing process. For example, you may not be ready to go out yet. Forcing yourself to cash in on the "new freedom" may cut short the very essential mourning process.

The antidote for "shoulds" is to avoid using the words *should, ought,* or *must.* Use flexible rules and expectations that always admit exceptions and special circumstances. For example, telling yourself "I should be independent and comfortable being alone" is like putting yourself inside a psychological straitjacket. You may end up denying important needs for security because you're stuck with an inflexible rule. It's better to say "I would like to learn how to become more independent" or "I hope to feel more comfortable alone." These statements admit that you're in a process and don't have to achieve your goals instantly. You may be more comfortable being alone in five months or five years. But right now it's OK to depend on others. Using the word *should* forces you to make premature and unhealthy demands on yourself.

Subscale 7: Blaming Others

Higher scores indicate a tendency to hold others responsible for any pain, loss, or failure. Your spouse is blamed for your loneliness, hurt, and fear. Blaming others has its roots in the belief that you are helpless to provide for your own emotional needs. You are a victim of the selfishness and insensitivity of others.

Blaming others keeps you from having to face your part in the breakup. As long as you focus on the failings of your ex-spouse, you can be protected from the awareness of your own failings. As long as you are angry, you don't have to be depressed. In the Divorce Awareness Scale, blaming also includes the use of global labels. Reducing your ex-spouse to a "bitch" or a "jerk" absolves you of any fault. He or she was bad and you are good.

In the Gosse-McKay survey, one-third of the respondents agreed with the statements, "S/he made me miserable and ruined our marriage" and "I was too good for him/her." These statements fuel your anger and will make it harder to cooperate if you continue to share parenting.

The antidote for blaming is to focus on your own choices. You chose to marry your ex-spouse, and you endured, for a time, an unhappy marriage. You chose characteristic ways of dealing with your mate and solving problems. These choices are your responsibility. And the pain you lived with must also be, in some measure, your responsibility.

Subscale 8: Catastrophizing

Higher scores indicate a tendency to exaggerate potential danger, You habitually focus on future scenarios of disaster. The divorcing person may use this cognitive trap to plan a future full of bleak and frightening possibilities. Catastrophic thoughts often start with the words "what if": "What if I'm rejected by my friends? What if my children are damaged? What if I have to live the rest of my life alone? These are frightening thoughts. The more airtime you give them, the more your anxiety grows.

In the Divorce Awareness Scale, catastrophizing includes overgeneralizing. "I'll *never* succeed in a marriage" is an unrealistic catastrophic fantasy. By saying *never,* you are falsely assuming that each new relationship must follow the same pattern.

In the survey of divorced people, one-quarter of the respondents reported believing "I'm not going to be able to stand this." Such catastrophic thoughts tend to increase an already high level of anxiety. Financial concerns may also lead to catastrophizing. One-quarter of respondents agreed with the statement, "I'm not going to survive financially." Divorce often begets serious financial problems, but almost everyone *survives*. Questioning your survival heightens your anxiety and inhibits problem solving.

Notice that catastrophic statements always focus on the future. Things are going to get worse, disaster is right around the bend. By envisioning a future full of danger and pain, you suffer anxiety in the present.

To end catastrophizing you must give up the "what ifs." Instead, think in terms of *percent probability*. Are the chances 1 in 100,000 (.001 percent) or 1 in 1,000 (.1 percent) or 1 in 100 (1 percent)? During the day, write down your worries when they are most intense and rate the percent probability that the catastrophe will come true. At night, go over the day's list of worries and rate the percent probability now that you are comfortably ensconced in bed. Seeing a disaster that was inevitable at three o'clock become unlikely at eleven helps distance you from the power of your catastrophic thoughts.

The opposite of catastrophizing can also be a problem. Some people nurture unreal expectations of life after divorce. They imagine being rescued by a new relationship. They fantasize about meeting the white knight or goddess. They anticipate exciting sex and stimulating people. The result of unrealistic expectations is often bitter disappointment. The knight never arrives, the sex is unfulfilling, and the new relationship may bear a strange resemblance to the old.

Thought Stopping

If you don't believe that cognitive traps cause emotional pain, you can prove it to yourself. Meditate for a few moments on all the things your spouse did which were "mean" or "unfair." Notice the feelings of anger that begin to rise. Now try some mind reading. Try to imagine the reaction of your in-laws, how they really think about you. Notice that these thoughts may stir guilt or depression. Now try some "what ifs." Look into the future and conjure up all the things that could go wrong. Notice how your anxiety increases. If focusing on your cognitive traps increases pain, turning them off should provide some relief. Try this exercise. Indulge in some more "what ifs." Think about the children or future loneliness. When you feel a little anxious, switch your thoughts to a favorite vacation spot and take three deep breaths. Notice how turning off your painful thoughts switches off your anxious feelings.

Getting proficient at turning off thoughts takes some time and practice—and some commitment. To begin, you will need to start monitoring your thoughts so that you are aware when you're falling into the old cognitive traps. Notice when you're scaring yourself with "what ifs." Listen to your inner dialogue of "shoulds" or self-blame or generalizations. Becoming sensitive to the things you say to yourself makes changing them possible.

One way you can remember to listen in on your inner dialogue is to use your emotions as cues. If you're feeling anxious, the emotion can function as a red flag to signal that you've been catastrophizing. If you're depressed, use that as a signal to see if you've been mind reading, filtering, or blaming yourself. If you're angry, notice if you've been blaming others or using global labels. Instead of being the helpless victim of your feelings, you can now use them as reminders of the powerful inner voice that influences your emotional life.

Once you've learned to monitor your thoughts, you can use one of two strategies to stop them. The first is a very simple method called *stop and breathe*. When you first notice painful thoughts, shout "Stop!" subvocally (inside your head) and take a very deep breath into your abdomen. Empty your mind for a minute and take two or three more deep breaths. Each time painful thoughts reoccur, use the stop and breathe technique: Subvocally shout "Stop!", empty your mind, and focus only on your breathing. If you find that you don't respond to the command "Stop!" place a rubber band around your wrist and snap it while you subvocally shout. Many people find that the minor pain caused by the rubber band is quite helpful in interrupting their thoughts.

Once you've stopped the painful thoughts, don't be discouraged when they come back. They always do. After all, those thoughts were a long-standing habit, and habits don't die easily. Nature abhors a vacuum, and the old, painful thoughts will come back more easily if you have no new thoughts to replace them. After you stop and breathe, make sure that you change your mental focus. Think about an upcoming vacation, fantasize about a new love affair, do some planning for your children. Focus on anything but the old "what ifs," blaming, or mind reading.

A second strategy to stop painful thoughts is the *three column technique*. Make three vertical columns on a piece of paper. Whenever you're hit by a painful emotion, do the following: Write down the major thoughts which preceded and accompanied the emotion in column A. If any of these thoughts reflect a cognitive distortion, name the distortion in column B. Now comes the most important part: in column C, rewrite the thought so that it becomes a more realistic statement. Rebecca used the three column technique during a period when she felt particularly anxious. She used the rewrites in column C to help replace her old distortions. When she caught herself catastrophizing, she quickly switched to her more realistic column C statements. Her three columns are listed below.

A	B	C
1. I'm not going to be able to stand the loneliness.	Catastrophizing	I can adjust to anything. I'll feel awful for awhile, but I'll slowly recover. Everyone who divorces goes through this.
2. I'm going to fall apart.	Catastrophizing	At times I will feel bad, but I know I'll continue functioning.

A	B	C
3. No one will help me now that Jim's gone.	Overgeneralization	Jim probably won't help much, but I have a father, a brother, and two good women friends. Also, I'll meet new people.
4. I'm not going to be able to function as a parent.	Catastrophizing	For a time I'll probably be somewhat depressed and irritable. I won't be quite as good a parent, but I won't be dysfunctional either.

BEHAVIORAL TRAPS

Each person responds in his or her own way to the stress of losing a marital partner. You try to cope with the pain as best you can, using adaptive strategies that may have worked for you in the past. If you survived previous emotional traumas by withdrawing, you may again use withdrawal to help you through the anger and loss. If you escaped pain in the past with compulsive eating, working, or TV watching, you are likely to try this strategy again. Your attempts at coping are normal and necessary. They only become a problem when carried to an extreme. For example, fighting your loneliness with sexual experimentation is only a problem if it turns into compulsive Don Juanism or a series of hurtful, high-risk relationships.

The following behavioral traps are useful coping strategies carried to extremes. Like a record that gets stuck and plays the same few notes over and over, you keep trying the same coping behaviors and never move on with your life.

Withdrawal

Following separation, many people have a very natural tendency to pull back from everybody. You may feel too exhausted to talk or answer questions. The nervous sympathy of friends may be more than you can bear. You'd like to wrap yourself in a cocoon and just let the world go by for awhile.

Many people, afraid of awkwardness or disapproval, withdraw from their own social network. They suddenly feel uncomfortable with married friends and prefer the safety and solitude of home. All this is normal. When you have suffered a trauma, when you're on the rollercoaster of anger, hurt, loss, and yearning, it can be exhausting to socialize. And because you don't feel up to it, pulling yourself together to be with people may provoke great anxiety. Said one woman, "People would call and I'd have to calm my voice and sound reasonable. It was like putting on an act, saying what was expected and keeping my voice from falling apart. Finally I unplugged the phone." *(53-year-old beautician)*

Withdrawal has become a trap when you find yourself isolated from friends and family or having difficulty functioning at home or work. The isolation may take place gradually. After you put in six months of not calling friends and begging off from lunch and dinner dates, people begin to leave you alone. A mother of three explained: "One day I realized that people weren't calling any more. I didn't really want to see anyone, but still it was a shock. I felt like I'd been written off just because I was too depressed for small talk. And that depressed me even more."

Sometimes the withdrawal is even more profound. "The only place I feel good is in bed. Sometimes I read and sometimes I don't. Anything else seems like too much. Shopping is too much. Talking to my ex-wife is too much. Talking to my clients is too much. I haven't been to work in a week, and frankly I'd like to just sleep through this." *(38-year-old lawyer)*

If you get to the point of feeling dysfunctional, it's probably time to seek professional help. If you withdraw to the point of isolation, and the isolation stretches over months, this may again indicate a need for assistance. What's important to remember is that withdrawal is a normal reaction to stress for many people. When it begins to get in the way of everyday functioning or is hampering your recovery and the building of a new life, then you need to take remedial steps. A prolonged period of withdrawal can leave you emotionally bankrupt. Without the emotional support of others, you may drain your own resources to a dangerously low level. It's like running on battery power: you can do it for awhile, but sooner or later everything just stops.

Dependency

While some people withdraw following a divorce, others rely more heavily on parents and friends. Increased dependency is a normal reaction to stress. Some newly divorced people move back in with parents or past roommates. Others depend on an ex-spouse or ex-lover to provide a sense of continuity and security.

Dependency only becomes a trap when it gets in the way of building new relationships and a new life. Even though it's a very comfortable routine, spending every evening watching TV with your folks can lead to a certain emotional numbness. Your parents are nice to you and may make few demands, but you only get some of your needs met. By staying home you may have to suppress your needs for touching, sex, and intimacy.

Depending on sympathetic friends to listen as you constantly rehash your marriage can lead to becoming an emotional junky. Over and over you express your anger, hurt, and sadness. It's a trap because you get consumed with negative feelings, your friends lose interest after awhile, and nothing changes in your life. "I spent every night with my roommate,

Susan. We talked about her marriage and my marriage. They were the bitterest conversations I've every heard. We had nothing good to say about any man. It was comforting. I felt safe there. But I never went out." *(27-year-old receptionist)*

Clinging to an Ex-Spouse

"I talk more now to my ex-wife than when we were married. But it's crazy. One minute we'll be reminiscing, and the next we'll be fighting over visitation rights. I have all these buttons she can push to get me angry in a second. After the fight I'm surprised to feel turned on. We've even gone to bed a few times. If I have a bad day at work, I call Jill. If I'm lonely, I call Jill. Sometimes I think we should be moving on, but there's no one else I'm close to." *(50-year-old executive)*

Some couples whose divorce was amicable manage to preserve an intimate friendship. Others stay attached, but unpleasantly so. The attachment can be expressed in many ways: a man will keep his key to the house and continue to do his laundry there. A woman, guilty about initiating the divorce, will continue to sleep with her ex-husband to ease the blow. Ex-partners can stay hooked through endless battles over custody and spousal support. Conversations can be a deadly mixture of solicitude and rejection, anger, and yearning.

Your bond to an ex-spouse becomes a trap when it prevents you from developing a satisfactory relationship with anyone else. If your emotional energy is wrapped up with your ex-wife or husband, there will be precious little left over for new friends and lovers. You need a balance. The old relationship provides continuity with the past; new relationships are your commitment to the future.

Living for Others

Some people react to divorce with a plunge into altruism. A man may spend his weekends fixing up his ex-wife's house. A woman may clean her ex-husband's apartment or do his laundry. Some parents turn all their energy and attention into meeting the needs of their children. The children always come first, every night and every weekend. There's never a thought for yourself; your own recreational and emotional needs seem insignificant by comparison. A 36-year-old mother of two described her struggle to break out of this pattern. "I felt worthless. I felt like a failure as a wife. I sure as hell didn't want to fail as a mother. My own needs didn't seem to count—it was like I didn't deserve anything. Within a month of separating, I signed up as a Bluebird leader and got very involved in my son's nursery school. Every weekend was carefully structured to provide enrichment and healthy recreation for the kids. I did everything. In the beginning I was too busy to be lonely. But now this ache has set in. I realize I need adults. I feel guilty, but I'm taking one night off from the kids each week."

Living for others often accompanies the feeling of emptiness which follows a divorce. There hardly seems any point in doing things for yourself. You wouldn't enjoy them anyway. You may feel bruised and hurt, unsure of your worth, uncertain of your social skills. It's natural to retreat for a time and think of others. "I couldn't do much for myself, so at least I wanted to make my wife comfortable," one man reported. "I rebuilt the engine on her car and was halfway through painting her house when it hit me that I was just filling up the emptiness." *(47-year-old carpenter)*

Living for others becomes a trap when you do it as a way of life. Acts of generosity and renewed efforts to nurture your children can help you through the trauma of separation. But you'll become malnourished if sooner or later you don't begin attending to your own needs. That means nights off to go bowling, dinner with friends, or joining a singles club. You need to nourish yourself in order to keep on caring for others.

Escape From Yourself

One way to deal with emotional pain is to bury it. Any compulsive activity will help. Overeating and drinking, compulsive reading or TV watching, or immersion in work may insulate you from the worst of the pain. This is very adaptive for some people and keeps them from being overwhelmed to the point of becoming dysfunctional. It becomes a trap when the eating, drinking, TV watching, or workaholism damages your health or undermines your recovery. "The night he left I had two glasses of white wine and it calmed the worst of the anxiety. Wine worked for awhile, and then my doctor gave me Valium. When I was scared I had a way of switching it off. I felt like I was in control. I wasn't aware that I was getting dependent." *(28-year-old secretary)*

One man, who had never watched much television, suddenly found himself glued to the tube. "I was at it six hours a night. I began making excuses about taking the children because it would cut into my television time. I felt safe when the TV was on. Just the sound of it was relaxing. I resented phone calls during my favorite programs. It's the worst addiction I've ever experienced."

It's best to regard any compulsive escape as a temporary crutch to get you through a bad night or a particularly low moment. The more often you turn to a compulsive escape, the more likely it is to trap you into unhealthy habits and cut you off from others.

Paradoxically, among the greatest forms of escape are self-improvement campaigns. The self-improvement addict signs up for six classes, two workshops, and joins a Jungian dream-analysis group. He or she is out every night of the week and frantically rushes from one activity to the next. There's no time to think or feel, only to do. "My ex-husband went completely nuts. He joined a gym and took a fitness class on Mondays.

On Tuesday he had a men's group, Wednesday he was in a cooking class, on Thursday it was a public speaking course, on Friday it was folk dancing, on Sunday he was in a tennis club. Saturday was a bummer because he couldn't find anything, so out of desperation he'd visit the kids." *(37-year-old saleswoman)*

Taking classes and joining a gym are healthy steps toward recovery. It's when the classes and groups are used as time-killers, when they're stuffed randomly into holes in your schedule like fingers in a dike, or when they leave no time for your children, that you should consider cutting back. You need time to try new things and to experiment, but you also need time to feel and listen to your inner self.

Don Juanism

Following a separation, it's natural to want to prove your attractiveness to the opposite sex. Both men and women have a tendency to go through a period of promiscuity to reestablish their confidence in the sexual arena. Men, in particular, are in danger of Don Juanism when their fear of commitment or remarriage chases them from one conquest to another. Looked back on, the old marriage seems like a prison. There is almost a reflexive shrinking from any relationship, no matter how promising, that includes expectations or commitment. The answer, it seems, is to keep moving—from woman to woman in a collage of brief, intense encounters.

Over and over the Don Juan reassures himself that he's still attractive. He meets his needs for touching and sexuality, he gives and takes affection, but without ever deepening the emotional bond. Said one ad executive, "I slept with half the regulars at the Pierce Street Annex *(a singles bar)*. It was exciting for awhile—the newness, the chase. I rarely slept with them again. We'd nod nervously at each other in the bar. After six months I was so empty that my doctor prescribed pills for depression."

Don Juanism is not the exclusive province of men. Changing sexual mores have made it possible for women to escape the divorce trauma through brief liaisons. Women, too, experience a growing emptiness after months of casual relationships.

Most of the recently divorced are initially cautious about starting a relationship. Don Juanism can be a brief but normal reaction to this fear. It becomes a trap when you develop symptoms in reaction to brief and broken intimacies.

One way out of Don Juanism is to strengthen your ability to say no. Fear of commitment is really the fear that you'll need to set limits or say no and won't be able to. So the Don Juan just disappears or never calls again. That's his way of not having to face the guilt or anxiety inherent in disappointing people. If you can learn to say no, it paradoxically gives you the security to say yes. Commitment is no longer a trap or nightmare. You can make limits, you can even leave when you need to.

Searching for the Other Half

Some divorced people regard themselves as incomplete without a partner. You may have come to think of yourself as a couple and now feel lost without your other half.

Feelings of incompleteness, of somehow being inadequate alone, may fuel a frantic search for another mate. Those who fall into this trap may run from one singles group to another. There is a quality of desperation in each social encounter.

The *belief* that being alone is a miserable, empty experience makes you *feel* miserable and empty. The belief that you are half a person without a spouse makes you yearn for the part that is missing. One man described his search in this way: "I keep thinking she's out there somewhere, the woman for me. I hate being alone. I feel like a pariah to my married friends. A wife would make me whole again."

Sometimes this trap leads to ill-fated, consuming loves. People pour their hearts and souls into affairs with inappropriate partners. They latch on to the first available person in order to erase feelings of loss. And it works. For awhile. When the affair breaks up, however, there is even greater pain and loss.

A far better course is to face the reality of the present—you are alone. Someday you may meet a new mate, but right now you have a life to live. There's no doubt that you might feel happier, safer, more alive with a new person in your life. But that takes time; pushing it may drive you to make a doomed and hurtful choice. Despite the emptiness, you can sculpt your life into something good and worth living. Keep trying new things, keep reaching out to new people. Take a workshop, join a neighborhood action committee, learn to cook, learn how to change your spark plugs, take up dancing, bike racing, *anything* that keeps you alive and moving and in touch with yourself.

3

The Leaver and the Left

Most marital separations do not result from mutual decisions. It's extremely rare for partners to simultaneously arrive at the point where they wish to end the relationship. As a result, there is usually a "leaver" and a "left." These roles produce certain characteristic emotional responses which this chapter will explore.

Although the actual separation is usually easier for the leaver, he or she has often endured a great deal of emotional turmoil in preparation for the break. The partner who is left must then "catch up" as he or she begins to face the anger and loss triggered by separation.

Very often, both parties have made an unconscious decision to end the marriage, but have colluded to assign the leaver role to one of them. The partner whose patience runs out first and who finally decides to leave gets blamed for the breakup. The partner who is left may express anger, but may also be secretly relieved to avoid the responsibility and guilt of ending the marriage. Regardless of who leaves and who is left, both partners have contributed to the marital chemistry. The following exercise may help increase your awareness of how each of you participated in drawing apart.

Draw a line down the center of a sheet of paper. Put your name on the left side of the page, and your ex's on the right. Now list all the desires, habits, traits, and characteristics that each of you contributed to the poor chemistry of the relationship. Although the actual number of items on either side may not be equal, it will soon become obvious that both of you were fully involved in the process. You may also find it useful to use the same exercise to make an honest assessment of the efforts each of you made to try to save the marriage.

THE LEAVER

There are those situations where one person is determined to leave, but is psychologically unable to do so. Often, that person will try to arrange for the other person to assume the leaver role.

Missy and Chuck were married for more than three years before Chuck fully realized that he wanted out. He had always been taught, however, that divorce was wrong. He knew that his parents and family would blame him if he called it quits. He was unhappy and dissatisfied, but couldn't make the break. Slowly, he began to withdraw from Missy. Sexual intimacy became less frequent. When Missy asked what was wrong, he replied, "Nothing, everything's fine. I'm just tired from work." He began to put her down in dozens of small ways, always denying that anything was going on.

Confused, sad, and angry, Missy took less than a year to throw in the towel. She left "the bastard," and took the rap for ending the marriage.

People rarely leave a marriage on the spur of the moment. The decision to separate is usually the end product of a long, agonizing process, characterized by much vacillation back and forth.

Althea, a 42-year-old woman, had realized for several years that her marriage was doomed, despite her best salvage efforts. She needed time to prepare herself and really think things through, so she developed an interest in photography which required her to spend a lot of time alone in the darkroom. After 18 months of thinking and planning in that darkroom, she was ready to confront her husband.

Sometimes a fortuitous event will bring a sudden clarity to a long-standing problem. Harry had been increasingly dissatisfied with his marriage for nearly ten years when circumstance dictated a five-month separation: his wife had to handle family business affairs on the East Coast while he continued to work as a consultant in Arizona. During this time, he found that his life was much more pleasant without her constant nagging and carping. He found himself dreading her return, and on the day her flight touched down he screwed up his courage and suggested a divorce.

Miriam had always wanted a baby. "What's a family without children?" she later asked her lawyer. But Sam had always found excuses for putting off starting a family. First it was graduate school, then setting up a business—something else always came first. One night while they were watching a TV program, Miriam noticed how uncomfortable Sam was during a particularly realistic childbirth scene. Right then, she realized that he was never going to want children. Nine months later she asked for a divorce, and Sam reluctantly agreed.

Being the one to initiate a marital separation requires courage and a willingness to act on your decision. It also means preparing yourself to face the inevitable feelings of guilt.

Guilt

Guilt has been defined in many different ways by different psychological theorists, but whether the feelings stem from a Judeo-Christian upbringing, tension between your ego and super-ego, or your next-door neighbor's opinion, the results are the same. It basically involves a sinking feeling in the gut and the sure knowledge that you've done something WRONG. Guilt contaminates the natural grief process which the leaver as well as the left must go through, and makes a clean separation more difficult to achieve.

Typical self-statements. Guilt is usually manifested through a set of characteristic statements you make to yourself. Here are some typical examples.

I should have tried harder...
("The separation was all my fault. I knew he wanted homecooked meals, but I kept pushing him to eat out.")

A married man must be faithful...
("I feel very wrong about having an affair. I could have stopped myself. I should have told her instead of having her catch me in my lies.")

I know I ought to...
("I ought to stick it out for his sake (he'll fall apart) and the children's (I've no right to deny them a father). I'm selfish for leaving.")

Rules. Guilt is often the result of inflexible rules. These are personal rules which tell you what is right and wrong. Invariably, these rules incorporate words like *should, ought,* or *must.*

One man felt guilty about leaving the relationship while his wife still very much loved and needed him. When he began to examine his thoughts and feelings, he found that he had some long-held rules which said he *should* always reciprocate feelings and under no circumstance should he hurt anyone.

Although desperately unhappy, a 35-year-old beautician was unable to leave her husband because she knew she *ought* to stay with her child. The father was quite willing and capable of assuming custody of the teen-aged boy. She hung on until the boy managed to escape by lying about his age when he was seventeen and joining the army. Only then did she allow herself to leave.

Healthy versus unhealthy guilt. Healthy guilt is appropriate. It is a signal that you have violated an important value. As a signal, it's useful because it's painful enough to help you stop or atone for destructive behavior.

Healthy guilt derives from healthy values. Healthy values are flexible (they make room for exceptions and let you have your quota of mistakes) and life enhancing (they have at their root the intention that you and others be happy). Healthy values encourage you to protect and provide for your own needs as well as the needs of others. And most important, healthy values are your own—not unexamined dictums handed down from parents and other authority figures. They are beliefs that you have thought about, questioned, and still hold true. When you violate such values and feel guilty, your guilt tells you it's time to take action.

Fred, a pathological gambler, squandered his wife's inheritance and even wiped out his children's college fund. When he hit rock bottom he was acutely guilty and remorseful. He joined Gamblers Anonymous and started the difficult road to recovery. Eight years later, he once again holds a respectable management position and is paying for his children's education. His marriage didn't survive the ordeal, but he has established a meaningful relationship with another "recovering" gambler.

Unhealthy guilt is inappropriate and does not motivate change. It is usually the result of inflexible, arbitrary rules that force you to deny certain basic needs. These rules allow no exceptions and leave you no quota of mistakes. The values that lie behind them have been passed down to you by a parent, church, or influential friend. But they don't work for you—they diminish rather than enhance your life. But even though they are not your rules, even though they force you to endure pain, you feel terrified of breaking them.

Deborah fell in love with an unemployed labor organizer she had met in a storefront legal aid office in Harlem during a sociological expedition, a trip assigned by her college professor. Her parents loudly disapproved: Deborah is Jewish, and her labor organizer happened to be Black. She was stuck. If she went ahead with the relationship, she would be emotionally (as well as economically) disowned by her parents. Inevitably, she would feel wrong and guilty. If she broke off her relationship, she would be pushing away a man she loved.

Solutions to the Problem of Guilt

Reframing. Perhaps the simplest solution to the problem of guilt is to reframe the strict rules which have produced it. Reframing is a psychological technique which allows you to see things in a new and more productive light.

> *You should be a good mother.* The inescapable implication is that you should *always* put your children's welfare first. That is, you should be a martyr.
> *Reframe:* In reality, a "good mother" models valuing and taking care of herself. She takes care of her own needs so she will have the emotional resources to provide for her kids. She teaches her children self-reliance.

You should be a good provider. It's the father's job to bring in lots of money, regardless of the personal cost. Even if it means that he is unable to spend time at home with his wife and family.

Reframe: A "good provider" provides his family with adequate amounts of affection and personal contact. Money isn't everything, and it can't replace the real value of a loving, available parent.

You should stick to your mate "until death do you part." This inflexible rule served a real purpose in the past when economic considerations mandated the preservation of the family unit at all costs.

Reframe: These days, the "death" of mutual love, respect, and caring is adequate and justifiable grounds for the dissolution of a disastrous marriage.

Reframing allows you to restate a rule or value so it more accurately protects your needs and the needs of your family. Notice that the reframe expands the rule so it is a more realistic, life-enhancing guide for behavior.

Atonement. In some cases, simply apologizing will serve to lessen guilt. Other ways of absolving guilt might include paying restitution or helping your ex-spouse to get off to a new start.

Charlene had wanted to be a psychologist, but had stopped her education at the B.A. level to have children. Her husband's career always came first, and she took care of the children. When he left her, he agreed to pay sufficient rehabilitative alimony to put her through school. It was, for him, an act of atonement. Seven years later, having survived the ordeal of graduate school (and single parenthood), Charlene is now working part-time at a family service agency and developing a private practice.

Figuring out *what* to do is usually the easy part of atonement. The hard part is actually *doing* what you've decided. A note of caution: indulging in self-flagellation or incessantly saying "mea culpa" is not a useful way of doing penance. If more than an apology is required, if there is a need for action or restitution, beating your breast will not work. Decide what needs to be done to absolve your guilt—then *do* it.

The Gestalt approach. Fritz Perls, the originator of Gestalt therapy, was the first person to postulate that the other side of guilt is *resentment.* He incorporated this insight into his style of "two-chair work." You can use this technique in your own home.

First, set aside some time when you can be by yourself and won't be disturbed. Place two chairs (or pillows) facing each other. Sit in one seat and center yourself by focusing your attention on your diaphragm and breathing deeply. Now imagine that your ex-spouse is sitting opposite you and start telling him or her about your feelings of guilt. If you get stuck, change seats and allow the "other person" to remind you of all your sins from his or her point of view.

Now return to your own seat and change your sentences. Instead of saying, "I feel guilty about. . ." now begin your sentences with the phrase, "I feel resentful. . ." or "I resent you for. . ." Continue saying these sentences until they feel right for you. Conclude the "session" by announcing to your ex-spouse that you have chosen not to feel guilty anymore.

Minimizing self-blame. The person leaving the relationship usually gets all the blame. The real problem occurs when the leaver accepts the negative judgments of others and begins to indulge in self-blame. While it is healthy to accept your own share of responsibility, it is important to achieve a balanced point of view. This can best be done by recognizing that both you and your spouse played a part in the death of your relationship. The leaver may have been the one to openly announce the end of the relationship, but the other person may have also been giving subtle or indirect messages for a long time. Love dies slowly, and its passing is usually the result of a relationship that was emotionally malnourishing for both people involved.

Their friends thought that the Merediths were an ideal couple, caring of each other and charming company to have around. But they slowly drifted apart as each became more and more involved in his or her own interests. There were no children to cement the relationship, and in time the marriage simply dissolved from its own lack of energy. Someone had to "do the deed"—and so Jim Meredith left.

What began as an amicable separation turned sour when Arlene Meredith's relatives began to blame Jim for all the problems. On top of it, his mother accused him of not "giving his all" to the marriage. Jim became increasingly depressed. Eventually, professional intervention was needed to stop his downward spiral.

Forgiving yourself. The hardest part of overcoming guilt is to forgive yourself. When you've gone through the rest of the process, when you understand clearly the mistakes you've made and have paid the appropriate price, it's time to stop. Even convicted felons get out of prison after serving their time. One way of forgiving yourself is to write yourself a letter of pardon. When guilt feelings reoccur, you can read the letter to yourself.

Michele was 17 years old and pregnant when she married Bob. Two kids and five years later, she realized that she wasn't happy. Bob wasn't home much. He was too busy working during the day and going to school at night. Michele spent her days washing clothes, cleaning the house, shopping and cooking, with the two kids in tow. She felt that she was being pushed further and further into a corner with no exit. She realized that she had to leave now or else forever give up any dream of leading a life of her own.

One evening Bob came home to find a baby-sitter and a letter from his wife. Michele had left for the West Coast to make a life for herself. Perhaps the most debilitating of the many problems that faced her there was guilt. She had always been taught that a good mother never abandons her children. And Bob loved her and wanted her to come back home.

Eventually, with the help of a support group, she was able to come to terms with herself. She had been too young to have children. Her resentment towards the kids was natural and normal. In time she realized that her leaving was really an expression of her deep need for self-worth. When her life stabilized with a job and an apartment, she arranged for the children to spend summers with her.

THE LEFT

Surprised, hurt, abandoned, angry, ashamed, rejected, betrayed, devastated—these are a few of the most common feelings experienced by those who have been left by their spouse. But sometimes the left also experiences a sense of relief; tension has been slowly growing for a long time and the declaration is like a breath of fresh air in a musty room.

The person who gets left is usually the one who was more committed to the relationship or dependent on it for emotional or physical support. Millie was a 38-year-old housewife with three children and a husband who was spending increasingly more time "working at the office" in the evenings. When he eventually told her of his affairs and his decision to move out, she was totally surprised. "I thought things were OK," she said, "we never fought or even argued much." After the shock wore off, she felt crushed and "for the first time in my life I almost hated someone."

Anger

The person who is left often feels devalued and hurt, betrayed by the selfishness of the leaver. Anger, even to the point of rage, is a normal reaction. The anger serves two purposes. First, it helps to mask the more painful feelings of being worthless and "not OK." The feeling of worthlessness is extremely disruptive psychologically. It can paralyze you, holding you back from making adaptive changes in your life, from reaching out or seeking those things which nourish you. Feelings of worthlessness are the royal road to depression. People who experience them don't take care of themselves and don't live as long. It's small wonder that the psyche has a natural protection from such a dangerous emotion: anger.

Rage wells up so quickly at an attack on your self-worth that you may not even notice the intermediate step where hurt and "not-OKness" start to overwhelm you. It's good to regard your anger as protective armor, but not something you should necessarily act on or use as a guide.

The second function of anger is to provide energy. There are two possible responses to feeling victimized and betrayed: you can collapse, or you can take care of yourself. Anger helps mobilize you to take the risks necessary for change. It gives you the energy to emotionally support your children and make adaptive decisions necessary to survive the crisis.

The anger you feel is natural, but it must be controlled. Control can be exercised, in terms of both duration and effect. Anger that fills your waking hours and continues unremittingly for weeks is doing more harm than good. The protection it provides is overshadowed by the stress to your somatic nervous system. But you can control the duration of your anger by controlling your thoughts. Focusing on the injustices of your marriage or your sense of being cheated or abused stirs up the rage. The best plan is to schedule an hour or so a day to review the things that anger you—and then to turn it off. Reserve your angry thoughts for the next scheduled period, but don't let them infect the whole day.

You can control the effects of your anger by resolving *never* to make a decision while caught in the grip of any strong emotion. Keep decision making for a time when you feel clearheaded and emotionally balanced. Remember that decisions made in the heat of anger can haunt you for a lifetime.

Self-Pity and Self-Condemnation

Feeling sorry for yourself, indulging in self-pity, or putting yourself down are dangerous traps for the person in the relationship who was left. While feeling abandoned and victimized are natural reactions, they will lead to problems—and can become crippling if you are in so much pain that you become socially paralyzed and can't reach out to others. What follows is a downward spiral of withdrawal and isolation.

Jan was going along, trying to be a good provider, with a family, a two-car garage, and a reasonable mortgage payment. His life wasn't exactly exciting, but with the outlet of Sunday football and the money set aside for the orthodontist bill, he thought things were under control. When his wife Cynthia "left" (actually, she kept the house, and he had to move out), at first he felt a kind of exhilaration. But soon his new "freedom" turned sour—a stale routine of TV dinners and lonely nights. Singles bars were scary; he'd get a little drunk and end up going home alone. Eventually, he stopped going out ("The beer is cheaper here") and began to dwell on how good it used to be. "If only I had done things differently."

Going With It

When you feel down, it's sometimes useful to exaggerate the feeling for awhile. In fact, healthy mourning for the death of your relationship requires that you thoroughly indulge yourself for a time. Some people bemoan their fate, while others complain that everyone else is out having a good time while they are sitting home alone. One man used to picture imaginary scenes of his ex's ecstatic happiness. He styled himself as the "born loser" for whom nothing had ever gone right.

Some people tend to romanticize their terminated relationship. They remember only the good times: the candlelight dinner five years ago, the walk on the beach in the summer of 1974, roses on the tenth anniversary. Others tend to indulge in fantasy. A good one is the "romantic tragedy," the ideal love affair doomed to a sorrowful end by the jealous gods. Many people are tempted by revenge fantasies. Your ex finally realizes his mistake and returns to you on his knees, begging for another chance. You are preoccupied with your new bear and order your servants to send him on his way.

However the mourning process affects you, you'll find that it's a process that can't be avoided or denied. Going into it and going with it will enable you to go through it, and to get on with the decisions you'll need to make in your new life.

Once the shock of the breakup diminishes, the roles of leaver and left become less significant for most couples. And they are ultimately temporary identities, taken up for a time in order to get through a crisis, and then put aside as each partner begins to absorb the long-term impact of separation. Grief, however, is likely to continue long after the initial guilt and outrage have dissipated. Chapter 4, "Mourning and Mending," presents the stages of grief that you are likely to encounter and suggests techniques for coping with them.

4

Mourning and Mending

There are many similarities between mourning the death of a loved one and mourning the death of a marriage. But the feelings of grief that the death of a marriage brings are seldom clean and unambiguous, as they are usually mixed with feelings of hurt, anger, bitterness, hatred, and perhaps even excitement. A first step toward learning how to mourn in a healthy fashion is to learn how to recognize and acknowledge the various stages of grief you are likely to experience.

STAGES OF GRIEF

The process of grief does not follow a logical progression; grief may come in waves, spasms, or pangs. No one grieves according to a rigid sequence, and the various "stages" are not presented below in the order of their occurrence. Many people repeat or recycle through several stages before their grief work is done.

Grief has a way of surfacing when you least expect it. It can be stirred up by a fragment of melody or a tantalizing aroma carried by a vagrant breeze. Martha had been divorced for over two years when she enrolled in a gourmet cooking class. She found tears welling up when she cooked soufflés: "He loved those kind of dishes. I remember cooking and waiting for him to come home during the good years."

The first stage of grief is inevitably *shock*. This natural protective mechanism of the body enables us to go on despite the impact of loss. The feeling of numbness may be over in a few hours or hang on for a week or more. Each of us has a different capacity for absorbing feelings of loss.

The second stage is often *release* through sobbing. Much stronger than crying, sobbing is a violent release of energy that may even assume the form of wailing. Many people are frightened by the loss of control it involves or are afraid that it will go on forever. It helps to have someone to hold you during this stage, and to remind yourself that when your body reaches a natural state of exhaustion the sobbing will pass. The exhaustion is a healthy way of turning off your feelings for a time.

Following a divorce, at least one of the partners usually experiences *relief.* The relief may be as strong or stronger than the sadness he or she feels. This is particularly true if the other spouse has been abusive or an alcoholic. As one woman put it, "I was always frightened and on guard. I never knew what would happen next. Now I can begin to relax."

The next stage may come unexpectedly. You've just begun to feel OK, and without warning a sudden *depression* takes over. The full impact of the loss hits you: you are alone, unloved, unlovable, doomed to a life of emptiness. "Those first few days were terrible, I couldn't stay focused on anything. And I kept crying and crying—I cried myself to sleep. Wherever I looked, there was emptiness. I had lost everything." *(30-year-old stenographer)*

Another early stage of grief is *craziness,* characterized by poor judgment and irrational behavior. It's a time when people tend to jump to conclusions or to make hasty decisions. A basic rule for the grief-stricken is never to make decisions involving moving or money while feeling overwhelmed by loss.

At some point in their grief, most people *panic*. When the pain becomes more than you can bear, a normal instinct urges you to drop everything and run away. At these times it's helpful to remember that feelings of panic are temporary. Find a quiet place to sit down and do some deep breathing. Focus on your diaphragm and notice your breath going in and out. Within a few minutes the panicky feelings will subside.

You may also experience *physical symptoms* related to unresolved grief. These may occur at any time and might include insomnia, trembling, diarrhea, or vomiting. Rare cases can involve a temporary paralysis or loss of feeling in a limb, loss of hearing, or blurred vision. It is always wise to check physical symptoms with a medical doctor, but keep in mind that their appearance during grief is a common reaction.

Feelings of *guilt* and self-blame are also common at times of grief. These usually take the form of thoughts beginning, "If only I had done. . ." or "I should have. . ." This form of self-torture should be indulged in sparingly, since it may be habit-forming.

An important part of the grieving process is *withdrawal,* taking time to be by yourself. Isolating yourself from others for a time can be very healing if you don't get stuck in endless rumination. Withdrawal can be a way of taking stock of yourself and examining your needs, wants, and goals.

Sooner or later your grief will include *anger.* The vehemence of your angry feelings may frighten you, but you will find it more helpful to express them than to keep them bottled up until they finally explode. Unresolved anger often gets displaced and taken out on others, sometimes years later. As one man said, "I could feel the loss and emptiness somehow turning into rage. How could this have happened to me? How could my life have been so scarred? After I said this outloud to a few people, the feeling slowly cooled down."

AVOIDING GRIEF WORK

It is a natural human tendency to want to avoid pain and unhappiness. People who are grieving are often willing to exhaust themselves pursuing unsatisfactory or unrealistic goals simply in order to avoid acknowledging what they're feeling. This may occur because a current grief has hooked onto the unfinished business of the past. The unfinished mourning for a loss suffered in childhood often comes back to contaminate the experience of marital separation. The following techniques show that all avoidance of grief work is based on either *hanging on* or *denial.*

Legal "Remedies"

Some of the best ways to avoid grief work are to use institutions like the courts to hang on. Legal battles may drag along for years, forcing continued contact between the ex-partners and postponing the inevitable need to start a new life.

Possessions may become the objective battleground of the divorce. People who did not get what they wanted emotionally may now decide to settle for things such as silverware, art objects, or the rocking chair. This process can become ludicrous, as it did in the case of the million dollar divorce settlement which became hopelessly deadlocked over the issue of who should get "custody" of the LEGO set.

Spousal support can be another way of hanging on, sometimes for the rest of a lifetime. The receiving spouse makes sure that the paying spouse is constantly reminded of the marriage by the size of the support check. While the point is not meant to discourage spouses from demanding and receiving legitimate support, it is important to recognize that support issues can be misused to keep old bitterness alive.

The other side of the game is for alimony checks to be mailed late, or not mailed at all. In fact, less than half (49 percent) of spouses who receive alimony get a "full" check each month. The receiving spouse is constantly forced to think about the ex and often to spend time and energy to make contact and collect.

Most feminists now recognize that punitive alimony settlements are tacit recognitions of the woman's subservience. The attempt to achieve financial equality after a marriage often acts as a handicap, perpetuating not only an economic but also a psychological dependency. *Rehabilitative alimony* is an alternative approach: the unskilled spouse receives enough money to provide for education or retraining. The payments are time-limited and clearly defined, both in scope and purpose.

Perhaps the saddest legal remedy is the use of children to avoid grief work. Some parents struggle over custody because they are unable to say goodbye. They go through lengthy court battles in a desperate attempt to maintain some kind of contact with each other, even if only a hostile and embittered one. A similar motive may also be behind many "ex-spouse kidnappings" which actually focus attention on the parents, not on the children.

Social "Solutions"

The following nonsolutions are additional ways of avoiding grief work. They involve other people or invite the collusion of the rest of the world.

Probably the most common method is to *get mutual friends to take sides.* Friends are good for many things, but they seldom serve well as judge and jury or postmortem analysts of who was right or wrong. Even if all your friends do agree that your ex was a jerk, it won't help you adjust to the separation or bring about a reconciliation. If you need someone to talk to about your feelings of self-worth—which are the real issue in these attempts to pin the blame—you're best off with a mental health professional.

Using others to keep tabs on your ex is also an exercise in futility. It's a very good way to lose friends who don't want to be caught in the middle. (There are people who enjoy these situations—they also chase ambulances and fire engines.) But the real problem is that you're setting yourself up for a future of no-win comparisons. If he's happy, then why aren't you? If she's depressed and lonely, then you should feel guilty.

The inability to tolerate being alone (and face your feelings) may result in a *frantic effort to fill up your free time.* Most newly separated people do all right during the week by focusing attention on their work. But when the weekend rolls around, they panic. Some people spend most of their free time during the week going to bars and trying to set up dates or find out about Saturday night parties to attend. Charter members of the T.G.I.M. (Thank God It's Monday) club, they straggle back to work again, relieved to find they've survived another weekend.

A related problem is the "rebound effect," or *falling in love with the first person you meet*. This usually results from a desperate search for someone to fill the vacuum left by the former spouse. The rebound can end in resounding disaster: if the new person doesn't work out, you'll be left to deal with the death of two intimate relationships and an increasing fear of making a commitment to someone new.

Another common solution these days is to *indulge in a succession of casual affairs*. "Pick-up" bars abound and offer the easy solace of a one-night stand. The empty bed is temporarily filled, but the long-term reaction is usually depression over the lack of intimacy or cynicism about future relationships.

Personal Pitfalls

There are a number of common reactions to divorce that should, if possible, be avoided. One is trying, at all costs, to maintain full intimacy with your ex. Everyone has heard stories of "friendly" divorces with a friendly aftermath: an idyllic picture of new wife and ex-wife at a picnic with all the children. . .and so on. In reality, this kind of détente is difficult to achieve unless two basic criteria are met: (1) *all* the wounds are healed, and (2) you no longer need the love your former partner provided. You might also do well to assess the emotional price it will cost you to maintain this friendship, and whether or not you are willing to pay it.

A similar pitfall lies in the impulse divorced partners often have to help each other through a crisis. This is a trap for nice, kind people who may be afraid of beginning a new life and indecisive about burying their dead relationships.

For many ex-spouses, there is the temptation to try to get back together again. Of all the hopeful fantasies, this is the least likely to come true. Most of the reasons for the original divorce are usually still there, and after a second honeymoon period most of them will inevitably resurface. Each member of the ex-partnership usually brings along a knapsack of old hurts and resentments which is hard to put down.

In an effort to fill the emptiness left by separation, many people fall back on reliving old memories. The lost past is often documented and preserved by a collection of old love letters and mementos. But it's difficult to reach out to someone new with hands (and heart) full of things from the past. Seen for what it is, your nostalgia is simply dissatisfaction with your current life. The best cure for being stuck with old memories is to make some new ones.

Many people succumb to the temptation to check up on their ex. This situation was poignantly depicted in the film, *Chilly Scenes of Winter*. The protagonist keeps driving by his ex-lover's new house (60 miles away), parking his car, and sitting in it until all the lights go out. This is a good way to avoid meeting someone new, except perhaps the milkman at three in the morning. If you find yourself "accidentally" cruising in your ex's neighborhood, make an immediate U-turn to the nearest friend's house.

You may find yourself wishing that the breakup had never happened—and feeling sorry for yourself because it has. Regret is a natural phenomenon, but it can become self-destructive if overdone. It won't if you put a limit on the time you'll allow yourself to wallow in self-pity before getting on with the rest of your life.

Be careful of "anniversary dates" and the feeling of devastation that returns for some people on the anniversary of a first date or wedding. Spending your time dwelling on "what if" rather than "what is" is a tremendous energy drain. A reasonable amount of sadness at these times is normal, even useful, but allowing yourself to become immobilized just serves to delay your recovery.

Using alcohol or other drugs is a particularly dangerous pitfall. These substances offer a seductively simple way out by providing immediate relief from painful emotions and enabling you to achieve blissful numbness. But in the long run, they simply add another problem to your life and delay the time when you have to face reality.

The final pitfall to take heed of is suicide. Many people toy with the idea of killing themselves as a way to end grief or "get even" with their former spouse. A passing thought of suicide is normal, but if you find yourself spending a lot of time on fantasies of killing yourself, it's best to get some professional help. If you feel in a crisis, call your local suicide prevention hot line; the people there are trained to help you.

SUCCESSFUL MOURNING

Only two basic tasks need to be completed for a successful mourning: letting go of the past and giving in to feelings in the present. As straightforward as these tasks may appear, success in completing them often follows a paradoxical path.

One model to look at is the Jewish custom of "sitting Shivah." When someone dies, the immediate family goes into a period of ritual mourning. For seven days they do nothing but devote themselves to thoughts of the departed. It is traditional for the mourners to sit on hard wooden benches all day. Friends and other family members come with food and drink; the mourners' job is to mourn, not to cook. The guests take turns sitting on the bench and talking about the deceased. They remember the good times *and* the bad times. They reminisce and weep (and also eat and drink, since mourning takes energy). At the end of a full week, the mourners are glad to be able to sit on a soft couch again, and to be able to think about the rest of their lives. This ritual serves several purposes: (a) it makes denial impossible, (b) it leaves room for anger as well as appreciation, and (c) it acknowledges depression, yet builds in a time limit to contain it.

Our society has no rites or customs for dealing with the death of a relationship. To get through the emotional aftermath of a divorce, you will have to design a ritual of your own.

Permission To Mourn

Most of us are victims of childhood injunctions such as "Big boys don't cry," "Don't worry about your lost watch, I'll buy you a new one," or "If you don't have something nice to say, don't say anything." We have been trained not to acknowledge our painful feelings even to ourselves, much less to share them with others. As psychologists have discovered, this situation often leads to chronic headaches, ulcers, or even heart attacks. Just as denying your feelings won't help, intellectualizing (thinking them through) will not provide the relief you need. The only answer is to acknowledge the hurt feelings. Only then can you begin to heal. Your legitimate sadness at the pain of separation gives you the inalienable right (if not the duty) to grieve over your loss.

Acknowledging Feelings (Giving In)

For many people, a helpful beginning is to understand why feelings are scary. We have all heard horror stories about people overwhelmed by depression, immobilized by self-pity, or driven insane by uncontrollable rage. These are stories of very unusual events. The reality is that you can take control over your experience of grief. You do have the strength to shut off feelings if they become excessive. And most significantly, you are able to grow by experiencing more of yourself than you did before.

Many people have been taught to be concerned only with other people's feelings, not their own. This is the time to question that ethic. You are important; you have the right to feel and to be aware of yourself.

Allowing yourself to feel pain is bound to hurt—that's why people avoid doing it. You have two choices: You can (1) experience the pain and learn to let it go, or (2) hang on to the pain and continue to suffer directly or indirectly for years. If you want to make the first choice but still feel stuck, review the techniques for avoiding grief work covered earlier in this chapter. Put a check mark next to any that you are still doing. Make a decision to stop doing one of them within ten days.

Dealing With Feelings (Letting Go)

Most professionals agree that in order to let go of pain you must first be willing to experience it fully. The first step is to "own" your pain—to take responsibility for its existence. No one is "doing it to you" or making you feel whatever it is that you are feeling. Certainly, things would be different if only he or she hadn't done such and such, but your feelings come from inside of you, and only you can do something about them.

When you are ready to get in touch with your feelings, begin by making some time for yourself—a time when you are alone and free from external pressures. Choose a quiet safe place (perhaps your own bedroom) and be sure to wear comfortable clothing. Now close your eyes, pay attention to your body, and try to relax. Notice where you feel residual tension: your neck and shoulders (a common place to carry tension to protect yourself) or perhaps a tightness in your throat or stomach (which may relate to having swallowed feelings for a long time). Now begin to make sounds, quietly at first, but then with increasing volume as the feelings rise. Let the feelings come up, as a wave comes into shore—allow them to crest, and then subside. Notice that feelings can ebb and flow, just as the ocean does on the beach.

An alternative is to allow words to spring up spontaneously. Repeat the words that come to you over and over again until you actually feel them in your body: "I'm sad...I'm sad...." Again, remember to respect your own body's natural rhythm. You will find that feelings come and go, intensify and diminish.

Strategies for Grieving

Once you are in touch with your feelings (pain, sadness, anger), you will probably want to get rid of them. Once again, the best way "out" is by the paradoxical approach of going further "into it." One method for minimizing the pain of separation is to establish a regular routine for mourning. First establish a focus for your attention. Many psychologists suggest that you make a "shrine" for your ex. Reserve a part of one room for putting up pictures and storing memorabilia, perhaps setting aside a beautiful lacquered box for old love letters. Keep a record player handy for playing those special songs that remind you of the good old times. Spend at least fifteen minutes (but no more than one hour) each day focusing your attention on the memory of the lost one.

Another useful strategy is to write a letter to your ex. Use large sheets of paper and write every other paragraph with your unaccustomed hand, using a crayon or a large pencil. It isn't necessary to mail this missive: just writing all your feelings down will help. Using the unaccustomed hand will let you speak from your deeper, simpler feelings. Take this opportunity to tell him or her all the things that you always wanted to say, but somehow never said.

As you ready yourself to go on to a new life, it will help you to bury the past. As a symbol that you are reaching the end of the mourning process, you can literally bury old love letters and mementos. Burning is often more satisfying than burying, since you can say goodbye to each piece as it goes up in smoke. Remember to *say* goodbye out loud, over and over again. Your objective is to finish up and go on with your life.

Getting Support

Support will plainly not be as easy to come by as it would be if you were mourning the death of a loved one. But most people find that there are friends they can reach out to for support. You will probably find relatives or people you know separately from your ex-spouse more capable of dealing with your grief than mutual friends or people affected by the death of your relationship are. These friends have some grief work of their own to do and may be threatened by your new status.

Some people can rely on their own bodies to tell them when to seek support (a phenomenon called *tactile hunger*). The "need" you feel for a hug is a very reliable signal. Remember, the moment you allow someone else to share your feelings, you are no longer alone.

CHILDREN AND GRIEF

Children are rarely afflicted with tension headaches and less often with ulcers. If left alone, children deal quite well with feelings, unlike their "socialized" parents. Problems arise when parents inhibit their children's expression of feelings: "Be brave. Don't cry." Parents who do not express their own emotions also serve as poor models for their children.

Children deal with their insecurities by asking questions over and over again. Parents are most helpful when they answer such questions as fully as possible. The process of requesting and receiving information in itself enables the children to be reassured that parents still care. Children may choose to spend a lot of time in fantasy or solitary play after a divorce. This is a healthy way of working through the mixed feelings that accompany a separation. Playing with dolls who are "going through a divorce" or baseball players who are "leaving their home team" helps children to understand and lessens the pain of separation.

Some sadness is normal in children of separated parents. Sometimes sadness is extended to depression characterized by loss of appetite, apathy, helplessness, hopelessness, irritability, withdrawal, or obsessive self-criticism. At this point, professional help may be indicated.

STARTING A NEW LIFE

Once you've finished the mourning process, it's time to move on. You can expect to have some relapses—further attempts to live in the past, days when you fall flat on your face and find yourself wishing "it" had never happened.

Now is a good time to take a personal inventory. Get paper and pencil out and make three lists. List A is for all the things that you don't like about yourself and your present situation. (This is probably what you have been focusing on for the past several days, weeks, or months.) This list might include things like "I lack self-confidence," "I spend too much time alone," or "I've gained too much weight." List B is for writing down things that you do like about yourself and your situation: your good sense of humor, the greater privacy you have now, your ability to cook gourmet meals, and so on. Take your time doing this task and go back and forth between lists as often as necessary. Be honest with yourself. This should provide you with a balanced picture of your assets and liabilities.

Now return to list A and pick out the dislikes that you want to change. Use list C to write down new goals for yourself. Some will be short-term goals: "Go to the movies with a friend this weekend" or "Reorganize the kitchen shelves." Others might be long-term goals such as "Go back to school and get a masters degree in Public Health" or "Become an interior decorator." Make your first draft as long as possible, including unrealistic as well as realistic goals. Some of your goals will require further investigation, such as finding out about entrance requirements for school. Others may be a little frightening, such as "Ask the new secretary out for a date." Taking risks is a scary business, but it can also be exciting and even fun. The important thing to be aware of is that as you go through this process you are beginning to gather new strength. You are putting the past behind you and looking forward to a better future.

MOURNING AND GROWTH

Every ending implies the possibility of a new beginning. Divorce is a painful process, but it can also offer an unprecedented opportunity for personal growth.

Irene was a housewife who always felt vaguely dissatisfied with her life. When her husband left, at first she felt devastated. Within a year she was able to establish a support system for herself and her children by sharing a house with another single mother. She decided to go back to school, got a law degree, and passed her bar exams with flying colors. She is currently working in a San Francisco law firm. She reports feeling a sense of purpose in her life and enjoys getting up each morning to face the challenge of a new day. Irene has been hurt. She grieved. But she also changed. She found that life could have new richness, despite the scars of a traumatic loss.

5

Friends and Relations

FRIENDS

Telling friends about your divorce is an awkward job at best, since you may approach the task with feelings of shame, guilt, hurt, anger, sadness, or some combination of these. The strategy you choose should be one that keeps you at a comfortable psychological distance and allows you to be in control of the amount of feelings you share. With some people, a telephone call may provide the appropriate context. You will prefer to tell others in person, making face-to-face contact over coffee or perhaps over a drink.

Initial Reactions

One way to prepare yourself for the difficult task of telling your friends is to review the typical initial responses people have to being told the news.

1. Many people are surprised at the positive response of certain old friends. Said one woman, "When I told them the news, many of them sounded relieved that I had finally gotten rid of the 'jerk.' The most common reaction was 'Well, it's about time.' I had no idea my unhappiness was so transparent." In reality, it's not easy to hide a bad marriage, and most friends will have sensed long ago that there was "trouble in paradise."

2. The other side of the coin is the response characterized by a gasp of disbelief and the phrase, "But you always seemed *so happy!*" One man reported that he became so tired of hearing the cliche, "But you were such a lovely couple. . ." that he finally decided to stop telling people he was separated. Responses like these usually come from people

who never bothered to find out who you really were; they preferred to see your relationship as they wanted it to be. While they were not really interested in your marriage, their sympathy may be helpful to you during the first bleak days following separation.

3. The middle-of-the-road response "If that's what you think will make you happy. . ." is one of the most frustrating, since it offers the least amount of support and tends to undermine your self-confidence. People who respond in this manner usually have ambivalent feelings towards divorce or being single that they are unwilling or unable to fully share with you.

4. Perhaps the best response you can expect from a nonintimate friend is "I hope things will work out for the best." Be prepared for awkwardness. One man described a typical interchange: "I finally said to these friends, 'There's something you ought to know.' Then I told them and there was SILENCE. Then they said, 'Oh, we're sorry.' What do you say next? 'Thanks for feeling sorry'?"

5. The most devastating responses come from people who try to make you feel guilty, reminding you of all the societal "shoulds" divorce goes against. Examples are "You should have tried harder, you could have made the marriage work" or "How could you leave her (or him) and the children for someone like that?" Rather than offering you their friendship and support, these people choose to remind you of the social taboos of our culture. It's a dirty job, but someone always does it. If you are unable to avoid these self-appointed moralists, you will be wise to give them as little fuel as possible—the less said to them about your marriage the better. Little that you say will be met with understanding or even an open hearing, and most will be seized on as evidence for accusation and judgment.

Types of Friendships

To some degree, how and how much you choose to tell people will be determined by the type of friendship you have established. The context of your friendship will also determine the kind of long-range effect your separation will have on your continuing relationships.

Intimate friendships are those characterized by mutual loyalty, complete trust, warmth, and affection. An intimate friend is a man or woman for all seasons who will stand by you in good times and bad. He or she is a caring and sharing person who will hold you when you cry as well as delight with you in your joys and triumphs. These are the people with whom you can open your heart and to whom you can tell everything. They won't go away. One or two such friendships can be a lifelong source of nurture during times of need.

Neighbors and carpool mates fall into the category of *proximity-based friendships*. These friendships are founded on similar life styles, daily routines, or shared problems in living. Friends like these are people you talk to about the problems of crabgrass and high taxes or share recipes with. Neighbors exchange favors such as loaning tools or trading off baby-sitting. While bonds of affection and loyalty are often formed, these are not fundamental to the friendship.

Maggie and Kathy were neighbors on a cul-de-sac for several years. Their children were always eating at each other's houses and playing together. The two women would spend at least an hour a day talking; the husbands worked on cars together and shared a cord of wood. Eventually the families moved apart. When Kathy got divorced she used Maggie as a confidante, someone to talk to when she needed a willing ear. They visited each other often at first, but now see each other only once or twice a year. Although genuine, this friendship relied heavily on geographical closeness.

Conjoint friendships occur when a husband and wife both establish an independent relationship with the same person. A real problem can develop if both ex-partners choose the same person as a confidant. Hurt and angry feelings inevitably result when the friend is finally forced to choose one or the other. This conflict was compounded even further in the case of one couple. During their separation, both confided in a long-time family friend. It turned out that he had always had a "crush" on the wife, and in this time of uncertain and shifting loyalties he ended up having an affair with her. The husband felt doubly betrayed, and only professional intervention kept him from an act of violence.

Casual friendships include those relationships which are related solely to work or interests. Co-workers and bowling team members present a sticky problem in terms of how and how much to tell about your separation. Common everyday conversations often include such questions as "How's the wife and kids?" or "Is Tom still working weekends?" In spite of your understandable reluctance to open up a "can of worms," it's probably best to let these people get the news of your separation from you, rather than from a third party. There's no need to go into great detail. Most people will respect your disclosure and not invade your privacy. Incidentally, friendships based on shared work or interests are commonly not affected by a separation and will usually continue as before.

Married Friends

Most separated people discover the hard way that their social circle has been largely composed of married couples. Friendships based on marital status are the most susceptible to change after a divorce. Although limited daytime activities such as luncheon dates or tennis partnerships may continue, evening and weekend events will be drastically affected. The change doesn't happen because people are uncaring or unfeeling. Married friends often feel awkward and embarrassed about another couple's breakup: no protocol exists for how a couple should socialize with a formerly married friend. The dynamics of a three-way friendship are more complex and hazardous than the interrelationships of two couples who meet to play bridge together.

Loyalty is also a question. Your old friends may be unwilling to invite you to a social gathering for fear of seeming to take sides against your ex-mate. During their marriage, Tim and Terri had both been friendly with the Smith family. Not long after the divorce, the oldest son of the Smith family was to be married. The parents didn't know how to handle the situation, and so they invited *neither* to the wedding. Both Tim and Terri were hurt when they were excluded.

Another factor is that the separated individual often no longer fits in easily to coupled social occasions. This is partly due to the different life situation of married and single persons: hearing the single person talk about how to cope with single parenting, loneliness, or a new sexual freedom may be faintly disturbing for old married friends.

In general, married friends will react to your new status as a single (and available) person in direct proportion to their own feelings of security. Unfortunately, a significant percentage will see you as a threat to their marriage. This is not simply due to your new sexual availability. Your example raises the spectre of their own marriage breaking up, especially if you now appear to be happy and thriving as a single person.

Some married friends attempt to deal with the problem of your new "singlehood" by doing some uninvited matchmaking—the "Hello Dolly syndrome." This situation usually ends in disaster, since few married people know many singles and therefore have a small sample to choose from. One man's friends invited him to dinner to meet someone named Sheila. The whole evening he felt like he was in a fishbowl, with his friends expectantly looking on. The next day his married buddy quizzed him extensively on all the details of how it went when he took her home. In truth, he was as attracted to Sheila as he was to a heart attack. Developing new relationships is difficult enough without this kind of "help."

In most cases the separating person is met at first by support from married friends who genuinely want to be helpful. They will offer dinner invitations, sympathy, and perhaps advice. Over time, some friends will become more associated with "him" or "her," based perhaps on who met whom first. Finally, and inevitably, the relationships between separated people and the majority of their married friends slowly fade away. There is usually no actual breaking point. Rather, people fail to call to arrange a visit or make a date, and time goes by . . . Sometimes the separated person blames the married friends for failing to initiate contact and chooses to feel rejected. Sometimes the married friends blame the separated person for withdrawing into isolation. Either way, married and separated people often feel increasingly uncomfortable in each other's presence, and a mutual distancing occurs. Most separated individuals do remain in touch with one or two couples, however. These friendships form the nucleus of a new social circle and are a stepping-stone to the future.

Special Problems

Soon after your separation, friends will begin to notice signs that you are making a transition into a new way of life. While these are healthy signs for you, they often cause your friends some special problems.

1. Because the implications of your changing status are uncertain, you will probably become the object of *fantasy* and *projection*. The various ways your friends picture your new life will tell you a lot about who they are and what they imagine their life would be if they were single again. Some friends may imagine that you are having a really "swinging" time, while others may be convinced that you are totally lonely and miserable. A 34-year-old carpenter named Tom reported the following disturbing experience, which happened a few months after his divorce. An old friend, the wife of a couple whose marriage was on somewhat shaky grounds, decided to come over one evening. Their friendly visit was repeatedly interrupted by telephone calls from her husband, who accused them of having a sexual orgy. (In reality, they were talking about recent movies and indulging in an orgy of chocolate-chip cookies.) Tom said. "The whole episode left me feeling at a loss. I didn't know whether to laugh or cry. But it sure spoiled the visit."

2. A friend who over-identifies with you can sometimes act more condescending or hostile to your ex than you do. These gratuitous champions of your cause will often go out of their way to be rude or nasty to your former spouse. Roberta remembered a time when her friend Sue came to visit while her ex-husband was there playing with the kids. Sue had brought a box of expensive candy as a present, but when she saw "him" she marched straight to the kitchen. Once there, she announced in a very loud voice, "These are for you and the kids, and make sure that *he* doesn't get any!"

3. Some of your friends may try to put you in the role of divorce counselor or experienced guide. Since you've "gone through with it," they will pump you for information about everything from lawyers to logistics ("How did you get him to move out?"), as well as the details of your finances. These people are not really interested in your life, although they hope to use it as a blueprint for their own futures.

Other friends may come to you hoping that you will tell them that they should divorce. These friends are trying to avoid taking responsibility for their own actions. In these situations, it's usually best to not give advice, since you will probably get blamed for any wrong decisions and rarely be praised for any right ones. People who are really in an unbearable situation can usually find their own way out.

4. Perhaps the most difficult problem you may face as a newly separated person is that of *unwanted sexual advances*. It is not uncommon for "happily married" friends to respond to your new "availability" with heightened sexual interest; a few may even propose a discreet affair. The offer may be flattering, but accepting it poses a high risk of destroying your friendships. While both men and women have reported the occurrence of this phenomenon, women are usually the ones who receive the late-night visitors: an unhappy husband who "just wants to talk" about his unsatisfying marriage, but ends up suggesting himself as a solution to your loneliness and need to be touched.

RELATIONS

Telling your family about your plans for a divorce is usually a lot harder than telling your neighbors or friends. One reason for this is that American families are more emotionally and geographically distant now than ever before. Since Americans currently move on the average of once every five years, they rely less on their extended families for support and a sense of belonging. While family members are told about the birth of a child, an illness, or a great new job, they are rarely told about day-to-day experiences and feelings. They are often the last to know about marital difficulties. This lack of intimacy makes it difficult to face the inevitable questions following your announced intention to divorce.

It's also hard to face the very real tendency of kin to evaluate and judge each other. Some family members feel that their responsibility to help one another in times of need implies a right to criticize and blame. Telling your family is a risk. It's likely that one or more of your kin will exercise their "right" to evaluate your behavior.

A third factor that makes telling your relatives difficult is that family reactions are so unpredictable. There is no socially approved way to respond to the news that a son or sister or nephew is getting a divorce. Reactions run the gamut from attacks on the ex-spouse to angry lectures about selfishness and "moral failure." The problem is that no one can agree on exactly what divorce is. Is it failure? A tragic mistake? A symptom of irresponsibility? Or is it a step toward growth and self-development? The way a particular family member interprets and defines divorce will very much determine his or her reaction. While you can make guesses, it's not always possible to predict what assumptions kin will make about divorce in general and about your divorce in particular.

The fourth reason it's hard to give the news to kin is that divorce stirs such strong feelings, particularly in people whose family identity is closely linked to yours. A father may feel disgraced, a mother may become depressed, a competitive brother may feel triumphant, a sister may fear that your divorce is contagious and a threat to the survival of her own family. Reactions such as these can intensify your hurt and guilt and make you want to withdraw from family contacts.

Putting It in Words

People often cope with impending divorce by denying it. You put it out of your mind and speak of it to no one. To say anything, to share your pain and anxiety, would be to somehow make it real. One woman described how denial literally choked off her words: "Bill and I agreed that we'd separate after the holidays. Even though I talked to my parents quite often on the phone, and we actually had Christmas dinner with them, I couldn't say anything. I was so depressed, I was just a zombie. In my mind I rehearsed a thousand ways of telling them. But I'd feel this choking sensation, almost like I was being strangled, if I tried to say anything. I think I was afraid that saying it would make it really come true. It would become a reality and not just my private nightmare."

When you finally overcome denial to the extent that you can say something, the first person you talk to is likely to be a brother or sister, not one of your parents. This is because siblings are usually less judgmental. They have a smaller stake in your living a "successful life."

Your parents' reactions to your plans for divorce are likely to be consistent with the kind of people they've always been. If they've had rigid rules about right and wrong behavior or have tended to disapprove of the way you've lived your life, then you stand a good chance of being criticized or even punished for your decision. If your parents have generally been flexible and supportive, then it's reasonable to expect that they will react to your divorce with sympathy and offers of help. Here are some of the problematic responses that you may get from parents and other relatives when they learn of your impending divorce:

- *"I told you so. You never should have married (him or her)."* One woman described her mother's reaction as "disgust": "Not at the divorce, but that I'd married Tom to begin with. She wanted to know what took me so long to 'see him for the loser he is.' "

- *The message that you've failed or disgraced your parents.* An insurance salesman put it this way: "They always set high standards for me. If I got a B in school it meant I wasn't trying hard enough. And they've been disappointed that I didn't do better professionally—they don't have much use for salesmen. So my divorce was the coup de grace in what they saw as a not very successful life."

- *Requests that you attempt a reconciliation.* Parents and relatives will sometimes begin unsolicited negotiations with a spouse to promote "another try at it." A mother of three young children reported being badgered for weeks to go back to her husband. "My mother kept saying, 'He's the father of your children, give him a chance.' She refused to acknowledge what I'd been through. She just saw him as 'a good man with a few problems.' She threatened to withdraw financial support if I didn't make another attempt."

- *"We were always so proud of you, but this. . . "* Here's a guilt-inducing message. One woman complained, "It's like all the good things I'd done were erased, like the failure of my marriage overshadowed everything. I felt like I'd lost their respect."

- *The message that you've been irresponsible or immoral in "breaking up the family."* This is very often the response of kin with a strict religious background. The family is seen as an inviolable unit. No amount of pain, yearning, or unhappiness can justify relinquishing your responsibilities. One woman's mother put it this way: "What has happiness got to do with it? You have children. You owe them a father and a home. If you want to know what a sin is, what you're doing is it." A father of two little girls reported this reaction: "My parents told me I was no better than Eddie Fisher when he left Debbie Reynolds. That killed me because they were always so down on him. So they were basically telling me that I was a scum."

- *The message that your parents have been made overwhelmingly sad by the breakup of your marriage.* This is particularly true of parents who have taken great vicarious pleasure in witnessing the growth of your young family. "My mother just collapsed. I swear to God, she cried harder than I did. She went on and on about how she'd known Bill for ten years and kept bringing up old reminiscences. She was so devastated herself, she was no comfort whatsoever to me." *(32-year-old housewife)* Sometimes a parent's sadness is so guilt-producing a divorcing couple will make another try at the marriage or seek counseling as a way of showing that no stone has been left unturned. "Basically I wanted to prove to her that it was hopeless, dead, defunct. I stayed in the marriage another six months, collecting horror stories like a personal injury lawyer, and repeating them to my mom. It was the only way I could cope with her sadness." *(30-year-old detail man for a pharmaceutical company)*

- *"We've failed."* This is the parent who takes full responsibility for your marital problems. "My father drank quite a bit during my teen years and he thought that had a lot to do with the breakup. I said 'I don't drink, I'm not an alcoholic, what could that have to do with it?' It didn't matter, he *knew* it had affected me in some way. He was convinced that he had scarred me." *(29-year-old school administrator)* "My mother says it's because she and my father were never close. She thinks their marriage set a lousy example. I keep telling her that's just bunk. But she keeps on repeating it like a broken record." *(23-year-old secretary)*

- *The inquisition.* You feel expected to answer the most probing personal questions about "what went wrong." "My mother wanted to know if I satisfied my husband sexually. She asked me if I made an effort to cook things he liked. Listen to this: the fact that Hal left me for a woman he works with gave my mother the idea that I might have been unfaithful first. Underneath she was saying Hal was so terrific I must have done something to drive him away." Sometimes the questions are quite solicitous and express a great interest in learning how sad, angry, or frightened you are. Of course, you may be perfectly comfortable sharing your feelings, particularly if your family has always been close. But if there has been little real intimacy with family members, probing questions may feel like an invasion of your privacy.

- *Invasive advice.* Parents and family members often cook up grossly inappropriate suggestions at the time of separation. Spouses have been advised to try saying the rosary, take up running, go on a vacation, or have a baby. One man, who was going through an off-again, on-again separation, was advised by his father to get his wife pregnant. "With a baby she'll look to you as the father. She'll stop worrying about this other stuff and think about the child." As well-meaning as the advice may be, it rarely has much to do with who you are or why the marriage isn't working.

- *"If you'd only. . ."* If you'd only been more interested in the home. . . worked fewer hours at the damn job. . .hadn't gotten involved with someone. . .helped a little around the house. . .and so on. Some family members can't wait to share their theory of what went wrong. But the blaming messages they contribute are like putting salt on an open wound.

- *Suffocating sympathy.* Parents sometimes go overboard in their condemnation of your ex-spouse and their cataloging of the wrongs you've suffered. This can be annoying because it unrealistically puts full blame on your ex-partner. Over-abundant sympathy may also carry the message that you are too incompetent or fragile to handle pain. "I felt infantalized. My mother kept worrying that I wasn't being taken care of. It was like she was saying I was a helpless child. The sympathy irritated more than it helped." *(32-year-old house painter)*

One obstacle that will make telling your parents especially hard is that your reasons for divorce may make no sense to them. As one man put it, "My folks could have understood if she'd been unfaithful or abused the kids or been a lush, but telling them that I felt empty and lonely meant nothing at all. Telling them that I had to change my life if I was going to have any chance at happiness meant even less. It was like preaching salvation to a Hindu—the message just didn't compute." In many cases, telling parents that you seek happiness and fulfillment or that you have grown to be a different person with different needs will produce very unsatisfying results. Your quest for personal happiness will be seen as an indulgence and your growth as a pretext for selfishness.

Coping With Disapproval

It's almost inevitable that certain relatives will disapprove of your divorce. Four groups are most likely to disapprove:

1. Those who idealize family life and family unity. Their value system places family unity above any private needs and concerns, and tales of your personal unhappiness will fall on deaf ears.

2. Relatives who have struggled through hard times, but have managed to salvage a decent marital relationship. Since their model is to "hang in there," they'll want you to do the same. Your decision to divorce may be seen as a lack of courage or commitment.

3. Relatives who've had a terrible marriage and have chosen to stay mired in it. These people will resent you for not sharing their suffering. Your choice to leave a damaging, painful relationship will be a disturbing reminder of their own decision to stay in pain. They are almost forced to reject you in order to deny their own wasted years.

4. Relatives who have never liked you and now have an excuse for their dislike. These are the people who never approved of your values or lifestyle, who were perhaps secretly jealous or harbored grudges for real or imagined injuries. Now you've given them a chance to really point the finger. They may take sides with your ex-spouse, or be content to catalogue your marital failings.

Here are the best ways of dealing with disapproving kin.

Keep your privacy. When relatives challenge you and push you to explain, tell them only what you are comfortable having them know. Don't share the intimate details of your life unless you feel a sense of support and caring.

Don't get drawn into conflict. Relatives who don't approve of your decision may actually go on the offensive. Getting angry and trying to defend yourself to them may only add fuel to the fire. The best policy is to state your point of view in one or two simple sentences. When attacked, simply repeat, and keep repeating, these few sentences. This is called the "broken record" technique.

DAD: Do you realize the economic disadvantages? There's a lot you won't be able to give your kids now.

JULIE: That's true, but the marriage was too painful and too lonely for me to go on with it.

DAD: Sometimes you have to make sacrifices to keep a home together.

JULIE: That's true, Dad, but in this case there was just too much pain and unhappiness to make me want to go on with the marriage.

DAD: Your happiness isn't the only thing that counts. The children have a right to a father and the best standard of living you can provide them.

JULIE: I want the best for them, and I want them to have contact with their dad. But the loneliness and pain I felt left me no choice other than separation.

Notice that Julie agrees with everything her dad says, but continues to reiterate her basic point. She isn't going to be drawn into an unproductive argument. She lets her dad know where she stands, while allowing him to express his concerns.

Don't ask family members to take sides. One of the saddest things about divorce is that families can become quite partisan. People who like and support you may feel obliged to reject your ex-spouse. Less supportive family members and in-laws may blame you for the breakup. If you encourage this process, you are only buying trouble. First, you are asking your family to collude with you in the *delusion* that you bear no responsibility for what happened. If everyone absolves you, then you never have to examine your own behavior—and you end up making the same mistakes. Second, if your family condemns your ex-spouse, this attitude will eventually rub off on your children. They too will be drawn into taking sides. Third, a once cordial relationship between two sets of grandparents may be lost. Fourth, you may blow the chance to develop a good working relationship with the father or mother of your children. A young mother described side-taking in her family: "I was so angry that I just wanted them to see what he'd done, to hate him as much as I did. And it worked. But now I've recovered and I have more of a relationship with him. Sometimes we actually go on dates; we do a lot of talking about Kimmie. My parents think I'm crazy. They think I should stay away from him, and keep their grandchild way from him."

Don't make decisions based on fear of disapproval. Many people put off divorce for months or years because they fear the disapproval of kin. They mind-read judgmental reactions from parents, siblings, and in-laws. The decision to stay or leave a marriage should be based on how you and your children are faring at home, not on the projected reactions of relatives. "What will they think?" is a common fear. But the disapproval of relatives is a relatively minor and transient problem compared to years of pain and longing spent in an unhappy marriage.

Don't ask for support from disapproving kin. It is unrealistic to expect that your family will give you unanimous support for a divorce. Counting on approval from everyone will make you extremely vulnerable to any anger or blame. It's best to expect a certain amount of flak. Get your support from family members who understand and approve, and give the others time to adjust. Don't feel that you have to win over and explain yourself to everyone. "My mother understood what I'd gone through, and to some extent so did my father. But my brother and his wife are very church-oriented. They felt my separation was an act of selfishness. It hurt, but I didn't fight it. I talked to my parents and they felt that my brother would come around in time." *(30-year-old merchant seaman)*

Getting Support

Following a separation, your family can be a major source of support. Help can range from the offer of a meal to assistance with child care and finances. For women with children this support can be crucial. A father or brother can help repair the house or the car or even aid in disciplining the kids.

Many people consider the possibility of moving back in with their parents at the time of separation. This option can be an attractive way of reducing the financial burden and getting help during a stressful life transition. One woman put it this way: "I just needed to put down the responsibility of the kids, the job hunting, and the cooking, and be taken care of for a while. There were adults to talk to in the evening, and I no longer felt that awful emptiness."

The problem with returning home is that it often implies a failure, a loss of status, or a return to an earlier life. When you first left home you may have been quite young, even in many ways still a child. Following a divorce, your parents may pressure you to return to the child role. You may be treated as if you are incompetent or ill and expected to observe the same rules you knew as an adolescent. Parents may keep track of how late you come in and who you date and begin to interfere in your management of the children.

If you live with your parents for more than two or three weeks, it is likely that you will experience increasing pressure to do things their way. There will be small recurring conflicts growing out of a clash of lifestyles and values. A 31-year-old woman described her first three months at home in this way: "In the beginning I was considerate and always watchful. I felt like I was walking on eggs. By the third week I was completely exhausted. They wanted me home by ten. And they wanted a full report on my activities. They complained if I left toothpaste in the sink. Finally I said, 'Look, I'm all grown up. I'm happy to keep the sink clean, but I don't want to have to keep the same hours I did when I was sixteen.' That was fine for awhile. But then they started complaining I didn't dress up enough for work and went out and bought me some perfectly hideous clothes. They had a hemorrhage when I spent the night with someone. It was just too much."

Establishing an adult relationship with your parents is often a difficult task. As a married person, you were protected from parental interference by the fact that you lived with your spouse. As a single person, you are fair game for complaints, suggestions, or demands. A 25-year-old barber described his change of status with his parents: "When I was married, I felt they treated me with a certain deference. Decisions about the kids, the shop, holidays, et cetera, were left up to my wife and I. Now I've suddenly become an incompetent. They've got a million suggestions. The implication is that I've suddenly lost the ability to handle my own life."

Here are some ways to get support without giving up your autonomy:

1. Ask for what you need. If you need help with the kids or you need to move home for awhile, be specific and direct. Explain exactly what you need and how long you will need it. Specificity and directness are hallmarks of adult communication. People know what you need and can say yes or no or make a counterproposal. You aren't being direct when you hint or just wait helplessly for assistance. This is the stance of the frightened child who must depend on adults to notice what's wrong and do something about it.

2. Give something back. If your brother fixes your car, invite him over for dinner. If you move home, offer to do the laundry and vacuuming or help out in the kitchen. If your mother assists you in fixing up a new apartment, buy her a thank-you gift. Reciprocity keeps you functioning as a grown-up.

3. If you need parental support, it's better to live *near,* rather than *with* your parents. That way you can get support and still remain independent. Living at home will make it much more difficult to function as an emotionally and sexually mature adult.

4. Before moving home, openly negotiate all expectations and limits. Be clear with your parents that you are grown up and expect to have adult privileges and responsibilities. Discuss what support you will get and what support you will give. Be clear about any rules and restrictions.

5. When living at home, schedule regular check-ins to see how the relationship is working. It's important to keep current with your parents so that each of you knows how the others are feeling. During a check-in, you can discover if your parents are feeling overburdened with child care, concerned about late-night dates, angry that you've been leaving the dishes, and so on. Check-in is also the time when you can ask that people knock before entering your room, that your kids' table manners not be criticized, and that your ex-spouse not be attacked within earshot of the children. Regular check-ins reduce friction and make it possible to work through problems before they explode into a major crisis.

6

Healthy Conflict

For most couples, their relationship immediately following separation is marked by conflicting needs and interests. Unresolved feelings of hurt and anger add an extra charge as negotiations begin over property, custody, and parenting issues. Typically, the high-income partner wants to provide as little spousal support as possible, while the low-income partner tries to maximize support. One partner may wish to postpone selling the country property for tax purposes, while the other needs cash and wants to liquidate everything. Both partners may want the antique bed, the oak desk, or the sailboat. Both may fight for custody of the children. As one woman put it, "For the first time we have completely different interests. Right now we're arguing about the house. I want Mary to stay here until she's finished high school, he wants to sell. We can't run away from the problem. We *have* to work it out."

Conflict over parenting styles intensifies during the postseparation period. Parents accuse each other of being too lax, too strict, careless, lazy, inattentive, and so on. The complaints often mask a sense of helplessness and loss. One man, whose wife had blocked joint custody, described his children as ". . . street urchins. She keeps them in rags. Literally. She thinks it's hip or something. She's too busy being a swinging single to care for them." Bitterness of this sort is common when parents feel they've lost control of their children's lives.

Because postseparation conflict is inevitable, the only real question is whether it will be healthy or destructive. In healthy conflict, issues are openly explored. In unhealthy conflict the issues are obscured beneath a torrent of rage and blame. Healthy conflict protects the children and makes their welfare the highest priority, while unhealthy conflict draws them deeper into the struggle. Healthy conflict generates solutions. Unhealthy conflict ends in a stalemate which forces the participants to seek redress in the courts.

The sad truth is that people usually do get what they want. If you want an attack-and-run guerrilla war, you will get it. If your highest priority is to hurt and wound, you can usually do that too. On the other hand, if you want to preserve the kind of communication that solves problems and protects the children, that too can be accomplished.

A THREE-STEP CONFLICT RESOLUTION MODEL

Healthy conflict resolution depends on three separate skills: the ability to express your needs, the ability to listen, and the ability to generate alternative solutions.

Expressing

The first step in conflict resolution is to make a clear statement of what you want and why you want it. If you are direct and specific about your needs, your ex-partner won't have to guess and mind-read.

Many people are passive communicators. Rather than spelling out their needs, they try to express them nonverbally by frowning, crying, or withdrawing. Coldness and sarcasm are often used as indirect expressions of hurt or anger. Passive communicators sometimes try to use others as messengers who will carry information to an ex-spouse. They may tell their lawyer, the children, or their sister-in-law about gripes and problems, but never talk directly to the one who needs to hear. As a result, conflicts either remain unsolved or escalate into court battles.

Aggressive communicators express conflicts openly, but use an attacking, blaming style. Sentences often begin with "You . . ." followed by some kind of negative judgment or label. The aggressive communicator uses absolute terms such as "always" and "never." Issues are framed in black or white, good or bad dichotomies. One woman described her husband's aggressive style: "If the kids aren't here at exactly the time he arrives to pick them up, he's in a rage. He says I always screw it up, that I'm trying to block the visits. But it's just a problem of the kids forgetting. We could solve it if the two of us could talk."

Assertive communication is a healthy alternative to the passive and aggressive styles. Being assertive means that you speak directly to an ex-partner, without blame or put-downs. You make an effort to explain the problem, how you feel about it, and what you want to do to resolve it.

Stating the problem. Stick to the facts: explain exactly what you think is going on. Try to discuss only one problem or situation, describing it as nonjudgmentally as possible. Joan, a mother of three small boys, wanted to discuss a daycare problem with her ex-husband. "I'm hoping to go to nursing school this fall. Child care for the kids will be about $350 each month."

Notice that Joan doesn't say something like "You've never carried your weight in child support payments." This might be true, but attacks won't solve the problem. She doesn't complain that support payments have sometimes been late. That's a different issue and will only obscure the problem at hand. There's no pulling for guilt either. Joan could talk about the infrequent overnights with dad, she could point out that she has almost exclusively carried the childcare burden. But an attack of any kind will only create defensiveness, and Joan really wants to solve the problem. She sticks to her simple, nonpejorative statement.

Stating your feelings. Use "I" messages to describe how you feel angry, hurt, disappointed, confused, and so on. Avoid "you" messages such as "You're exhausting me," "You're cheating me," "You're making me crazy." Instead take responsibility for your feelings and say, "I feel exhausted," "I feel angry," "I feel confused and upset."

Notice how "I" statements are inherently nonblaming. Some people turn their feelings into disguised "you" statements. "I feel that you are being selfish" is an attack, not a feeling. There is an important distinction between *expressing* and *dumping* your feelings. Expressing means that you acknowledge and report what you feel. Dumping means that you use your feelings as a club to attack and hurt the other person.

Joan expressed her feelings about the daycare problem in this way: "I feel depressed and frightened, thinking about how little I'd have for food and expenses if I paid the entire daycare bill." Once again, she doesn't express her anger about insufficient or late support payments or the excessive childcare burden. Those are other issues and must be dealt with separately.

Stating your wants. This is where you propose your solution to the problem. Be specific. Avoid talking in terms of attitudes, as in "I want you to be more considerate" or "Just care a little more about your kids." State what you want in objective or behavioral terms. For example: "I need you to pick the children up before six o'clock on Saturday," "I'd like to defer selling the house for three years," "I would like unlimited visitation privileges." You should also include at this point any advantages that might accrue from your proposed change.

Joan suggested this solution to her childcare problem: "I'd like you to pay half the child care. If you help me with the child care, in two years I'll be through nursing school and can begin to support myself. Then you'll be able to reduce or eliminate spousal support."

Here is a summary of the basic elements of assertive communication.

I think
- Describe the situation objectively
- State the facts without slipping into blame or negative judgments
- Don't make a long-winded argument

I feel
- Use "I" statements which show that the feelings belong to you
- Express rather than dump your feelings
- Don't make accusing "you" statements

I want
- Propose a specific solution to the problem
- Propose an objective or behavioral change, not a change in attitude
- Point out the advantages of your solution.

Rehearsing. It's hard to make an assertive statement without preparation. This is especially true when your feelings are running strong and you find yourself easily upset.

Before trying to confront your ex-partner, write out what you think, feel, and want in the situation. Read it over, being sure to eliminate any taint of judgment or blame. Now rehearse what you've written in a calm, neutral voice. Keep practicing until you can say it from memory in a natural way.

Arnie, whose ex-wife wanted him to continue helping with the maintenance of her house, prepared this assertive statement:

> *I think:* "Right now I'm spending about two weekend days a month fixing the house."
>
> *I feel:* "Because the house is yours now, I'm starting to feel used . . ." He crossed out the word "used" as pejorative. "I'm starting to feel unwilling to work that hard on something that isn't mine. I feel depressed at the end of the day, like somehow I've wasted my time."
>
> *I want:* "I'd like you to get someone for the painting and heavy work. If you do, I'll still be happy to help with the simple fix-it jobs."

Arnie's script starts with a clear statement of the problem. There are no complaints or suggestions that he's been victimized. Arnie takes clear responsibility for his feelings and makes no attacking "you" statements. He explicitly spells out his wants and provides an incentive for agreement.

Susan, mother of a six-year-old, wanted her ex-husband to take more responsibility for laundering the child's clothes during overnights. She also wanted the boy's father to buy some pajamas and playclothes for use during the three nights a week her son lived at dad's house. She prepared the following assertive statement:

I think: "Right now Jimmy's clothes go back and forth between our houses in a suitcase. All the laundry is done at my house. There's quite a bit of work involved in packing and laundering his clothes."

I feel: "I feel rushed and tired when I have to do this packing all the time. And I notice I've been irritated when the clothes come back from your house dirty and I have to wash them."

I want: "I'd like for you to have a separate set of pajamas, underwear, and playclothes at your house so we wouldn't have to carry them back and forth. I'd also appreciate it if you'd wash any clothes that do come back to my house. If you want, I'd be glad to help you shop for the new clothes."

The problem, once again, is simply stated and contains no "you're bad" messages. Susan takes clear responsibility for being exhausted and irritated. Her statement of wants is specific and contains an incentive (help with the shopping).

When there's no time to rehearse. If a conflict spontaneously develops and you have no time to prepare an assertive statement, you can still organize a response using "I think, I feel, I want." Take it one step at a time. Think things through before answering. Pause between sentences and mentally rehearse the next thing you're going to say. Keep it simple and stay away from blaming "you" statements.

You'll be surprised how a little practice can make assertiveness almost second nature. "I think, I feel, I want" will become an automatic structure that you turn to for conflict resolution. One woman put it this way: "When I say the first thing that comes into my head, I always get in trouble. Now I separate the problem from my feelings, and I separate the feelings from my needs. By saying stuff clearly and not putting the blame on Jim, I find we have an easier time making parenting decisions."

Principles of assertive expression. The following six principles will help you design your assertive statements.

1. *Focus on a single issue only.* If you want to discuss a problem of late or cancelled visits, you will only confuse the issue by bringing up the children's need for health insurance. If you want to clarify who will purchase the children's winter clothes, don't simultaneously discuss child care for your upcoming vacation. By staying with one topic at a time, you remain focused on specific solutions to specific problems.

2. *Don't drag up the past.* We all keep a psychiatric museum of old hurts and betrayals. Current problems are often disturbingly reminiscent of these painful relics from the past. A late support payment, for example, may trigger a whole chain of memories about old money conflicts. There's a certain amount of pleasure and catharsis in raking over old sins, but they won't help you solve the problem now. The current conflict will only intensify as each of you digs in to defend your position.

3. *Hit above the belt.* Everyone has a "beltline" that is his or her limit of hurt tolerance. If you say something "above the belt," the other person is likely to hear you and be able to tolerate the emotional pain involved. "Below the belt" statements are ones that are too painful to hear. Hitting someone below the emotional belt paralyzes his or her ability to think and reason clearly. People differ in how much and what kind of criticism they can take. Be aware of the other person's beltline. Hitting too low or too hard will only delay resolution of the conflict.

4. *Practice good timing.* Choose a time for conflict resolution when both parties feel relatively stress-free. Don't try to solve problems when either one of you is tired, angry, or has just experienced some kind of trauma. Conversely, good timing means that you deal with issues soon after they come up. Don't store away or "gunnysack" your hurts and irritations until they explode. Storing up grievances results in the most destructive kind of fighting. The wounds are deep and the scars are often permanent.

5. *Be clear.* State your gripes simply without making an elaborate argument. Use "I" statements to make it clear that you are expressing *your* feelings. Stay away from inflammatory "you" accusations.

6. *Be specific.* Focus on objective or behavioral issues. Don't ask for respect, consideration, fairness, or emotional support. These vague concepts rarely translate into any specific action. The other person still won't know what you want changed.

Listening

The second step in conflict resolution is effective listening. This means finding out what the other person wants and why he or she wants it. Effective listening is not an innate ability, but it is a skill which can be learned. Listening requires a commitment to understanding how your ex-partner feels, how he or she sees the world. For a moment you put aside your own prejudices and beliefs, your anxieties and self-interest. You attempt to really look through the other person's eyes.

Listening actively. Listening is more than just keeping quiet. It is an active process that requires your participation. One of the best ways of listening actively is to *paraphrase* what the other person says. Typically, paraphrasing involves saying in your own words what you think your ex-partner has just expressed. "In other words, you're willing to spend every other weekend with the kids and pay half of the orthodontist's bill," or "When you say 'share equally,' do you mean. . .?" The best thing about paraphrasing is that it allows you to check out your perceptions and get immediate feedback. It lets both parties correct errors and misconceptions so that they can avoid major confrontations later on.

A second way to listen actively is to *ask questions* which clarify what's going on. "Are you cutting down on overnight visits for a particular reason?" "With you working more hours, how will we handle child care?" Clarifying questions such as these tend to move a dialogue from vagueness to greater specificity.

An active listener pays attention to the whole message. This means not merely listening to the content, but also focusing on the *nonverbal* aspects of the communication. If a person says "I'm open to hearing your suggestions" while sitting with arms folded and legs tightly crossed, you might do well to question the sincerity of the statement. Someone leaning forward is usually interested in what you're saying, while someone leaning back and looking off to the side is not. Tone of voice, inflection, rhythm of speech, and facial expressions all give you additional information and help you understand more fully what is really being communicated.

Your listening response. After the other person has expressed his or her thoughts, feelings, and wants, you can make your listening response. This means paraphrasing in your own words what was said and asking questions to clarify what you don't understand. This is not yet the time to express your own point of view. The goal is to understand and feed back what you've heard.

The listening response keeps negotiations from turning into arguments. You try to understand, not to refute. The other person feels heard and as a result less likely to go on the attack.

Listening blocks. There are several common pitfalls to avoid if you want to be an effective listener. The first is *rehearsing a response*. Halfway through the other person's statement you begin to prepare your answer, thereby missing half of what is said. This situation is epitomized by the person with a chess-player mentality who is constantly playing out alternative strategies while the other is talking: "If she says that, then I'll counter with this, but if she responds with that, then. . . ."

Another pitfall is the tendency to make *assumptions* about what your ex-partner is *really* saying. This is sometimes called "mind reading," since you are trying to guess the secret meaning of a communication by focusing entirely on the nonverbal level of intonation and body language.

You can combat the tendency to mind-read by checking out assumptions. Ask questions, and find out if your guesses are right. "I imagine that you want to sell the furniture, is that true?"

People who are extremely set in their ways or who possess collection of predigested opinions have a hard time listening. They have a small but well-thumbed encyclopedia of *judgmental statements* such as "All men are controlling," "You can't trust the *(fill in any group)* because they're all *(fill in a negative label)*," or "Women don't know how to handle money." Making such prejudgments saves a great deal of time, since you can write someone off without having to pay attention to what they're actually saying. Effective listening is more time consuming. It involves hearing and evaluating the content of a message before making a judgment.

Some people find it hard to listen because they're always drifting off into their own fantasy or *daydreaming* about being someplace else. This usually means that they don't want to stay in the interaction, perhaps because it's too threatening or anxiety provoking. If this happens to you, see if you can find out exactly what the threat or anxiety is that's triggering your "side trips." You'll also find it helpful to limit how far you go: let your mind wander for only a few seconds at a time and then come right back to the conversation at hand.

"*Comparisons* are odious," said Cervantes, and they are particularly problematical when you are trying to listen to someone else. It's easy to get carried away by thoughts like "She'll probably do a better job of raising the kids," "Things are much harder for me," or "I'm suffering more than he is." When you're focusing on keeping score it's difficult to really listen to the other person.

Generating Alternative Solutions

The third step in conflict resolution is either to agree on the proposed solution or to generate new alternatives. If you agree with the proposed solution, negotiations are at an end. If you disagree, it's now appropriate to express your thoughts and feelings about the initial proposal and begin to look for alternatives.

There are two ways to find alternatives. (1) *Make a counterproposal* outlining your solution to the problem. Suggest some reasons why your solution may be preferable. (2) *Have a brainstorming session.* Sit down together and come up with as many alternative solutions as possible. The more the merrier, the crazier the better. Say anything that comes to mind. It doesn't have to make sense. When you have a long list, look for ways to combine or modify some of the ideas. Only when you've finished brainstorming should you evaluate the alternatives. Think about the financial and emotional consequences of each possibility. Look at long-term and short-term consequences. How will the children be affected? What impact will it have on your relationship? These considerations will help you narrow down the list of alternative solutions to a likely candidate. Agree to try it for a set period of time and then reevaluate. Since the new plan has a time limit, neither of you should have to feel stuck with it.

PUTTING IT ALL TOGETHER

Al and Marcia have been separated for six months, and an issue has arisen over visitation. Al wants scheduled visits twice a week, while Marcia wants Al to arrange visits informally with the kids.

Expressing

MARCIA: *(Stating the problem)* The way it is now, you see the kids one evening a week and on Saturday. They want to see you, but the schedule isn't flexible enough for them to ever do something else that falls on your day. They're missing out on things and in time they might start resenting it. *(Stating her feelings)* I feel worried and concerned about both you and the children. I see their disappointment when they can't do certain things that fall on your day. I worry that they'll turn-off to the visits and that you'll end up terrifically hurt. *(Stating her wants)* I'm happy that you see the kids a lot, but I'd like you to arrange each visit on an appointment basis, rather than by schedule. I'd make every effort to help you see them just as often.

Listening

AL: You're saying that the twice-a-week schedule doesn't allow the kids enough flexibility. It bothers you to see them miss out on things, and you're worried that they'll start resenting me and I'll be hurt. You want me to call the kids up and make appointments for our visits, rather than just having it on a schedule. Am I understanding you?

MARCIA: Yes, that's the arrangement I'd prefer.

Generating Alternative Solutions

AL: I'm worried that after awhile I won't see much of the kids if I have to initiate every single visit. I imagine myself getting discouraged when I hear them saying "No, I can't do it Monday...No, busy Tuesday ...How about sometime next week, dad?" I think I could get very hurt by that. How would you feel about keeping the Saturday visit on a regular schedule, but negotiating with the kids about which night during the week we'll get together? Also, I could let them know it's OK with me if they cancel Saturday for something they really want to do. What do you think of that?

MARCIA: I think it's an improvement over the way things are. I'm comfortable with it.

Notice that Marcia clearly separates her feelings from the statement of the problem. Her feelings are in the form of "I" messages, not attacks. She states her wants specifically so that Al knows exactly what changes she prefers. Al carefully repeats back, in his own words, what Marcia thought, felt, and wanted. He checks it out to make sure that he heard her accurately. He then goes ahead to share his own thoughts and feelings about Marcia's proposal and to make a counterproposal. Both Al and Marcia have the achievement of a mutually satisfactory solution as their highest priority. There are no hidden agendas of hurt or blame.

COMMON NEGOTIATING ERRORS

There are several classic ways to sabotage the conflict resolution process. First and foremost is a *judgmental attitude.* This is communicated through the use of guilt-producing "should" and "you" messages. One negotiation got stalled when Ted started saying things like "You're vain, you spend all your money on cosmetics, you should learn to budget your money more wisely." Naturally, Alice got mad and began defending herself by accusing Ted of not caring about his appearance and of being in general a despicable slob. Using the "should" is a sure button-pusher, since it often evokes childhood memories of parents lecturing you on what is right and wrong.

Another good way to sabotage negotiations is to use *absolute terms* at the slightest provocation. This escalates the conflict to the atomic bomb level. "Your alimony check is *always* a week late, I *never* want that to happen again because if it does I will immediately call the police and have you arrested." The use of exaggeration and generalization which this process involves tends to irritate the other person and may invite a retaliatory response. "Oh yeah, well you *never* have the children ready when I come to pick them up, and I intend to go to my lawyer to reduce my alimony payments because you're living with your boyfriend."

A sure turn-off to negotiating is being subjected to a *lecture.* The usual response, learned at home or in school, is to want to escape—anywhere but here! This is also true for *nagging,* a carping or hypercritical attitude which is guaranteed to bring negotiations to a grinding halt. As much as you believe that your comments are designed to be genuinely informative and helpful, if they are repeated several times and accompanied by pejorative remarks, they are bound to be misinterpreted. A common response is the *autocratic termination:* "That's it, I've had it—end of discussion."

The use of *blaming statements* will also lead to stalled conflict resolution. Accusing the other person, telling them that they are bad and responsible for all the wrong things going on, is sure to increase conflict. Often, the other person will get back by *discounting:* "I'm tired of hearing this stuff, you don't know what you're talking about; besides, I don't care what you say anymore anyway . . ." Another response might be the *psychologizing* put-down. "I know why you're saying that, your mother was always harassing your father, and now you're trying to do the same to me."

These maladaptive communication styles are usually the result of unresolved grief reactions due to feelings of loss and separation. The hurt and anger get played out in the negotiation process. By following the suggestions for expressing what you want and using effective listening, you can minimize these problems and maximize your chances for achieving a mutually satisfying resolution.

II

7

Means of Divorcing

Even when the turmoil of the breakup feels overwhelming, the pain usually seems understandable. You look back on your marriage, remember the emotional commitment you made, and expect to pay a heavy emotional price to release yourself from it. But the price you pay to undo your legal commitment may not seem reasonable at all: months or even years of paperwork and negotiations, court procedures and expenses, attorneys and other costly outside help . . . all to cancel out a single legal document, the certificate of marriage that probably took up less than fifteen minutes of your wedding day to complete.

No matter how you go about resolving the legal issues of your divorce, two emotions you are likely to experience are anxiety and frustration. Even if you find a completely supportive and reassuring attorney to handle all the complications for you, there'll still be times when you doubt the rightness of the decisions you make. And even the most streamlined of do-it-yourself divorces will have its moments of impatience and delay.

Other emotions will join in too: the residual anger you feel toward your spouse, your grief and guilt and hurt. And there'll be moments when you'll be tempted to use the negotiating table or your attorney's office or the courtroom itself to act out—or act on—the emotions welling up inside you at the time.

Some couples find that the formality of the dissolution process can be a help. "When Mike and I split up, all we had left of our marriage was a lot of loose ends. The court stuff gave us a timetable and even a kind of structure for deciding things. In a way it was depressing—seeing our marriage reduced to a pile of bureaucratic forms. But it also helped give me some distance from the relationship. Getting the agreement down on paper was a way of getting clear." *(30-year-old rehabilitation counselor)*

Your reaction to the process will depend very much on how well you and your ex-spouse can cooperate in going through it. The chapters in this section present your legal options—the methods you can use to come to an agreement and the issues that must be agreed upon. As you read through them and choose the ones that you think will work for your situation, you will also be taking a first step toward creating the kind of divorce you want to have.

There are three main ways to get divorced:

1. Doing your own (often with the help of a book or typing service)
2. Hiring attorneys to negotiate or litigate your divorce
3. Using a mediator to help you mediate the divorce

Each method has advantages and disadvantages. This chapter will help you determine which may be best for you.

DOING YOUR OWN

Doing your own divorce means that you represent yourself, rather than use attorneys to represent you. In legal jargon, you are filing for the divorce "in pro per." You negotiate your own settlement and file your own papers. The couples who take this approach are already in basic agreement about how they will divide their assets and provide for the children. They don't want to pay attorneys when the major decisions have already been made.

Couples who do their own divorce typically use a divorce manual or kit to explain the process and get them started. Because each state has different laws and procedures and some counties have variations on the state procedures (for example, extra forms to file), each state needs its own divorce manual.

How can you tell if doing your own divorce is right for you? There are a number of factors to consider.

1. What issues do you have to make decisions about? Property? Spousal support? Child custody and visitation? Child support? Do you suspect or know of any serious differences of opinion regarding these issues? If you do, you may need the help of a mediator or attorney.

2. After reading the divorce laws that will be affecting you, do you feel confident that you understand them? Often tax considerations, property division, or support guidelines are confusing or unclear. If you feel hesitant, further reading or consultation with an attorney or mediator may be helpful.

3. Are you prepared to negotiate with your spouse? Some people are simply too emotionally distraught to sit down and negotiate a settlement in a businesslike fashion. Couples who are in no hurry to get a

divorce sometimes wait a year or more before they finally address the technical requirements of dissolution. During this time, spouses begin to adjust to separation and often acquire a much better idea of what they need from the settlement to carry on their new lives. Some partners spend a few months going to counseling separately or together in order to speed the adjustment process and facilitate negotiations. If you simply can't talk to each other, or if you have strong needs for revenge, it will be impossible for you to do your own divorce. You will need a good attorney who is committed to protecting your interests.

4. Do you trust your spouse to deal with you honestly? If not, doing your own divorce is unlikely to succeed. You won't trust your spouse to fully disclose all assets, income, and so on. You'll expect to be cheated.

Couples who have no children, few assets, and short marriages that will require no spousal support often have little to dispute about. For them, getting a divorce is primarily a matter of paperwork. Some states have simplified divorce procedures for couples with short marriages and no children. These procedures make it easy for you to do the divorce yourself and cheaper for both you and the state because there are fewer forms for the state to process. Recently, California introduced a divorce procedure called a *Summary Dissolution* for people who have been married under five years, have no children, no real estate, less than $3,000 in community debts (not including car loans), own less than $10,000 in community assets (not counting cars), and own less than $10,000 separately (not counting cars). Couples that meet these requirements can follow a simple procedure that involves filling out and filing only two forms and does not require a court appearance. If you have been married for only a short period of time, check to see if there is an equivalent procedure in your state.

Having children and assets doesn't automatically bar you from doing your own divorce. But it does mean the process will be more difficult. You'll have to do more research on laws, taxes, and custody options, and you will probably have to do a lot more negotiating. But couples who take the initiative and responsibility for their own divorce spend much less money and often have a more satisfying result. What follows is an example of the process you might go through if you do the divorce yourself.

An Uncontested Divorce

Beth and Sam decided to use a divorce manual called *Do Your Own Divorce in California.* They agreed on how they would divide their property, who would have the children, and how much support Beth would need until she found a good job.

Beth prepared the *Petition,* which tells the court basic facts about the marriage and what she wants done, and the *Summons,* which is a notice from the court to Sam that a petition has been filed. Because Beth lives in a county that requires couples to file a *Confidential Counseling Statement* stipulating whether they want counseling, she filled this out as well. Beth brought the Petition, the Summons, and the Confidential Counseling Statement, along with a money order for the filing fee, to the court clerk. She then sent a copy of the Summons, the Petition, a blank Counseling Statement, and a *Notice and Acknowledgment of Receipt* (which assures the court that Sam has received these papers) to Sam. Sam filled out the Notice and Acknowledgment of Receipt when he received the papers and sent it to Beth. He did nothing else. By not responding, he was making it possible for them to have an uncontested "default" divorce.

Thirty days after the date Sam signed the Notice and Acknowledgment of Receipt, Beth filed the *Proof of Service* (which assures the court that Sam has been notified), a *Request for Entry of Default* (which tells the court that Sam is not contesting the case), and a *Financial Declaration* (which tells the court about Beth's and Sam's assets and liabilities). Beth got a date to go to court two months later. When she went to court she took the *Interlocutory Judgment* and *Notice of Entry of Judgment* forms with her (these forms describe the terms of the divorce and must be approved by the judge). The judge signed the Interlocutory Judgment, which made all of her agreements with Sam official and readied things for the final judgment. Six months after the day Sam signed the Notice and Acknowledgment of Receipt, Beth filed the *Request for Final Judgment, Final Judgment,* and *Notice of Entry of Judgment* papers, all of which are simple forms that must be filed to finalize the divorce. Beth and Sam waived the two-month appeals period that normally runs before the final decree.

Beth and Sam's divorce was simple to do and cost under $200. The only expenses were $10 for the divorce book, $3 for copies of official papers, and $112 filing fees.

Professional Resources

When you do your own divorce, don't be afraid to use professional resources. Some couples consult attorneys either to better understand their rights or to receive help with tax planning. In some counties, legal services conduct divorce seminars and support groups for spouses unable to afford professional help. An increasing number of divorcing partners are now also turning to mediators to help resolve issues where they feel stuck.

Meg and Hal were in the midst of a do-it-yourself divorce when negotiations broke down over spousal support. Meg earned $800 per month, and Hal earned $2,000. When Meg asked for $400 per month in support, Hal hit the roof. A friend recommended a mediator. The mediator explained how other couples handled similar situations and suggested some options. A review of the county's support schedule put the issue into perspective. Both Meg and Hal could see the range of spousal support courts in their area tended to award. With the help of the mediator, they agreed on the original $400 support figure. They had spent four hours with a mediator ($200) and were once again in a position to do their own divorce.

Divorce services have sprung up in some states. These are really specialized typing services for couples who have agreed on all of the issues of their divorce, wish to avoid the expense of paying an attorney to do the paperwork, and don't want to do the paperwork themselves. As a rule, nonattorneys who run these services are careful to avoid giving legal advice for fear that the local bar association will sue them for engaging in the unauthorized practice of law. Their function is to provide you with the forms and see that they are properly filled out, fees are paid, and everything is filed on time. Couples who don't have the time or patience to do all the paperwork find this method a simple and relatively inexpensive alternative. Technically, they are doing their own divorce. They have simply hired a clerk to fill out and send forms.

Divorce services tend to be found only in larger metropolitan centers in highly populated states. Anyone looking for a divorce service should look up *Divorce* in the yellow pages of the phone book. If no divorce service is listed, try calling a few of the attorneys or mental health professionals who advertise divorce counseling and asking them for a referral. You might also call the local bar association and ask if they are aware of any divorce services in your area.

HIRING AN ATTORNEY

There are situations in which a couple should not even try to do their own divorce. This is so when either spouse isn't sufficiently versed in the law to fully understand his or her rights and options. John and Kate did their own divorce two years ago and have been in constant contact with their attorneys ever since. Kate discovered one month after the divorce was final that she had unknowingly given up over $10,000 worth of pension rights. When she agreed to give up her rights to John's pension she didn't understand its value, nor did she comprehend her need for support. She has attacked the final judgment and it looks as if she will be awarded some more money, but she has already spent a sustantial sum in attorneys' fees.

An imbalance of power between spouses is a second situation where it's advantageous to hire an attorney. If one spouse is far more sophisticated or assertive than the other, the second spouse may need the protection of a trained advocate. Selma and Ron had been married for 30 years.

When Ron asked for a divorce because he was seeing another woman, Selma was devastated. Her role had always been that of a traditional, somewhat dependent housewife, and she had relied on Ron's judgment for most financial decision making. Ron brought home a divorce book and began dividing their marital assets. Selma listened and agreed to Ron's suggestions. Ron was trying to be fair, but just as always he was making all the decisions. As a result, the agreement Ron put together failed to meet many of Selma's needs. In particular, Selma wanted to get some technical training, but no allowance had been made for any of her educational expenses. Ron had left Selma the house, in what he considered an act of generosity. But the truth was she didn't want to live in the house; there were too many memories. Selma was unhappy with the agreement, but she didn't know how to tell Ron. Four days before Ron was going to file for the divorce, Selma went to an attorney. Ron was shocked. He decided that Selma must be trying to "bleed him white" and got an attorney who was known as a courtroom "heavyweight" to protect his interests.

A third situation where you might need an attorney is when you feel so guilty about the divorce that you're tempted to "give everything away." Mary and Ted had been married eight years and were just beginning to do well financially. Ted wanted a friendly divorce above all things and he was determined to keep attorneys out of the picture as much as possible. He and Mary negotiated their entire agreement with very little effort. Ted was willing to give up anything to satisfy Mary because he felt deeply guilty about initiating the breakup. Mary wanted to punish Ted, so she took whatever she could get. She got the car, the furniture, and most of their savings, and she stayed in the apartment. Ted took a single bed, a few pots, and $500. Today, five years later, he regrets his lack of concern for himself. He wishes he had secured the help of an attorney or mediator who could have provided some balance to the negotiations. Ted shudders when he thinks of what he might have given away if there had been a lot more money at stake.

If you seriously distrust your spouse, you should hire an attorney. Don't attempt a do-it-yourself or mediated divorce: these approaches require mutual respect and honesty. Mat suspected his wife of hiding marital assets. Examination of their small business's books revealed a great deal of activity in the accounts and large sums of money being moved from one account to another for no apparent reason. Mat wanted his books evaluated by a professional. The attorney he hired was able to use discovery procedures to determine exactly how much money needed to be divided. It was an expensive process, but Mat felt protected by his lawyer's efforts.

Couples who have a great deal of money or complicated issues to resolve when they divorce are well advised to seek professional assistance. Attorneys, mediators, appraisers, and accountants may be necessary.

Consider the couple with a small business, $200,000 in property, and three young children. They need an attorney to supervise the appraisal of the business and division of the property. They may also need an accountant to advise them about the possible tax consequences of each method of property division they consider. A mediator might also be of help with custody issues. Remember, creating a well-written, well-researched agreement will save you considerable future anxiety and expense.

There are good reasons and bad reasons to hire an attorney. Many individuals have a hard time facing the realities of the divorce: the loneliness, the lower standard of living, the changed social status, and the abandonment of dreams. Being in the same room with their ex-mate is just too painful. Handing the divorce to an attorney who will orchestrate and guide them through the process is precisely what these spouses want. Other couples know that they do not want to cooperate. They are angry and want to fight. They want the opportunity to unleash their anger for many years of frustration and pain. The attorney, in these cases, often acts as a paid thug who legally beats up on the other spouse. The divorce is likely to be an expensive process, both financially and emotionally. But in the heat of anger, expense is no object. What counts is grabbing as much and hurting as much as one can.

However bad you feel or however deeply you've been hurt, avoid litigation if at all possible. A court battle will consume the very assets you are seeking to protect. Homes get mortgaged to pay attorneys' fees, and college funds get eaten up by court costs. And worst of all, your children will be traumatized by the anger and blame which litigation always brings.

MEDIATED DIVORCE

Mediation can be used either as the primary means of getting a divorce or as a tool when you are negotiating your own divorce and issues become too complex or emotional for you to continue without help. Mediation is also recommended by attorneys in hotly contended divorces when a cooperative solution is the only way for either party to win—as is often the case when a couple is fighting over their children. Sally and Jim have one major stumbling block to an otherwise peaceful divorce: Sally is moving to another state and she wants to take their only son. Jim wants to keep their son with him. Mediation is the only hope they have to find a solution that both of them can live with.

Much like couples who do their own divorce, couples who go to mediators have a variety of motivations. They may do it for the children, to save money, to avoid adversarial proceedings, or to preserve the remaining good feelings they do have toward one another. Many people have known friends who began divorce proceedings bearing a minimal amount of ill will and ended $10,000 poorer and unable to calmly hear their spouse's name. No one knows exactly when it all went wrong. Couples who choose to go to a mediator want to be sure it won't happen to them.

Some couples who mediate have already fought in court, spent thousands of dollars in attorneys' fees, and see no end to the fighting. These couples are particularly bitter, but many also see mediation as the last hope to end a mutilating legal war.

Considering the benefits of mediation, it is surprising more couples don't mediate. But people going through a divorce are often more unstable than at any other time in their lives, and mediation requires a great deal of determination and commitment from the couple. In the short run, negotiating a fair settlement can be far more demanding than accepting the judgment of a neutral third party like a judge. Some couples do not want to shoulder the responsibility of deciding what a fair distribution of their marital assets might be. The choices are simply too hard and too painful to make.

There's no doubt that mediation is difficult. It's very hard to negotiate openly with a spouse when you're swamped with feelings of animosity, grief, suspicion, or guilt. But many couples prefer the uncomfortable mediation process to an exhausting adversarial contest. Sara and Ben got divorced after 17 years of marriage. They had done well financially over the course of their marriage, and together they owned a chain of weight reduction spas that had begun to do very well indeed over the last five years. Ben was extremely bitter about the divorce and did not want to work with Sara at all in coming to an agreement—but he knew that for the sake of their business he *had* to work with her. Sara and Ben chose a mediator who was willing to do a bit of shuttle diplomacy as well as mediate with them both in the room. As a result of their cooperative agreement, Sara and Ben are both quite wealthy today.

When choosing the means of divorce best suited to your needs, evaluate your situation carefully. Read the chapters on professional mediation and choosing an attorney. Can you discuss any of these options with your spouse? If you can't, you may have limited choices about how you separate. If you can, you are taking your first cooperative step and have a good chance of saving yourself both money and emotional trauma.

8

Your Attorney

Choosing an attorney can be the most important decision you make after you decide to separate. The attorney you hire will guide you through the divorce. He or she will have a great deal of effect upon the attitude you adopt toward that process, influencing both your actions and perceptions.

Attorneys have a mixed reputation in our society. They evoke the respect associated with the law and figures such as Abraham Lincoln. They are also distrusted, because of figures such as Richard Nixon and images of lawyers as ambulance chasers and shysters.

> CHICO: You're pretty shy for a lawyer.
> GROUCHO: That's because I'm a shyster lawyer.

Many people who divorce are dissatisfied with the legal representation they receive, and attorneys are aware of that fact. When a group of psychiatrists asked twenty attorneys who practice family law how satisfied clients are with legal services received during a divorce, 45 percent responded that most clients are dissatisfied.*

Some lawyers maintain the unquestioning trust of their clients. "My lawyer is like my therapist. He sits me down, asks me what is wrong, listens to my woes till I'm calm, and then we work on the problem." *(29-year-old florist)* Other clients never want to see an attorney again:

> When my husband and I went to an attorney, we were on pretty good terms and wanted to use just one attorney. She told us she could only represent one of us. My husband got another attorney and the situation went downhill from there. We had bought two

---

*Margaret S. Hermann, Patrick C. McKenry, and Ruth E. Weber. "Attorneys' Perceptions of Their Role in Divorce." *Journal of Divorce*, Vol. 2(3), Spring, 1979.

houses in the same neighborhood so that the children would have easy access to each of us. It was a nice plan, but once we had two attorneys things ran amok. The legal fees cost so much that we had to sell the second house and I almost lost my house as well. My husband worked for the city and was on leave. His attorney had him remain on leave so that his income would look low. I hadn't asked for any spousal support, and now even the child support is ridiculously low. The whole thing was a fiasco and I'm still mad. *(36-year-old store manager)*

When we separated we were at least civil. That's before the lawyers got involved. Her lawyer told her to take all the money out of our joint checking account. Mine told me to cancel her name on the credit cards. I ended up bouncing some checks, and I later learned she was very embarrassed one day at Sears. The lawyers advised us not to speak to each other any more than absolutely necessary, so we couldn't even try to work anything out. We just did what they told us, and what they told us made us enemies. *(40-year-old realtor)*

A shortage of material resources will often result in dissatisfaction with any divorce settlement the separating couple makes. When there is only a limited amount of disposable income available to a family, no matter how equitable the settlement is, both parties will be in difficult financial condition after separating. The attorney is not only the bearer of this bad news, but also an additional expense diminishing already limited resources.

THE FAMILY LAW PRACTITIONER'S ROLE

The traditional role of the family law attorney has serious and potentially disastrous limitations. Our courts' adversarial system was not designed to resolve family conflicts. Taking a client's side in a contest of wits and discovery, the average attorney may be able to use the system to reveal the truth in a criminal or personal injury matter. But the same aggressive attitude wreaks havoc in a divorce. Cases that could have been negotiated to a successful conclusion may end up in a protracted court battle because one of the lawyers has a focus on "winning." Such disasters are a primary reason why divorce work has been viewed as the dregs of legal practice by both attorneys and lay people.

It is to the attorneys' credit that 80 to 90 percent of divorces are negotiated out of court. Negotiated divorce settlements are clearly more desirable than litigated settlements. Going to court is extremely expensive. For a major struggle, you can expect to pay $5,000 to $100,000 in legal fees and court costs. And the emotional cost in anxiety, hostility, and delay is even greater. Nevertheless, while an attorney is negotiating for a client he or she must always be prepared to take the case to court should negotiations fail. The attorney's ability to threaten and potentially win a court battle often gives him or her the leverage needed to bring about an effective and fair out-of-court settlement.

The introduction of no-fault divorce in every state except Illinois and South Dakota reflects a liberalized public opinion regarding divorce. No-fault divorce laws allow couples to divorce on the grounds of irreparable breakdown in the marital relationship. No blame is placed on either party. No one has to be proved guilty of mental cruelty or infidelity. Property is divided in an equitable fashion; since no one is deemed at fault, no one is punished.

Although adversarial divorce proceedings are now being discouraged by mental health professionals, courts, and some attorneys, the system has not changed to the extent its critics see as necessary. Most divorcing couples continue to use separate attorneys.

Adversarial Relationships

In obvious and in subtle ways, the legal system and many attorneys direct divorcing spouses to see each other as adversaries. One likely result of this new orientation is a further widening of the emotional split between the already divided couple.

Communication problems are a common complaint. Attorneys frequently advise divorcing clients not to communicate with each other or with opposing counsel. This protects the spouses from making ill-advised bargains and revealing information that may work to their disadvantage, but it also promotes an adversarial relationship between the partners. Spouses' needs and intentions may become distorted as information gets passed down the chain from wife to wife's attorney, to husband's attorney, to husband. Arlene wants to live in the house for the *next year*. She tells her attorney. Her attorney tells John's attorney Arlene wants to *live in the house*. John's attorney tells John that Arlene *wants the house*. John becomes irate and yells that the house is half his. John may never find out that Arlene was only asking to live in the house for a year. He will react to what his attorney told him and begin fighting for the house.

Attorneys often find themselves functioning as paid gladiators in custody wars. This is unfortunate because custody disputes are the most destructive conflict any divorce can cause. Once parents begin to fight for the children, accusations, blame, and disparagement of the other parent seem inevitable. The adversarial system actually encourages each parent to spell out the faults of the other. Parents emerge from the fray psychologically tattered, insecure, and likely to never completely forgive each other. Ironically, the disputing parents not only hurt each other, but also do enormous damage to the kids they have been battling over. The children feel torn and responsible for the fighting.

Legal training supplies lawyers with little guidance for helping clients with their nonlegal problems. Some lawyers are natural counselors and make great efforts to attend to their client's emotional as well as legal needs. Many attorneys actively encourage clients to seek therapy or join support groups. Other attorneys prefer to regard their function as strictly that of a legal technician. Your attorney's orientation toward divorce will have a significant impact on the emotional as well as legal outcome.

Your "Best Interests"

The lawyer's obligation to look after a client's "best interests" creates the family law quandary. This rather ambiguous ethical obligation can be interpreted as a responsibility to guard the client's monetary interests, to satisfy his or her emotional needs, or to influence the client toward some course of action the attorney thinks is best. Unfortunately, these three criteria often require contradictory actions. The pursuit of a client's monetary interests may result in a loss of family harmony. Children have been "traded" for monetary considerations having nothing to do with the children's welfare. For example, one man offered his wife this bargain: he would not block her wish for sole custody of their son if she would accept a lower alimony payment. Disputes over the family house or a special piece of furniture can be the catalyst for a fight that destroys the last remnants of spousal cooperation. Yet many lawyers are reluctant to intervene to stop a property dispute because the client has apparently made the choice that property is a priority in the divorce—and a lawyer is paid to fight for a client's wishes.

When clients do not know what they want, cannot communicate, or cannot get what they want, the attorney has little hope of pleasing them and misses the gratification of doing so. Jake is an attorney who takes great pride in doing a good job for this clients. He finds divorce work terribly difficult because clients keep changing their minds about what they want as the divorce continues:

> I had this one guy who came to me and said, "Give her the house, I don't want it!" I talked to him about the future and about his rights, and he still insisted I help him give her the house. Six months later he came in with a new tune. He'd met a woman, decided his ex-wife had always been pushy, and didn't want her to have anything more than necessary. What a mess! How can I do a good job in that kind of situation?

Many clients abdicate responsibility for their case once they have an attorney. While it is important to listen to your attorney's advice, you should never lose sight of the fact that it is your divorce and that you are the only one who can negotiate, agree to a settlement, or choose to fight. You are better able to assess your needs than any third party can. The attorney you hire to represent you should carry out your wishes and reflect your attitude toward divorce.

HOW TO FIND AN ATTORNEY

Locating an attorney to help with a divorce is often a haphazard affair. Many people consult their own attorney or a friend's attorney. If they don't have any such ready contact, they may turn to the yellow pages or a local bar association. Attorneys who want to do divorce work frequently advertise in the commercial section of the phone book. The bar association may have a special listing for family law practitioners.

If a friend or family member refers you to an attorney, find out what you can about the attorney from that source. What kind of experience did your Uncle Max have with his attorney?

a. *He wrote a will for Max and Max was satisfied. The hourly fee was $80 and the initial half-hour consultation was free.* Writing a will is not particularly relevant to how the attorney would handle a divorce, yet Max was satisfied. This attorney is worth checking, especially with a free consultation.

b. *She handled an insurance claim for him. A real tiger in court. Max takes her all his business now.* Watch out! If she is a tiger with your divorce action your money may be eaten up and your children may be mauled. But go ahead and talk to her. She might have a very different attitude toward divorce and be a good negotiator as well. Any attorney that satisfies clients is worth investigating.

c. *She is an old school chum and a very nice person.* This doesn't tell you a thing about her legal abilities. However, if Max knows her to be an intelligent and sensitive woman she might be just what you want.

d. *He helped Max with his divorce. Max wasn't thrilled, but he did OK.* Max can give you an accurate idea of how this attorney works. Did he negotiate? Did Max feel sufficiently involved? How much did it cost? Did the attorney return calls reliably? Was he good about explaining what was happening?

Before You Interview Attorneys

To find the right attorney, first ask yourself what kind of divorce you want. Amicable, the least possible fighting, you just want out? Mediated, you want to work it out yourself fairly with the help of a third party? Angry, you are still mad at your spouse and you want to punish him or her by taking all you can? Uninvolved, you don't want to deal with it, you want a good attorney you can trust who will take care of everything? Sit down, if possible with a friend who has been through a divorce, and list what you want from an attorney.

1. Do you want a sympathetic listener, or would you prefer a no-nonsense business-like attitude?

2. Are you going to try to negotiate some of the settlement with your spouse? Do you want an attorney to give you legal information so you can mediate the issues of your divorce in an informed manner, or will you want to let your attorney negotiate for you? If your spouse has hired an aggressive attorney who is already talking about going to court, perhaps you need a good litigator.

3. Do you have a great deal of property or a high income? If you do, you'll probably want some tax advice. Good tax planning in divorce can give both spouses more spendable cash, if they cooperate. For example, alimony and a new type of payment, family support, are deducted from the income of the spouse who pays it and added to the income of the spouse who receives it. On the other hand, child support is not deductible for the payor, nor is it treated as income to the custodial parent. Characterizing such payments wisely can save significant tax dollars.

4. Many clients like to stay informed about the progress of their case. If this is a priority for you, make sure the attorney you choose is willing to send you copies of letters sent and received and can explain legal procedures clearly. Many more attorneys are now encouraging clients to participate in resolving their cases. This means that clients must take a more active role, rather than leaving all the work to the lawyer. Client involvement tends to reduce fees and increase client satisfaction.

5. Clients of over-extended attorneys frequently complain about the attorney's lack of interest and availability. "I can never reach him!" is a common report. Keep this in mind when interviewing an attorney. Some people insist on talking to several of the attorney's clients for insight into how well other clients have been treated.

6. How important is the fee? Do you want the best attorney money can buy or a moderately priced general practitioner? Attorneys who charge higher fees generally have well-established practices and may be particularly skilled in a specialty area such as litigation or taxation. Often an attorney who has practiced from four to ten years is less expensive and may have more time for you and your case. Don't pay for more expertise than you need. Don't settle for less either.

If money is a major concern for you, there are attorneys who do divorces for a flat fee. You can call a number of attorneys from the phone book and just ask prices. If you are tempted by a flat fee, find out what services will be charged as extras. Sometimes the flat fee is only for mandatory paperwork, while every additional letter or phone call generates additional charges.

Don't forget the things you want in a lawyer just because you find an inexpensive attorney. You're likely to be sorry. Changing attorneys mid-divorce is costly and messy. Some attorneys are reluctant to take cases from other attorneys, particularly when clients are dissatisfied. Even if the attorneys welcome the change, the new attorney will have to spend time catching up on your case and still will not have the first-hand information and experience of the personalities involved. You will be paying for this time and for this lack of information.

If your spouse has already chosen an attorney, it might be advisable for you to consider that attorney's reputation when deciding what kind of lawyer you need. If the attorney has a reputation as a fine negotiator or a courtroom wizard, you may wish to find an attorney with a compatible orientation.

When lawyers with different approaches to divorce must work together to create a settlement, their conflicting belief systems frequently escalate hostility. Attorney A, who regards herself as a legal technician hired to get the best settlement possible for her client, may have a hard time working with attorney B, who regards his role as helping the parties create a settlement that is emotionally healthy and fair for both parties. Neither attorney will be playing according to the other's rules. Attorney B will be angered by attorney A's exorbitant request for property. Attorney A won't understand Attorney B's unwillingness to map out an aggressive strategy for his client.

When one attorney is doing a quickie divorce for a fixed fee, and the other is being paid by the hour because he or she believes in doing a thorough job, time may be wasted finding a set of ground rules acceptable to both. Helen's attorney was thorough and wrote Joe's attorney numerous letters requesting information. Helen's attorney got terse, unsatisfying replies, often accompanied by unrelated questions which her attorney would then spend more time answering in further letters. Joe's attorney was doing the divorce for a fixed fee and therefore spending a minimum of time on the case, while Helen paid her attorney to write each letter.

On the Phone and in the Office

Once you have gathered a few names, found out all you can about the lawyers you're considering, and have started to think about what you want, you are ready to talk to some attorneys.

The phone interview is your opportunity to begin crossing people off your list. A brief conversation can help you determine whether an attorney is within your price range, has an attitude toward divorce that is compatible with your own, and is able to provide the kind of lawyering you want.

You are hiring this professional, so make sure that you are comfortable asking questions and that you understand the answers given. Is the attorney able to understand what you want and willing to help you achieve it? Do you have confidence in this attorney? Do you like his or her attitude toward divorce? Is he or she concerned about the children?

Concerned about minimizing your legal fees? Does this attorney prefer to negotiate or fight? What proportion of his or her divorce cases are settled out of court? How long has the attorney been practicing family law in your jurisdiction?

Having a local attorney is important. Judges are human and often have biases, and you want an attorney who has an accurate idea of how your local judges decide issues. Which judges tend to grant custody to fathers? Who is more generous in deciding the amount of child support? Which judges are likely to follow the local support schedule faithfully?

Many people feel more comfortable with a lawyer who specializes in divorce work. Some state bar associations recognize family law as a field of specialization. Attorneys who practice a great deal of family law or want to specialize in it can apply for this special certification. Depending on the state, certification may require the attorney to take a certain number of hours of continuing education classes or to pass a test. Attorneys who are certified as family law practitioners may or may not be more experienced or more competent than those who are not. A family law certification is merely an indication that the attorney has a special interest in family law.

Phone Checklist

1. Are the fees hourly, or is there a flat fee? If a flat fee, are there extras? Is there a special price for the first hour?
2. How long has the attorney been in practice? Where has he or she practiced?
3. How much of his or her practice consists of family law? Is he or she a specialist in family law?
4. What kind of tax experience does he or she have?
5. Does this attorney prefer to negotiate or litigate (fight it out in court)? Does the attorney specialize in courtroom law?
6. Will the attorney keep you informed, explain technicalities, and send copies of all letters?
7. Will it be OK with the attorney if you work out problems and conflicts directly with your ex-spouse? Will the attorney help you mediate if you get stuck?

ONCE YOU HAVE AN ATTORNEY

After you have picked an attorney, use him or her to your advantage. The attorney has the legal knowledge, but you have the personal knowledge of your situation. Remember that you are the employer and that the attorney is working for your best interests. Be sure he or she understands your priorities. Go in with a list in your hand, so that even if you're nervous you don't forget. One man described his needs to an attorney in this way:

> I want this divorce to be as painless and inexpensive as possible, I am angry at my ex-wife, but I don't want to take that out in the courtroom if I can help it. What I really want out of this is (1) continued stability for the children, (2) continued contact with the children, (3) sole rights to my pension, (4) no alimony, and (5) a fair division of property. I'm willing to do some trading and compromising, particularly around property and pension issues.

The attorney was grateful for the client's clarity.

LITIGATION

"The court system is only for people who can't settle their disputes in any other way."—*Anonymous judge*

When you walk into court with your attorney, you abdicate the last vestige of your decision-making power. Your divorce is now in the judge's hands. The judge is probably overworked and less informed about what is a fair settlement than you or your spouse are. Assuming that you don't unduly antagonize the judge, he or she will most probably assume that both parties have polarized their positions and split the visible assets as fairly as possible and will make a good decision. However, remember that in court "a good decision is one in which both parties feel shortchanged."

It is unlikely that you or your spouse will be pleased with a litigated settlement. The costs are astronomical, results are questionable, and if there are children the parental bond suffers further strain. If your spouse's attorney refuses to negotiate fairly, you may have no choice. In that case, assist your attorney as best you can by providing information promptly and staying abreast of the case.

9

Divorce Mediation

Divorce mediation has been hailed by Warren Burger, Chief Justice of the United States, as "the Brave New World of settling marital disputes." It offers separating couples an alternative means of making joint decisions without going through the bitter struggle of legal conflict. The separating spouses agree to negotiate a dissolution agreement with the help of a mediator, or mediation team, rather than employing legal gladiators to slug the settlement out in the courts. This chapter will help you to decide if professional mediation is for you and which specific type or style of divorce mediation is best suited to your individual needs.

MEDIATION BASICS

Advantages of Divorce Mediation

1. Reduced financial costs. The average contested divorce may cost anywhere between $6,000 and $10,000 in legal fees alone. The adversarial process consumes the very assets which the partners are attempting to divide. A mediated divorce costs a small fraction of the amount required for a litigated divorce.

2. Reduced emotional costs. Adversarial divorce tends to assume failure and assign blame. Anger and dissension are often exacerbated. Because family members may be deeply traumatized, the recovery process is slower and harder. Mediated divorce focuses on compromise rather than confrontation and seeks to protect *both* partners from unnecessary further hurt.

3. Protection for the children. Many of the thirteen million American children involved in divorce proceedings have paid a high price. Traditional divorce often divides their loyalties, forcing them to suffer the loss of a parent. In court, children have been used as emotional hostages. A mediated divorce lays the groundwork for mutual cooperation and subsequent coparenting.

4. A sense of empowerment. In a traditional divorce, the power to make decisions is in the hands of the court and the power to negotiate and propose solutions is held by the attorneys. A mediated divorce gives the separating partners the privilege (and responsibility) of making their own decisions. Rather than being an agent of conflict, the attorney functions as a consultant and an educator.

Principles of Divorce Mediation

1. The *couple* is the client, not the husband or wife as individuals. Protection of the family is the highest priority. Mediators are committed to doing what is in the "best interest of the children."

2. Mediation provides a forum for cooperative solutions in which everyone can have his or her needs considered. This is especially important where children are involved and joint custody (shared parenting) is antitipated.

3. Mediation respects and supports the participants' ability to make decisions that affect their lives. The separating partners control the results, taking responsibility for the final outcome, rather than handing decisions over to the courts or the attorneys.

4. The mediator acts as an adviser who suggests options and can describe the range of decisions that courts are likely to make about a given issue.

5. Mediation allows for maximum exploration of all options and alternatives and requires full disclosure. It encourages brainstorming, compromise, and unique solutions that are handcrafted to fit the needs of a particular family.

6. The mediator is an advocate for each party's well-being, but carefully maintains neutrality. Neutrality is important, since a mediator who is perceived as biased can no longer work effectively with the couple.

7. All proceedings are subject to full confidentiality. The legal consultant/educator will not testify on either partner's behalf in the case of a court hearing.

8. Personal growth is a secondary goal of mediation. In the process of working out an equitable dissolution agreement, couples often learn how to cooperate for their mutual interest and how to avoid past mistakes.

Who Can Mediate

The following is a list of considerations generally agreed upon by professional mediators. If you and your spouse can agree on all or most of these points, then divorce mediation is probably a viable option for you.

1. Are both partners willing to divorce? In all but a few rare cases, one spouse is more anxious for the divorce to occur (this spouse usually initiates the proceedings). It is natural for the other spouse to be somewhat resistant, perhaps hoping there will be a change of heart. When both parties accept the reality of the divorce, mediation is possible.

Jack and Anita were a young Asian-American couple who were married for three years. Anita was unhappy, and after several attempts to make the marriage work she brought her husband to a divorce mediation team for help. Jack was a Nisei (first generation Japanese-American) who described his parents as "traditional and old fashioned." During the initial assessment session, he was able to acknowledge his own dissatisfaction with the relationship and his willingness to separate. However, he reported feeling unable to tell his parents of this shameful "failure." To admit to a divorce would have meant a devastating loss of self-respect both to him and his parents. Mediation couldn't proceed. Anita eventually had to retain her own attorney so she could go ahead with the divorce.

2. Are both parties willing to work together to achieve an equitable dissolution agreement? Divorce inevitably means pain, often accompanied by resentment, anger, and bitterness. This emotional climate makes it difficult to imagine cooperating, but cooperation is exactly what is necessary. Professional mediators will provide the partners with a safe place in which to negotiate.

Bob and Mary had been married for twenty years. The marriage had been difficult throughout the past ten years, and divorce had become inevitable for the last five. Mary had used these final years to establish a small consulting firm. Bob had supported her financially and paid all the taxes. When she was ready, Mary made her move and announced that she wanted a divorce. Bob felt used and hurt and was at first reluctant to cooperate with mediation. He needed time to recover from the shock and to ventilate his feelings before accepting the reality of the divorce. He was eventually able to participate in the mediation, but Mary had to be protected from his verbal attacks.

3. Are both partners willing to consent to full disclosure? This doesn't mean that the partners are required to share all their thoughts and feelings during a time when both are vulnerable to being hurt. A willingness to share feelings is helpful, but the disclosure required here means that all assets must be put on the table. This refers specifically to bank accounts and business holdings, as well as insurance policies, retirement plans, pensions, real estate, securities, jewelry, and so on.

Sally had always let her husband handle the finances in the household. When Mike announced that he wanted a divorce, she realized how little she knew about their community assets. Mike reluctantly agreed to full disclosure at the insistence of the mediator. Sally was completely surprised to discover that they owned a number of valuable securities. She also learned that a service station owned by Mike and his brother was plowing profits into the brother's liquor store. Discovery of this information made it possible for them to reach a fairer settlement.

4. Do the divorcing partners have any common goals? Examples of shared goals are a mutual concern for the children, a wish to preserve a friendship, or a desire to protect the community assets that might be wiped out by an adversarial contest.

After five years of marriage, Sam and Agnes had no children, a small bank account, and two old cars. They lived in a rented apartment. Although irreconcilable differences made them want to separate, they planned to remain friends. They concluded that an adversarial divorce would consume their meager savings and undermine the trust necessary to begin their new relationship.

5. Are the divorcing partners planning to do joint parenting? This issue goes beyond the legal concept of joint custody. Increasingly, both spouses want to maintain an active parenting role after the separation. For these couples, a mediated divorce that lays the groundwork for future goodwill and cooperation is essential.

Al and Michele had two young children. Although both spouses were devoted parents, they weren't very good at being either friends or lovers: Al worked long hours in his TV repair shop, and Michele was consumed by the stress of graduate school. They wanted to separate and agreed to do joint parenting. Both respected the other's rights and wishes to continue a relationship with the children. The mediators helped this couple to work out a coparenting agreement which met their unique requirements. Mediation covered the issues of how much time the children would spend at each house (two weeks on, two weeks off) and how to handle holidays, child support, child care, and insurance. A specific written agreement protected Al and Michele from much postdivorce bickering.

What To Expect in the Mediation Process

Most mediators begin with an assessment session to see if mediation is actually the most appropriate course to follow. Assessment may lead the mediators to suggest that family therapy would be more helpful or that divorce is not inevitable. If divorce is the most appropriate option, there is usually an exploration of the five points discussed above. This is followed by the "paperwork." Each participant is asked to fill out information sheets and monthly budget projections which result in full financial disclosure. This phase may require the assistance of an accountant, a property appraiser, or a tax consultant, depending on the complexity of your situation.

You may be asked to get independent appraisals of the house, automobiles, or valuable antiques. In this way a monetary value can be assigned to each item, making it possible to form two "piles" of approximately equal value. If sessions get acrimonious and the couple starts to yell and scream or trade insults, some mediators have been known to resort to a referee's whistle to maintain order. When there is a lot of "old business" (unresolved feelings), it often takes a mediation *team,* with one of the mediators working exclusively on the emotional issues, to separate the feelings from the facts of the divorce. Acting as traffic cops, they may require the participants to alternatively talk and listen, ventilate feelings and communicate wishes.

Mediators usually seek areas of agreement to build on. They will help you to resolve disputes by encouraging bargaining and making trade-offs. Each partner is asked to state what he or she wants, and then negotiate toward compromise. Major disagreements may be left for later, to be resolved after a pattern of cooperation and good will has been established.

Mediation sessions do not necessarily occur on a weekly basis. Sometimes meetings may be separated by several weeks in order to allow participants to compile additional information or to digest a difficult decision.

After the issues are resolved, the attorney involved prepares a dissolution agreement. Most mediators suggest that both participants have an independent attorney review this document before it is signed. The actual filing may be done by the attorney, or you may be asked to file the papers yourself ("in pro per") to save additional money.

MEDIATION STYLES

Once you have decided that a mediated divorce will work for you, you will need to determine which of the many mediation styles will best suit your situation. Mediation may be done (1) by a single mental health professional, (2) by a single lawyer-mediator, (3) by a lawyer-therapist interdisciplinary team, (4) through "structured mediation," or (5) through a court-sponsored public mediation program.

The Single Mental Health Professional

This option is most attractive to people who are primarily looking for assistance in "working through" the painful emotional difficulties inherent in separation and divorce. The mental health professional (usually a licensed psychologist or marriage counselor) is qualified to help couples cope effectively with the marriage breakup. Typically, the mental health professional attempts to create a safe environment in which the couple may express feelings without destroying each other.

The focus of the counseling is often on patterns of communication. For example, the mental health professional might insist that the couple use "I messages," a technique which requires them to start sentences with the phrase "I think. . ." or "I feel. . ." rather than "You did such and such. . ." This technique helps each spouse to accept personal responsibility and tends to minimize blaming and verbal abuse.

The process is usually culminated by the mental health professional "talking the couple through" the divorce, step by step. The couple is often referred to a "divorce kit" which lists all forms and gives explanatory data for filling them out and information regarding relevant divorce law.

This approach is inherently limited by the mental health professional's inability to deal conclusively with the legal issues. In a 1962 opinion, the Los Angeles County Bar Association cautioned that marriage counselors who advise clients on legal issues may be engaging in an illegal activity: the unlawful practice of law. Some mental health professionals believe that any legal advice given or legal instruments prepared in mediation are "incidental" to their profession and therefore fall outside of the "unauthorized practice" prohibition.

The Single Lawyer-Mediator

In this option, both divorcing partners use a single attorney. The entire family (or marital partnership) is the "client," and the attorney will not give legal counsel which supports either party individually.

The basic problem faced by a lawyer who wishes to do divorce mediation is the legal prohibition preventing representation of conflicting interests. Single lawyer-mediators usually have the couple sign a statement stating that they are aware that neither party is being represented and that the final agreement should be reviewed by independent attorneys. The lawyer also makes it clear that he or she can only give legal advice to both parties in the presence of each other and cannot represent either party in later legal proceedings.

The major advantage of using a single lawyer-mediator is the obvious reduction in cost. Henry Elson, a lawyer-mediator in the San Francisco Bay Area, has estimated that the typical total cost of mediation is no more than one-third of that paid out by parties engaging in a standard adversarial dissolution process.

An experienced family law practitioner has a wealth of background and experience in dealing with complex issues involving ownership of residences, retirement rights, and inequities of spousal income. The lawyer-mediator can therefore offer valuable advice regarding decisions relating to valuation, taxation, finance, and support. However, as pointed out by

O. J. Coogler, author of the leading text on mediation, while lawyers have much to offer as mediators, they often lack counseling skills. In fact, many lawyers routinely send their divorcing couples to mental health professionals for emotional support.

The Lawyer-Therapist Interdisciplinary Team

While "team mediation" may involve two mental health professionals or two attorneys, the team is usually composed of complementary professionals. A lawyer and a mental health professional jointly participate in mediation so that both can bring their own particular expertise to the mediation process. The attorney informs the couple of their legal rights and prepares the draft of the separation agreement. The mental health professional deals with the emotional elements which might block an effective settlement.

Three of the authors of this text (McKay, Rogers, Blades) work at Families in Transition, a San Francisco based group of licensed psychologists and family lawyers. F.I.T. makes a point of balancing any power inequities in the divorcing couple's relationship. After the initial assessment interview, during which the mediation process is outlined and basic agreements are obtained, the couple is always seen by a male-female team. The female member of the team is the attorney, giving the wife a strong authority figure with whom she can relate.

Most mediations at F.I.T. are completed within four sessions of two hours each. Time is kept down by requiring the couple to do "homework," such as compiling financial information and filling out the *Divorce Awareness Scale,* a psychological inventory which allows the mediators to avoid stepping on hidden "land mines" (see chapter 2 for discussion of this scale). As a matter of policy, the children of the divorcing couple are not involved in any decision making, but are usually seen for an assessment session by one of the psychologists. Where potential problems are uncovered, appropriate referrals are made. The couple is encouraged to make a joint parenting agreement of their own, an agreement that addresses the best interests of the children as well as the needs and wishes of the parents.

Families in Transition is unique in its insistence on following an "open process" model. The interdisciplinary team talks openly together in front of the divorcing couple, sharing concerns, reservations, and even disagreements they have as mediators.

Structured Mediation

Structured mediation, perhaps the best known form of divorce mediation, was developed by O. J. Coogler. The dedication of his *Structured Mediation in Divorce* states: "I am indebted to my former wife and the two attorneys who represented us in our divorce for making me aware of the critical need for a more rational, more civilized way of arranging a parting of the ways."

As in the interdisciplinary approach, structured mediation uses both family mediators and attorneys. Their roles, however, are sharply defined, with the attorney acting solely as a legal consultant. The couple is seen for the initial sessions by a marital mediator, educated in the behavioral sciences and specially trained in the mediation of family disputes.

The mediation takes place within a context of rules derived from recent divorce and property laws. Participants are required to agree to 40 structured mediation rules which delineate the mediator's role and require a commitment from the couple. The couple is specifically required to mediate on a weekly basis and to agree to binding arbitration if an impasse occurs. They are also subject to a forfeiture of their retainer fee if they refuse to proceed with mediation or arbitration after ten days written notice. While this strict approach may dissuade some couples from attempting this style of mediation, others may derive a sense of security from the clear structure it provides.

Once the couple is in substantial agreement, a single attorney (selected from a panel of impartial advisory attorneys) is brought in to answer legal questions, finalize the tentative agreement reached by the couple, and draft the dissolution document. It is this concept of the impartial advisory attorney that makes Coogler's plan different from other forms of mediation. Attorneys on the panel are required to complete a mediation orientation program and must be well-qualified in the field of family law.

Public Mediation

Although many states established conciliation courts in the early 1900s, it was not until the mid-1970s that these courts began offering divorce mediation services. As court-connected and court-supported organizations, these services are free to the divorcing couple.

Several judges in California have developed over the past several years a policy of referring contested custody and visitation issues to conciliation court. The goals of this court are to provide a nonadversarial means of settling conflicts while maximizing the participation and responsibility of the parties involved. In addition, the conciliation court tries to help families going through the divorce process settle their differences in an amicable fashion that will help them survive the crisis of dissolution.

Since January, 1981, all custody and visitation disputes in California are *required* to be mediated before going to a judge. In San Francisco, court mediators exercise a great deal of control; both the couple and their attorneys are asked to sign a stipulation to mediate, as well as an authorization allowing the gathering of relevant information from school and medical sources. In the vast majority of cases, a public mediator's recommendation will be followed by the court. Nationwide, public mediation services are now available in nearly half the states, although power to make recommendations varies considerably.

While court mediation programs are an economically attractive alternative, most suffer from time limitations (sometimes as little as one hour prior to the court hearing) and restricted areas of jurisdiction (for example, in some courts only custody and visitation issues are considered). Many important issues such as support or alimony may never be addressed by public mediators. An additional drawback is that no real effort is made to work with the feelings of hurt, guilt, and anger which accompany divorce, so that tension between the spouses often continues even after the court decree is final. The resulting animosity often means that parts of the settlement are not honored. Support checks arrive late or not at all. Sometimes the separating spouse skips town and the custodial spouse is left to flounder helplessly.

HOW TO FIND AND CHOOSE A MEDIATOR

If you don't know someone who can recommend a mediator to you, the next best alternative is to consult the yellow pages of your local telephone directory. Check under the headings of *Divorce Assistance, Marriage and Family Counselors,* or the "Divorce/Family Law" subheading under *Attorneys.* (See the appendix for a partial listing of divorce mediation services available throughout the United States.)

Choosing an appropriate mediator or mediation team is a crucial decision, so you will want to interview or call several before making a commitment. Check fee schedules and ask for details of their track records, such as what percentage of clients successfully complete mediation. Above all, try to get a feeling for the style or attitude of the mediators as well as the type of mediation model they are committed to. Does the mediator appear to stress a mechanistic approach with no-nonsense problem solving, or do "people values" and an interest in underlying issues seem important? Has the mediator had adequate training and experience in the field? Remember, once you've made your decision it will be best to stick to it and stay the course even if the going gets rough.

Divorce mediation is not for everyone, but it does provide an attractive option for those couples who are willing and able to take the risks and make the effort necessary to achieve an amicable dissolution. The prime advantages are reduced economic and emotional costs. When children are involved and joint parenting is contemplated, divorce mediation is clearly the best solution for all concerned.

10

Legal Issues of Divorce

In addition to the emotional upheaval and the uprooting changes in their life situation that divorcing couples experience, they must also take on the responsibility of resolving a number of concrete legal issues. Two questions must be answered by every couple:

1. How shall we divide the marital property?
2. Should one of us provide the other with spousal support?

A third question will have to be answered whenever the family includes children under the age of eighteen:

3. How will our parental rights and responsibilities be divided?

This chapter is designed to help you define these issues in the context of your own divorce: the marriage that was, the ex-couple that you now are, and the new lives that you hope to build once the process is done.

The previous chapters have explored the various methods you can use to decide these issues. No matter what means you choose, the laws and legal precedents of your state will have a determinative influence on the resolution you reach. Your state's divorce laws will define the upper and lower limits of what you can expect if a judge decides your case. Your attorney or a mediator will view your individual circumstances within the context of the law and the many cases that have been decided under it. If you decide to negotiate property, support, and custody issues on your own, you will also need to be aware of the way the law works in your state.

Consider this example. You haven't been married long, and you want support because you helped pay for your spouse's education. If you were doing your own research, your first step would be to examine your state's legislated laws. If there is no law stating a minimum number of years of marriage before support will be granted, your next step would be to research *precedents* (all the cases involving similar situations that have been decided in your state). You may find that no support has ever been awarded in your state to a spouse who has been married under five years. Or that support awards have ranged between $100 and $500 per month for marriages of from two to five years. Or that in other cases where a contribution to a spouse's education was made, compensatory support awards have been made. In any case, this information would give you a good idea of what you could expect from a court decision and would help you to decide whether to ask or how much to ask for in support.

Anything that you and your spouse agree to should be at least as favorable as the lower limit of what you could expect in court—unless you choose to give up certain rights in order to achieve other goals or advantages (protecting the children, keeping a good relationship with your ex-spouse, postponing selling the house, and so on). But remember that a man or woman who gives too much away in order to get custody of the children or maintain a friendly relationship with an ex-spouse is apt to feel resentful in the long run. Any decision you make now will have long-term as well as short-term consequences.

PROPERTY

No matter what state you live in or how you are handling your divorce, you will have to divide all of your marital property. The first step of this process is to decide which of your possessions are marital property. Doing this may take some research and negotiation.

Begin by taking an inventory of all your property and classifying it as separate property, jointly owned, or undetermined. In most states, separate property is defined as property that you owned before you were married or that was given specifically to you during your marriage as an inheritance or gift. In some states, property that you acquired in your own name while you were married will also be classified as separate property, especially if that property was paid for with your own separate funds. One couple's list and classification of their property is given below.

Separate (hers)	Separate (his)	Joint	Part separate, part joint
Jewelry Piano	Indian rug Antique bed	Home Appliances China Two cars (one apiece) Furniture Three acres of land $1,000 in bonds Savings accounts	Stamp collection

Many couples find that reaching a basic agreement on how to classify most of the property is a fairly simple task. Even when there are substantial differences, a preliminary list at least helps to define the areas of disagreement.

Once you have listed your jointly owned property, you will need to establish guidelines for dividing it. Here you will need to become familiar with the marital property laws in your state. Most U.S. citizens live in either an *equitable distribution state,* whose laws descend from English common law, or in a *community property state,* whose laws come down from Spanish civil law.

Equitable distribution states. English common law divided marital property according to whose name the property was in. As other laws required that title to property be held in a man's name, marital property was invariably awarded to the husbands, and divorced wives were left with very little. Alimony was often the only means available under common law to balance the inequities of the system.

The legislatures of most common law states have now enacted some kind of equitable distribution system to protect against this historical injustice. But the departure from English common law has eliminated one unjust system only to replace it with a system that gives judges too much discretionary power in deciding how property should be divided. In most of these states, judges have been given few specific guidelines, and as a result judgments are unpredictable and sometimes even capricious.

Consider the case of Debbie, a mother of three children. She and her husband tried to work out a marital settlement agreement, turned to attorneys for help, and became so alienated they ended up fighting the divorce out in court. Her attorney was new to the county where the trial took place and didn't know that the presiding judge was infamous in the legal community for his bias in favor of men in divorce cases. Debbie found out the hard way: she receives no spousal support and the county's minimum amount of child support, although she and her husband had been married for over ten years.

Community property states. Usually found in the western U.S., these states hold that all property acquired during the marriage (excluding gifts to or inheritances by individuals) is a product of community effort and is to be divided equally between the two spouses. Even with these clear guidelines, an astounding amount of variation appears in court decisions. Discrepancies occur because *characterization* of assets as community or separate and *valuation* of assets are both often hotly contested issues.

Cathy owned a small dress shop that was doing very well when she and Tom got married. The shop did so well while they were married that she was able to buy 100 shares of IBM stock, worth $100,000 today.

Cathy claims that the stock is her separate property because it was bought from the proceeds of her store—which she owned before she was married. Tom claims that the stock and some of the value of the store are marital property: the store became so profitable because of the work that Cathy put into it while they were married, and this increased value should be considered the product of community effort. Cathy counters that she really did very little, she could have hired someone to do it for her for $5,000 a year, and she'd be happy to give Tom half of that. . . And the argument rages on.

Many couples get bogged down because separate and community funds have become commingled, and it's hard to remember what the two partners' original intentions were—if they were ever made clear. Bill and Sue live in California, a community property state. By law, all the money that they earn is marital property, unless they agree to keep their salaries as separate property or agree to use them to buy separate property. Sue inherited $5,000, which she used to buy land in her own name. The original cost of the land was $8,000, and she paid off the $3,000 loan for the purchase price with her salary—which was community property. She believed at the time that she and Bill had an understanding that the land was hers: title was taken in her name, and they had always regarded her salary as "supplemental income." But Bill now argues that he had no intention of making his portion of the community property she used to pay the debt a gift to Sue. He claims that he has an interest in the land—which is now worth $15,000.

The property issues your divorce raises may not be as complex as the examples given here, or they may present even more intricate characterization problems. In either event, no thumbnail sketch or overview of marital property law can give you adequate guidelines for making a fair division of your property. If you plan to divide your property without help from an attorney, you will need to take a close look at the specific laws of your state. Do-it-yourself divorce books often contain simple explanations of state property laws. But remember that the "fairness" of any division can best be determined by the two people affected by it. Any suggestions you get from attorneys or books should be measured against your own sense of what an equitable solution would be.

Determining Value

Before attempting to divide any substantial marital property, you and your spouse will need to agree on the value it should be given. How much is it worth? There are three commonly accepted techniques of valuing property:

1. *Replacement value:* what the property would cost if purchased new (based on current labor and material costs)
2. *Fair market value:* what a willing buyer would pay a willing seller for it

3. *Liquidation value:* what the property would sell for at a garage sale or auction

In court, furniture and equipment are generally valued at their fair market value, although many items may be worth considerably more to either spouse. Houses and real estate are also appraised at fair market value. Liquidation value may be used to value items that neither party wants, and replacement value may be used to value items that both parties want or need.

When you value your property yourself, you can choose the valuation scheme that seems most fair or agree to a compromise between two methods if none quite fits. Tom and Cathy owned a favorite desk which they had bought together when it was new for $800. They both wanted it. It had a few dings and was obviously used, but both of them were ready to take it at a fair market value of $500. They decided to split the difference and buy a second desk for $800. Tom got the new desk and gave Cathy $150 to make up for the difference between the two desks.

For help in valuing your property you may wish to use appraisers, check the want ads to see what equivalent goods are selling for, or consult "blue books" for car valuations. A local gallery or museum can give you a good idea of what your artwork is worth, and a jeweler can appraise your jewelry. Your life insurance agent should be able to tell you the value of your policy. The more valuable the asset, the more accurate you will want an appraisal to be. Naturally, you don't want to use up a great deal of money on valuing your property, so use your discretion in the amount and kind of outside help you employ.

1. *Household property* such as furniture, kitchen utensils, work tools, appliances, and pictures should all be listed and valued if including them will contribute to a fairer overall division. Some couples don't bother to value household property and simply divide it up informally on the basis of who needs what. Others set a value on only the most important items: a piano, antiques, large appliances, and so on.

2. List and value any *assets* such as bank accounts, savings and loan accounts, credit union accounts, money market funds, treasury bills, certificates of deposit, mutual funds, bonds, limited partnership interests, stocks, individual retirement accounts, Keogh accounts, life insurance policies, pension plans, profit-sharing or retirement benefits, and interests in any business, professional practice, or corporation. Outstanding accounts receivable that were earned during the marriage should also be listed, including money recovered from injuries, prizes and awards and any tax refunds due to you or your spouse.

3. *Real property* should be listed at its appraised value, including the family home and any investment property you might own: rental

properties, unimproved land, farms, ranches, or commercial property. Whose name is the property in? Even if the property is in only one spouse's name, it still may be marital property. Is it held in joint tenancy, tenancy in common, or as community property? Property held in *joint tenancy* can remain that way after the divorce, but you should know that the death of either of you will leave the other joint tenant as sole owner. If you hold a *tenancy in common,* you can bequeath your share of the property to whomever you like. If you are in a community property state, all *community property* must now become separate property or held jointly under another form of tenancy.

4. List *debts and obligations* according to who the creditor is, the purpose of the loan, who has signed for it, what portion of the debt was incurred during the marriage, the annual interest rate, the monthly payment, the balance of the loan now, and the balance of the loan at separation, as these facts are relevant to deciding what is fair. If the loan was for Tom's car and Tom is keeping that car, he will probably assume responsibility for the loan . . . particularly if he also signed for it. If Cathy took out a loan before the marriage in order to buy stock which has now been classified as her separate property, she should now assume responsibility for the loan payment. If the loan has been paid for with community funds during the marriage, she should probably also reimburse Tom for the marital property which was spent. If the loan was for the house and the house is now to be split equally, then the debt should also be split equally.

5. List any *personal possessions* (jewelry, artworks, collections, and so on) that were not gifts and are jointly owned.

Tom and Cathy ended up with a list that looked like the one given below.

Assets	Real property	Household and other items	Debts
Cash in bank 1. checking 2. savings Money market funds Treasury bills Stocks Life insurance policy Equity in pension plan Accounts receivable	House Store	Autos Furniture 1. living room 2. dining room 3. kitchen stuff 4. bedroom 5. study 6. other Phone machine TV Artwork Silver China Records Coin collection Plants Stereo Books	Outstanding bills 1. Mastercard 2. Sears 3. Diner's club Taxes Car loan Other

Take note of the specific laws your state has regarding contributions to education (recent cases have contested the issue of whether a spouse who has been put through medical school or any other kind of intensive training should repay his or her spouse for the support provided), awards for injuries that occurred during the marriage, or laws covering other special circumstances. For instance, in some states, if one spouse has a "gambling habit," resulting losses may be deducted from the marital property to reimburse the spouse without the habit. List any such losses.

Dividing Your Property

Once you have listed all your property and come to at least a preliminary agreement regarding its classification and valuation, you are ready to begin either dividing your property yourself or doing so with the help of an attorney. There are bound to be some disagreements remaining over whether some items are separate or jointly owned property. Set aside any items that you have not been able to classify.

Take a close look at the possible tax consequences of any division you consider. Tom and Cathy agreed that each would take stock worth $100,000 at fair market value. However, the *basis* (the money spent to buy the stock) for Tom's stock is $50,000, and the *basis* for Cathy's stock is $150,000. As a result, Tom will have to pay tax on the increased value of his stock, while Cathy will be able to report a loss for tax purposes. Certain *exchanges* of property may also have immediate taxable consequences. If Cathy pays Tom $50,000 from her separate assets so that she can retain ownership of a piece of land they bought together for $20,000, Tom will have to pay taxes on the sale of the property and his profit. Contact your local Internal Revenue Service office and ask for Publication 504: *Tax Information for Divorced and Separated Individuals.* However, do not rely exclusively on information provided by the IRS to interpret the tax consequences if a substantial amount of property is involved. The professional advice of an independent-minded tax attorney or accountant could save you a great deal of money. (See also the discussion of tax consequences in chapter 11, "The House.")

If you have agreed that you want to divide your marital property yourselves, there are a number of approaches you can use to find an equal basis for doing so. First, work with the items that you agree are marital property. Start out small. Each agreement that you make will save you attorneys' fees, reinforce your cooperative efforts, and probably give both of you a more satisfying result than someone else's decision would.

It is unusual for couples to fight over personal property. Typically, each party takes his or her own personal possessions. Still, it is probably best to discuss any items of major value to make sure that there are no disagreements. For example, if one spouse wears a very expensive piece of jewelry that was purchased as an investment as well as for ornamentation, its value may need to be included in order to arrive at a fair division of assets.

Household items can often be separated with little difficulty, as many couples are in substantial agreement about most of the items involved. When each spouse drives his or her own car or when there are shop tools that only one spouse knows how to operate, there may be no question of who will keep what. A reimbursement scheme ("I'll take the tools and give you $600" or "I'll take the tools and give you the piano") can usually equalize any disparity in the value of items exchanged. If Sue drives a valuable MG and Bill drives an old Datsun, they may equalize the exchange by having Bill take the Indian rug or the washing machine. Publicly traded stocks and deposit accounts are easy to divide because their value is clear. When there is no obvious way to divide property which both spouses want, a number of methods can be employed:

1. *The auction* is a good way to value and divide property when the ulitmate objective is to have each spouse end up with the property most important to him or her. The party willing to give an item the highest value puts it on his or her side of the tally sheet and any difference in the final balance can be equalized through the division of the liquid assets. Ted and Cher had five items they just could not decide who should get or how to price: two paintings, two antique pieces of furniture, and a flute. They thought about what each item was worth to them and bid accordingly. Ted felt that the flute was worth $500 while Cher was willing to credit $550 against her side of the tally sheet to get it, so she put the flute on her side. Ted wanted both the paintings and thought they were worth $400. Cher agreed. Now Cher had $550 on her side of the sheet and Ted had $400. They agreed that Ted should take the piece of furniture he liked best and they would call it even.

2. *The two pile system* or "You cut the pie and I'll pick the piece I want" is best for the little stuff like household furnishings and kitchenware. Cher and Ted agreed that she would divide all the kitchen items into two equal bunches and Ted would have his choice of either bunch. Ted agreed to divide the household furnishings into two equal bunches, giving Cher her choice of either one. After each had chosen, they then traded for any items they particularly wanted that were in the other's pile.

3. *Choosing alternate items* from a list is another method of dividing property that offers both spouses a chance to claim the personal possessions and household property they want. John and Judith simply went through their house and kitchen taking turns claiming items for themselves.

4. For valuable and hard to evaluate property, *hiring an appraiser* is advisable. If you decide to hire one appraiser together, agree in advance to abide by the valuations made. If you each hire your own appraiser, agree in advance to value property half-way between any two different appraisals.

5. Finding a third party to *arbitrate* property division may be a more economical option than going to court, but it takes the decision out of your hands almost as much as a judge's ruling would. You may not be as satisfied with the result as you would be with division schemes where you have more input into the decision-making process.

6. When you are in too much conflict to agree on the division of property, you may choose to *sell it all,* or at least the portion that appears to be indivisible. This practice is usually very wasteful. Herb and Beth could not decide who should get the oriental rug, so they sold it. They were both sad to lose it and both felt that they had been unable to get a good price for it because neither of them was particularly familiar with the market. An alternative might be *auctioning* the disputed items by having each of you submit sealed bids.

7. A final way to handle items in dispute is to simply *donate* them to the children or a charitable institution.

Wedding gifts are frequently divided so that spouses keep gifts from each of their respective family and friends.

Children's items should generally be considered the children's property.

Family photographs and slides are easy to divide. Any photos desired by both spouses should be reproduced at the expense of both.

Pensions and retirement plans (terms used interchangeably in this section) have a messy history in divorce. Social Security, military pensions, federal pensions, and the like have been handled in a wide variety of ways over the last twenty years and the subject of much controversy at both the federal and state levels. Railroad pensions have been distinguished from federal pensions, which have been distinguished from Army pensions, which have been distinguished from state pensions, which have been distinguished from private pensions. At one time railroad pensions were determined to be the sole property of the spouse who earned them, while federal pensions were called marital property. Army pensions have been batted around by state determinations that they are or are not marital property, federal decisions reversing state decisions, and new congressional legislation changing the outcome of federal decisions. As the law is often confusing and a great deal of money can be involved, pensions can cause more animosity than any other property issue.

Any pension or retirement plan, vested or not, may be marital property and should be thoroughly researched. (A vested pension plan is one in which the beneficiary has put in time enough to earn some kind of return even if he or she quits working today.) Hiring an attorney or actuary to help with this one issue is often advisable: it's enormously upsetting to find out after the final agreement has been signed that a pension worth thousands of dollars has not been considered. Remember that omitting any item from your property settlement agreement will increase the likelihood that you will have to reopen it in the future.

If the pension has vested and you were married the whole time the pension was accumulating, a 50/50 split may be appropriate. If you were only married for part of the time that the pension was vesting, you should divide the pension in proportion to the contributions made before and during the marriage. On the other hand, if the pension has not yet vested and will not vest unless the beneficiary works for a stated number of years, or if the pension will not be collectible until some time in the future, or if the pension payments will end when the employee dies, you may have a harder time determining its present value. In general, if a pension is not yet collectible, you will need help to assess its actual value at the time of the divorce. A professional actuary who specializes in pensions can give you the best idea of the pension's value. Some lawyers and accountants may be able to provide rough estimates. You can talk to whomever manages the plan and find out how much the employer has contributed over the years, any amounts due to the employee at the present time, and the plan manager's figures for the estimated value of the plan. Don't be surprised if the valuations you receive are very different from those provided by your spouse. Try to agree on a value that seems fair to both of you. Some court systems permit the judge to reserve jurisdiction until some time in the future when the value of the pension will be more clear, typically the date when the employee spouse becomes eligible to receive benefits.

If your pension or retirement plan is property that has to be divided and both spouses have their own pension or retirement plan, it may be easiest to do a straight trade. When this is not possible, couples often trade other community assets of equivalent value. If Sue wants to buy Bill's half of the house and they have agreed that Sue has a $6,000 interest in Bill's pension, she may take a $6,000 credit toward her purchase of the house.

If you have a *will,* you will want to consider altering it. At your death, any property you hold in joint tenancy with your ex-spouse will automatically become his or her property, and if you wish a different outcome, you must change the title of any such property now. Many marital settlement agreements and state divorce laws assume that divorced spouses will no longer inherit under a will made before the divorce. If you still want your ex-spouse to inherit some of your property, you should investigate your state's laws and make a new will in accordance with them.

One advantage of starting with the easiest issues is that when you go back to the thornier questions that you skipped over in the beginning you may have some new ideas that will help you get unstuck. Once you have divided as much of the property as you feel able to, you may wish to take any unresolved issues to a mediator, an attorney, or an arbitrator.

SPOUSAL SUPPORT

Spousal support or alimony is a political as well as a financial issue. Ninety-nine percent of the time it is women who receive spousal support. These are frequently women who have chosen to forego careers, follow their husbands, and raise children. What is a fair price for a lost career? For how long after a marriage should a man be expected to pay for the choices his wife made during it? How can a divorcing couple's goal of separation be reconciled with a life-long financial dependence?

Divorced women are the newest lower economic class in America, often retaining this status until they marry again. Many lack skills to find jobs. For those who have young children, the expense of child care, transportation, and business attire hardly makes a job worthwhile. Some women actually find themselves worse off with a job than if they'd stayed home and collected support or welfare. Delinquent alimony payments are epidemic and burdensome to enforce.

More and more often, courts and spouses prefer to sever the marital bond as quickly and completely as possible in order to avoid the post-divorce hassles caused by late or nonexistent support payments. Many women are so reluctant to rely on the man they have divorced that they give up substantial financial rights in order to free themselves from the relationship. Some wives negotiate for a greater portion of the marital property so that they can afford to waive their right to support. *Rehabilitative alimony* has become increasingly popular. The unskilled spouse receives sufficient funds to provide for training and self-sufficiency, and the payments have a cut-off date so that the contributing spouse does not feel forever burdened.

When determining what amount of alimony is appropriate, courts consider a list of factors.

1. How long was the marriage?
2. Does one spouse depend on the other for support?
3. What skills does the dependent spouse have and what are his or her chances of finding employment?
4. Are there health problems?
5. Are there very young children to be cared for?
6. What was the family's standard of living?
7. What can the contributing spouse reasonably afford?

Find out how your state courts treat these various issues. Some are reluctant to grant alimony to spouses married for under five years. The legislature may have passed a law denying spousal support to any able-bodied spouse who has been married for under ten years, or perhaps it is merely common practice for judges to deny spousal support when a marriage has been fairly short and the law does not state a specific number of years. One formula currently in use suggests that alimony should be awarded for one-half of the length of the marriage. During her 15-year marriage with Ted, Ruth had done some part-time work outside the home. Ted made $30,000 per year, and the best that Ruth could expect to make in the next year was $12,000. She was awarded $300 per month for the next eight years and was allowed to trade other property for the ownership of the house, which was half paid for. Other guidelines suggest that a woman who has been married over 25 years should be given support sufficient to make her secure for the rest of her life.

Once you understand your state laws, think about how you feel. Work out a budget so that you have a concrete idea of how much support will actually be needed (see the sample budget given in chapter 18, "Surviving as a Single"). What seems fair to you? A mediated or negotiated support decision is usually far preferable to a court order because of the continued contact alimony requires. If the paying spouse resents the decision, a court order may be meaningless. There are many men who would rather leave their community or go to jail than pay alimony to a woman they have come to despise.

The tax consequences of any arrangement you make should be explored. Depending upon your particular circumstances, it may be to your mutual advantage to characterize monthly payments as a "buy-out" period for certain marital assets rather than as support. Expert tax advice could result in substantial savings.

CHILD SUPPORT

Like spousal support, child support requires the cooperation of the paying parent to work. When both parents do feel responsible for the children, they can come to an agreement by working out a detailed budget of how much per month each child costs and then agreeing to pay according to ability, on a straight fifty-fifty basis, or in any other manner that makes sense to their circumstances. (See the chapters on coparenting for ideas.) Many counties have support schedules that suggest appropriate amounts of child support based on both parents' incomes. Some couples find it simpler to follow the court schedule than to work out their own more personalized payment scheme.

When children are young, parents sometimes decide that they would prefer to have the mother remain home with the children. Ron chose to take on a greater support burden and Sue chose to make do with a significantly smaller income so that she could stay home with their one-year-old son for the first two years after their divorce.

Don't forget to consider the tax consequences of the support schedule you establish. In a marital settlement agreement you have the opportunity to characterize your payments as child support, spousal support, or family support (a combination of family and spousal support). Child support is not deductible to the one who pays it, while both family support and spousal support are. If one parent has a significantly higher income than the other, support can be characterized so that both parents end up with more spendable cash. Once Ron became single again, the $40,000 a year he earned placed him in a very high tax bracket. He and Sue agreed to characterize the support he paid her as family support so that he could deduct it from his income, thus saving thousands of dollars in taxes. Of course, Sue had to report all the money she received from him as income, but because she was in a very low bracket her taxes were considerably less than Ron's would have been. You should also agree now about who will claim the child or children as deductions. Clarifying this issue can avert much future controversy.

CUSTODY AND VISITATION

There are three commonly recognized forms of child custody: sole custody, joint legal custody, and joint physical custody.

Sole custody. By far the most common type of custody arrangement up until five years ago, sole custody traditionally meant that the mother received full responsibility for the child and the father was given visitation rights. Few families were satisfied by it. The mother was overburdened, the father felt cut off, and the children felt deserted. Everyone has heard about the every-other-weekend daddy, and often the father simply dropped out of sight within a few years because the situation was so painful for everyone. More successful visitation schedules generally mean more time with the noncustodial parent: several evenings a week with him or her, long summer vacations, and so on.

Men's liberation and the equal rights movement have promoted increasing interest in and use of joint custody arrangements. Evidence indicates that children need fathers as well as mothers and mourn the loss of a dad who has ceased to function as a parent. (See chapter 13, "The Effects of Divorce on Children.")

Joint Legal Custody. Although often vaguely defined, joint legal custody generally implies the continued sharing of parental rights and responsibilities: both parents make decisions concerning schooling, major medical issues, and religious training. The children continue to live at one primary residence and are visited by the second parent. Parents seeking joint legal custody should avert future controversy by clearly defining its meaning in their marital settlement agreement.

Joint Physical Custody. While it does denote a significant sharing of parenting time as well as parental responsibilities, joint physical custody does not mean that the children must be shuffled back and forth between two homes on a strict 50/50 time schedule. The parents can work out whatever arrangement makes sense, be it 60/40 or 20/80. Some children spend summers with one parent and the school year with the other, some live with each parent on alternate years (particularly when great distances are involved), and some children transfer houses on a weekly basis. The real issue is what is best for the child. Some children need more stability than others do. For others, frequent access to both parents is far more important. One of the primary benefits of joint physical custody is that it eliminates the feeling that children "visit" their parents. No child should feel like a visitor at his or her parent's house, and no parent should feel like a host rather than a parent.

The real question for couples with children is how to create the best custody arrangement for them and the children. This is one situation in which the judge's order may be terribly inappropriate to your situation. Too many parents have used their children as bargaining chips to trade for more property or less support, and many thousands of children have been irreparably harmed as a result of parents warring in the courts. Studies are beginning to show that those children who adjust most successfully to divorce have parents who are able to cooperate and continue to maintain close relationships with the child.

State laws are responding to the studies that have been made in a number of ways. California has been the first state to put into effect a mandatory mediation law: before any couple can take a custody dispute before a judge, they are required to attempt a mediated settlement. Mandatory mediation has been very successful. Other states, such as Washington, award the child to the parent who offers the other parent the most generous visitation rights.

Depending upon the age of your children, you may or may not want to include them in the negotiation of your custody arrangements. No child should be asked to choose which parent he prefers to live with, but he can give input about scheduling and the things he will need at each parent's house. By discussing arrangement in some detail before including the children, you can spare them exposure to the more torturous negotiations. (Many parents also find that a mediator can be extremely useful with custody issues by presenting a broad variety of options and helping them to visualize the consequences of each decision.)

Creative custody arrangements can benefit everyone. For example, parents with two or more children can arrange to see their children on an individual basis and still get some time to themselves. Frank has been divorced three years, and he shares his two children with their mother. He has each child approximately half of the week, but he has both together only one-quarter of the week. The children are doing very well.

They still have each other's company half of the time, but they also get to see each parent alone one-quarter of the time. The older child, who had been feeling a bit overshadowed by his younger sister, has developed a deeper relationship with both parents. The children's mother is experiencing a new sense of leisure from her two nights a week alone. Frank is enjoying his increased participation in raising the children.

Parents who have different work schedules frequently find that joint physical custody is a method of sharing the children that can also save on childcare expenses. Ruth is a nurse who works an afternoon-through-early-evening shift. Ron has an 8:00 a.m. to 4:00 p.m. job. During the workweek, Ruth spends the mornings with June, their four-year-old. She takes her to a daycare center at 1:00 p.m. Ron picks June up at 5:00 p.m., feeds her, and plays with her until Ruth picks her up on the way home from the hospital at 8:00 and puts her to bed.

Chapters 15 and 16 on coparenting offer many more ideas for designing a schedule and resolving the other details of a joint custody agreement. When you do come to an agreement, be sure to get it in writing. A written agreement will help you avoid a lot of arguments and provide a clear structure you can use to weather future emotional storms.

11

The House

For many couples, the family home is their one major asset. All of the other assets combined don't approach its value. If it is a home you have lived in for many years, there may also be strong emotional attachments. Neither of you may want to leave a place in which you feel secure and comfortable. Handling the division of the house in a manner that satisfies everyone is a demanding, but not an impossible task.

Whose House Is It?

The first step is to establish whether the house is entirely or partially marital property. If it is separate property, division is probably not an issue unless the house is being traded for marital property. If it is marital property, most states' laws provide that each spouse has a one-half interest in the house.

In some cases, the house may be part separate property and part marital property. Sue owned her own home before her marriage, and she assumes that the house is hers. But since marital assets were used to pay the mortgage and improve the house, her ex-husband feels that he should be reimbursed or awarded ownership of a percentage of the home.

Sue's house cost $60,000 in 1970, with $10,000 down and a 30-year loan for the remainder. Sue and Bill got married in 1972. When they got divorced in 1982, the house was worth $120,000, and the principal due on the loan was $39,000. Bill can argue that he should have a 50 percent interest in the house, minus the $10,000 investment and the first two years' mortgage payments, because he and Sue have been paying for the house together for most of the time. Certainly they would have bought a house together otherwise. He considered the house their investment during the marriage.

In rebuttal, Sue can argue that the house is in her name, that she never intended for the house to be marital property, that the money paid on the mortgage was less than they would have paid in rent over the years, and that the loan is in her name, reliant on her ability to pay it.

It is easy to see how couples can get into terrible fights over who owns the house and how much each one's share is worth. Each state has a slightly different way of evaluating these factors in order to reach a fair solution.

In many states, the fact that Sue's name alone is on the deed clearly establishes her ownership. But it's also significant that marital assets were used to pay the mortgage or improve the house. Was this money a gift to Sue, or should it be reimbursed? Perhaps the nonowner spouse bought an interest in the house. Was there any verbal or written understanding between the parties? If Sue and Bill agreed to pool all their assets when they got married, and Bill contributed $15,000 to their joint bank account at that time (which is now being split as a community asset), it would be unjust to allow Sue to disregard Bill's claim to equal ownership of the house.

If you merely made contributions to the house during the course of the marriage, it may or may not be in your best interests to own a percentage of it. Generally, in cases where the house has not increased in value, you are better off calling your contributions a loan, rather than claiming part ownership. In the absence of guidelines spelled out by laws in your state, or a clear prior agreement, the exact nature of this interest must be negotiated.

Title. If you bought your home together after you were married, how does the deed to the property describe your ownership: co-owned, joint tenancy, or community property? The state in which you live may draw different conclusions from the deed about a proper division of the property. Joint tenancy and community property imply a 50/50 ownership, while co-owned property may be 40/60 or 10/90. Community property can only be the property of married couples and must assume a new title upon divorce, even if you choose to continue to own it together. Some forms of title automatically determine how the property is disposed of should one spouse die. For instance, any property in joint tenancy automatically becomes the property of the other joint tenant upon death. If you plan to keep the house in joint tenancy following a divorce, you should consider whether you want your ex-spouse to become sole owner upon your death. If you don't, you should be able to change the form of ownership fairly easily, either on your own or with the help of a title insurance company or attorney.

Commingling. Marital property and separate property often become inextricably intermingled over the years of a marriage. In California, money and property that cannot be shown to be from a separate source are assumed to be marital property. Did you pay the down payment with separate or marital property? Have you paid the mortgage with separate or marital property? Did the bank making the loan rely on your separate property or your joint salary as security for the loan? In California, if you answered "separate property" to all of these questions, the house would be separate property. A mixed response would require some balancing and negotiating. Each state will weigh factors differently.

When marital income is used to maintain separate property, it may be important to ask who was writing the checks: the spouse who owned the property or the spouse who did not? If the nonowner spouse did not realize that marital income was being used to maintain separate property, he or she should probably be compensated. Conversely, if the house is clearly separate property, shouldn't the owner-spouse be entitled to some sort of rental value? Now consider the down payment. Was the money used a wedding present to one spouse, or to both? Did each spouse contribute equal or unequal percentages of the down payment? Depending upon the laws of your state, any of these factors may influence your legal position.

Explicit agreements between couples about the status of the house can be helpful—but only when the couple agrees what the agreement entailed. Jim and Anne own a home in California, a community property state. They bought the house the year they were married for $60,000, and it was worth $122,000 when they got divorced. The $10,000 down payment was made with money that Anne had saved. The house is in both their names as community property. Anne argues that she told Jim at the time they bought the house that the down payment was not intended to be a gift to the community. According to California law, if this is true, she should get a larger share of the house. If she can't have a percentage of the house that reflects the money she invested, she wants to be reimbursed for the $10,000, plus interest. Jim states that he has no recollection of any agreement about the down payment and that he wants a full 50 percent interest in the house.

If you investigate your state's property laws and are confused about what kind of interest you have in your house, consult an attorney. In addition to explaining the nuances of your state's marital property law, an attorney can also save you money when it comes time to pay the IRS.

Coping With Taxes

Taxes are an important consideration when deciding how to divide property. For example, a spouse who exchanges his or her interest in the house for a note or other property or rights may be flabbergasted when the IRS taxes him or her for a hefty capital gain. Yes, the house has appreciated, and the spouse is realizing the value of the appreciation. Very often, however, the tax wasn't taken into consideration when the division of assets was made, and no money has been set aside to pay it.

If only marital property is divided and exchanged, you should be able to orchestrate a nontaxable event—that is, you should be able to divide things in such a way that there is no taxable capital gain. If separate property is used as part of the repayment, it is probable that there will be some taxation, and you should be prepared for it.

One way out is to immediately roll the money over into another piece of property. Even a simple installment sale of the house will provide some leeway to spread out the taxable gain over more than one year.

When it becomes obvious that a specific amount of money will be lost to taxes, try to take this into account in your property division agreement. You may be able to do something to shelter the money before it gets taxed, or you can plan to realize the gain in a year when other losses can help offset it. An attorney or accountant can help you create a separation agreement that (1) provides you both with more spendable dollars by choosing the most favorable time to transfer ownership of the house and (2) arranges things so that taxable transfers of property are minimal.

Valuation

Once you decide what kind of interest you have in the house, you will need to determine what it is worth. If you have owned the house for some time, a determination of its market value often requires a professional real estate appraisal. If you bought the house recently, or house values are fairly predictable in your neighborhood, you may not feel that you need an appraiser. Some couples can agree to a price just by talking to several real estate agents.

The second step in determining a house's worth is to calculate your equity. Subtract the amount still owing on the home and the cost of selling it from the current market value. The remainder is your equity, the actual dollars you could net from sale of your house.

Sale

Selling your house is a simple way of dividing property. Each of you takes the percentage of the equity to which you are entitled.

However, many people don't want to sell their home. One or both spouses may prefer to remain in the house, or there may be young children who need the continuity of a familiar home and school. Another consideration is the real estate market. If the housing market is bad, it might be financially unsound to sell the house, and a delay of sale may be in the best interest of both parties.

When One Spouse Wants the House

When only one spouse is interested in keeping the house, your first concern is to decide how to fairly divide the marital assets so as to leave that spouse with the house.

If the spouse interested in keeping the house has sufficient separate assets, he or she can simply buy the other spouse's half of the house. Consider this example: the house cost $50,000, it is paid in full, and its current value is $70,000. The couple has stocks worth $70,000, for which they also paid $50,000. In this case the division is quite easy: one partner gets the stocks, the other gets the house.

However, even when assets have currently equal values, the gains or losses from their original purchase price can have important tax consequences. Suppose that $80,000 had been paid for the stocks, and they are now worth $50,000. The partner ending up with the house will be able to report a $30,000 loss if he or she sells them. If $20,000 was paid for the house, and it is now worth $50,000, the owner will have to report a $30,000 gain if he or she sells it. In other words, what appears to be a fair distribution of assets at first glance may be quite unfair after taxes.

Frequently, there are insufficient marital assets for one spouse to buy the other's interest in the house, even when marital assets are supplemented by separate assets. In this case, more creative planning is necessary. If the house has appreciated in value, or a good part of the first mortgage has already been paid, the partner keeping the house may take a second mortgage to purchase the other partner's share.

For Seth and Judy, a second mortgage wasn't possible. They were turned down by the bank because their house was in poor repair. Instead, Seth gave Judy a long-term personal loan. There was a set interest rate, and Judy paid Seth back in regular monthly installments.

Some couples prefer to structure the buy-out of the house so that the spouse living in the house pays rent for a specified number of years while he or she accrues enough assets to pay for the rest of the house or to secure a loan. If you choose this alternative, be sure to specify the rights and responsibilities of the rentee and the rentor. You don't want to end up squabbling over maintenance and repair bills.

The primary goal when creating any agreement is to make it responsive to both spouses' needs. Do you need cash now, or would a regular income be more useful? Do your best to address those needs and then create an agreement that you both understand and both can live up to. Mary wanted to buy the house and agreed to pay the $500 mortgage as well as $400 per month to her ex-spouse—which left her only $200 per month to live on. Rather than give up the house, she decided to take on a couple of housemates.

Once you have arranged for one partner to have ownership of the home, you must decide on the most advantageous way to transfer that ownership. You can make the transfer before initiating the divorce or as part of it, depending upon the laws of your state and the potential tax advantages. For instance, if one partner had a major loss in another investment this year, he or she may want to include the gain from the house on this year's taxes.

Many parents and judges prefer that the custodial parent retain the home so that the children are spared a second significant loss so soon after their parents separate. The noncustodial parent will often accept a deferred payment or less than his or her full share to ensure that the children remain in the same neighborhood and school for a few years—as was the case for John and Sandra.

Sandra did not have enough capital to buy John's share of their house, but John was willing to let her remain in the house until the children were 18. They agreed to maintain co-ownership of the house for the next eight years or until Sandra remarried. They talked about what would happen if Sandra should ask a man to move in with her: John was uncomfortable with the idea, but he finally decided that Sandra's relationships were not his concern unless the other man's presence was clearly affecting the children badly. Sandra agreed to pay the mortgage, taxes, insurance, and maintenance for the home, and also to credit John with $100 per month for child support. If John found a house during this period that he wanted to purchase, Sandra agreed to help him finance it as best she could, possibly by taking out a second mortgage on their home. At the end of the eight-year period, both of them would have an option to buy the house. The price of the house would be determined by an appraiser whom they mutually agreed upon. If they both wanted the house, the highest bidder over the appraised price would keep it.

When Both Spouses Want To Keep the House

When both spouses want to keep the house, deciding who gets it can be a hurdle. If one partner wants to maintain an interest in the house for investment purposes, a co-ownership arrangement allowing the other partner to live in it may be quite satisfactory. When both spouses want a house of their own as a residence, some couples try to find a second house to buy cooperatively. When both spouses insist that they wish to live in the house, the couple can try the auction technique: the spouse willing to pay the most for the house buys the other's share for that price.

Often, however, neither partner has the money to buy out the other. If one spouse does have enough money to pay for half of the house, the spouse lacking sufficient funds may protest. Arguably, the partner with less money may be more deserving of the house because the other spouse can better afford to buy a second home.

If neither party is willing to allow the other to buy him or her out, other options are available. Couples may choose to live in the house on alternate years until one or the other finds a living situation they prefer or becomes tired of moving. A few couples give the house to the children, moving in and out on a weekly or monthly basis while maintaining one or two separate apartments. For many couples, this arrangement is simply too costly. Most ex-spouses also find that such an agreement makes it difficult to develop a life of their own. But the arrangement does give each parent a chance to work on more options, and as time passes new solutions often present themselves.

When the credit and housing markets are tight, couples have been known to convert their home into a duplex. This solution poses a wealth of potential complications. What would it be like to live in such close proximity to your ex-spouse? How would you deal with his or her new relationships? Any couple considering this possibility should arrange buy-out options.

Dinah and Ralph lived together for five years before they married and five years as man and wife. When they divorced, neither wanted to sell their house to the other. They decided that making the house into a duplex would actually increase its value. They realized that they might not want to be co-owners of the house forever, so they specified what they should do if one or both of them wanted to sell their interest in the duplex: they would have the house appraised, and each would then have the option of buying the duplex at the appraised price, allowing 90 days to find financing. If both wanted sole ownership, the one willing and able to pay the most for the duplex would get it. If neither wanted sole owner-ship, or it was not possible to get financing, the house would be put on the market after the 90 days had passed.

Whatever arrangement you do work out, be sure that it is practical. Can you honestly afford to maintain the house in terms of the time and money it requires? Would you be happier with a bit more freedom and a bit less responsibility? Do you want to be committed to living in the same neighborhood for the next eight years? If you or your spouse remarry, how will that affect the agreement you make? If you agree to a long-term loan, how will you feel if you remarry and need capital to make a down payment on a new home? A contingency plan for this situation may belong in your agreement.

Many couples create loose or unclear agreements that lead to diffi-culties in the years to come. The more businesslike your arrangement is, the better. Continued good will between you and your ex-spouse is im-portant, but if that good will should break down, your agreement should be capable of standing up without it.

III

12

Telling the Children

In the course of interviewing more than 300 children for his book, *Divorced Kids,* Warner Troyer found that in almost every case the children had received no warning of any kind that their parents were planning to separate. This remarkable discovery was echoed in the findings of the California Children of Divorce Project, a landmark study by Judith Wallerstein and Joan Kelly. After following 131 children of divorce over a period of five years, Wallerstein and Kelly reported that 80 percent of the youngest children studied were completely unprepared for their parents' separations. They were given no assurances of how they would continue to be cared for. In a disturbingly high number of cases, a parent would simply disappear while a child was sleeping or away from home.

One child reported that she had been sent to a neighbor's house on a particular afternoon to play. "They were fighting and I was sent to Martha's. I came home after dinner and mom said daddy was gone. I didn't believe her, so she showed me his empty closet." Another child, who had experienced great trouble sleeping since the divorce, told how she'd been awakened one night to a lot of banging and loud whispers. In the morning her father's chair was gone, her parents' bed, and "a lot of other stuff." A week later, her father came to say goodbye. He had moved to a town some seventy miles away.

Why Parents Fear Telling Their Children

Many parents fear that their children are "too young" to be told. As one mother put it, "How could we tell a three-year-old about the pain we felt? How could we burden her with our own fear and anger?" Most professionals agree that if a child is old enough to recognize a parent's existence and has some grasp of language, he is old enough to be told.

Even preschoolers can understand that mommy and daddy have been angry and unhappy. They can grasp that one of you will move, and that both of you will continue to provide care, attention, and love. Some parents use the excuse that a child is too young to understand as a way of putting off a painful confrontation. The truth is that a child is almost always aware that something is wrong. And sooner or later the child must endure the trauma of a disrupted family. Your child needs to know what is going to happen and how it will affect him.

Many parents delay telling their children because they can't decide on the appropriate time. Should they talk about the separation a day, a week, a month before the actual departure? Should they wait until one parent has actually moved out? The following two guidelines may help with the time element:

1. The best time to tell the children is when a *definite* decision for separation has been made. Usually the final decision is made a few weeks to a month prior to the event. This allows the children time to ask questions, express feelings, and get important reassurance from both parents. If you only decide the night before, tell the children then. Don't make them wake up to a fait accompli the next day. Telling the children too soon, when you are only fantasizing or considering a separation, is also a mistake. Too much lead time contributes to denial. The children will tend to "forget" about the separation and be traumatized all over again when your plans are finally complete.

2. Tell your children when they ask. If they are old enough and concerned enough to ask, they deserve real answers. Without definite information from you, a child will simply make up his own answers. And very often the answer will be that he has done something wrong or is being rejected. A little girl named Ginny, in the absence of any definite information, decided that mommy had left because she was tired of washing the sheets after Ginny wet the bed. George felt that his father had decided to replace him "with a better family somewhere else."

Many parents are confused about *how* to tell the children—separately or all together, with one or both parents present. The ideal way to tell the children is at a "family meeting" where everyone is present. When both parents participate in telling the children, it gives the message that mom and dad will both continue to act as parents despite the separation. As one 12-year-old put it, "We asked them a lot of questions. We were screaming 'How could you?' and everything. But they hung in and you could tell they were really worried about us."

Telling all of the children at the same time also helps them develop a sense of closeness as they share feelings and ask questions. They can learn how their reactions are similar and different and can begin to give each other a measure of support. Your goal should be to create an ethic of "This is painful, but we're all in it together."

A family meeting to tell the children will obviously not be the final word. Discussions will continue—between the children, between parent and child. In later conversations with individual children, you can make separate explanations that take into account age and personality differences. A very young child may need to hear over and over exactly what arrangements are being made for his care. Because safety needs are uppermost for preschoolers, this emphasis on who will feed him, where he will live, how often he will see the second parent, and so on is of primary importance. Older children may need to hear more about your efforts to save the marriage and to be reassured that you won't force them to take sides.

Perhaps the greatest inhibition when trying to explain separation is the fear of saying too much. Parents are uncertain how to explain the erosion of love or how to describe their hurt and distrust. Sexual problems, affairs, the yearning for growth or freedom, the loneliness, the large and small betrayals all seem too complex and "grown-up" to share with children. The time of separation is also typified by a good measure of anger and blame, and it may seem an impossible task to describe your marital problems to the kids nonpejoratively.

Wallerstein and Kelly found that children coped better with divorce when they understood the event which led to the decision. The child's ability to deal with trauma was strengthened when he saw that the divorce was purposeful and rationally undertaken and that it was a carefully considered solution to the family's problems.

Telling your child the truth about what led to the separation enhances trust. Deceiving the child or "dressing up" your conflicts leads to confusion and distrust. It's OK to tell a child that mommy and daddy had problems in their sexual relationship, or that daddy became involved with someone else, or that mommy felt lonely. The description of the problems should be straightforward and nonjudgmental. You should also include information about your attempts to improve and save the marriage.

Jean, a 30-year-old computer programmer, told how she dealt with the difficult issue of her husband's homosexuality. "We told them that Bob had always been attracted to other men and that sometimes he'd had brief relationships with them. We said that it had affected our own sexual relationship and that I'd withdrawn because I didn't know how to cope with it. Bob said he needed to be free to explore his feelings toward men. We said we'd been in a lot of pain, and while we couldn't stay together, we'd both continue to love and take care of our kids." Notice that

Jean didn't blame Bob or turn him into a bad person. She simply stated the facts, while reassuring the children that they wouldn't lose either parent.

You don't need to be *explicit* about affairs, impotence, or homosexuality, but you can acknowledge these problems if they exist. It's better for a child to hear things directly from his parents than to fantasize his own nightmare or hear it from someone else. Your goal should be to give as much accurate information to children as possible, to create an atmosphere of open communication where children can ask questions and get real answers.

A particularly ticklish issue is whether you should reveal which parent initiated the divorce. The initiating parent naturally fears that the children will place all the blame on him or her and that the parent who opposed separation will have an opportunity to appear as the blameless victim. The best policy once again is to be open. Sooner or later the children are bound to learn who precipitated the divorce. And if you don't choose when to tell them, they will probably learn in the context of an angry or resentful attack. Discussing the issue openly, with both parents present, takes away some of its sting. As one child put it, "I know it was Daddy who decided to leave, but he still loves us."

Almost every parent fears the inevitable pain a child will feel when he learns of the separation. The most dreaded reaction is anger. A rejecting, enraged child adds enormous stress at a time when emotions are already raw. Wallerstein and Kelly found that fewer than 10 percent of children welcomed the divorce, while 75 percent strongly opposed it. There's no doubt that the children will be unhappy. Some will run screaming through the house, some will retreat to their rooms, some will cry and beg you to reconsider, some will threaten and berate. Fully a third of the younger children will simply deny or ignore what they've been told.

No matter how raw you feel, no matter how hard it is to face your children, it is a job that must be done—not just as an announcement that must be made, but as the beginning of a process where children can express feelings, get reassurance, and gradually integrate this enormously important change into their lives.

Guidelines for Telling the Children

Here are eight specific suggestions for telling children about your separation plans:

1. Tell the children *clearly* and *directly* what divorce means. Tell them in an understandable way what problems and issues have led you to the decision. Be prepared to repeat this information several times before the younger children really acknowledge what's happened. Try to show them that your decision comes from much careful thought about the marriage and not from whim or impulse.

2. Describe some of your attempts to protect and improve your marriage. One woman explained to her children how four months of counseling had led her to the inescapable feeling that very little would ever change in the marriage.

3. Emphasize that both parents will continue to love and care for the children. Be specific. Share your tentative decisions about visitation or shared custody.

4. Do not assess blame. If the children are told that there was an affair, acknowledge that it was a symptom of the marital unhappiness. Stress that each parent has been hurt in his or her own way and that each has felt pain. If you're angry, acknowledge it, but don't express your rage and blame to the kids. When you blame, you are tacitly asking your children to choose sides, to form a pathological alliance that labels one parent good and the other bad. As a result of such an alliance, a child may not only lose a parent, but may also begin rejecting parts of himself that are "just like daddy" or "just like mommy."

5. Try to describe any changes the children can expect in their day-to-day experience. Let them know where they will live, whether they will continue at the same school, how often they will visit or spend the night with the second (noncustodial) parent. Children often appear to worry a great deal about money, so let them know if finances will be pinched in any way that may affect them (guitar lessons, summer camp, mommy going off to work or working more hours). Warn the children if it looks like their primary parent may be in some way less available (going into a school or training program, returning to work, and so on). Give specific reassurance about who will buy and cook the meals, who will drive them to school, who will tuck them into bed. Little children, especially, worry about not having enough to eat and being left alone. Addressing these concerns is very comforting for them. If any living arrangements remain indefinite, frankly admit it. But reassure the children that all decisions will be immediately and openly discussed with them. Let them know that both parents are working to solve the inevitable problems and that order will be restored just as soon as possible.

6. It is important to emphasize that the children in no way caused the divorce and are not responsible for problems between their parents. Explain that you are divorcing each other, not your kids. It is equally important to let children know that nothing they can do can bring about a reconciliation. Little children often harbor fantasies of mending your broken marriage. They plot and scheme and hope. One six-year-old kept moving his father's picture onto his mother's night table. This daily ritual continued until the picture was hidden away. Tell your children very directly that you have made a careful, adult decision to separate and are unlikely to change your minds.

7. Assure your children that they will always remain free to love both parents. No pressure will be brought to reject one parent in order to continue getting nurtured by the other.

8. Encourage your children to ask questions. Not just at the beginning, but throughout the long process of adjusting to a separation. Allow them to express their feelings. Let them know you are listening by repeating back in your own words the concerns they express to you.

13

Effects of Divorce on Children

Over 60 percent of couples seeking a divorce have children still living at home. For these children, the breakup of the family begins a period of unparalleled stress and psychological pain. The first acute shock is often followed by intense fears, anger, and grieving. Wallerstein and Kelly, in their California study, found that one-half of all children experienced serious distress and felt their lives to be "completely disrupted" at the time of separation.

Few children in the study were relieved by the decision to separate. This was true despite the fact that 40 percent of the father/child relationships and 25 percent of the mother/child relationships were characterized as extremely poor, marked by neglect and threats of abuse. No matter how bad the family was, children felt it gave them vital support and protection. Even when children witnessed repeated spouse abuse (as was the case for 25 percent), most still preferred a bitter and violent family to the unknown terrors of a "broken home."

Divorce trauma for children involves far more than the removal of one parent from the house. Many children suffer a sudden and disturbing remoteness from the parent who stays behind. As one mother reported, "I'm depressed, I'm anxious, I'm overwhelmed. It never lets up. And Leah gets the short end of it." Tasks that had been shared by two are now the responsibility of one. As the primary parent struggles to keep emotional balance and still manage the home, children receive less attention and energy. During a time when they need more support and nurturing, they often do without.

Following separation, an income that was sufficient for one household must now be stretched over two. Many women feel compelled either to train for new careers or to resume an old one. The effect on children is that mom is suddenly much less available. She's not there after school. And all the little afternoon rituals, all those important and nourishing interactions get lost.

The noncustodial parent is also obviously less available. Despite the critical importance of staying involved, the vast majority of fathers tend to visit infrequently. University of Pennsylvania sociologists Frank Furstenberg and Christina Nord surveyed children between the ages of eleven and sixteen. They found that only 16 percent were visited by their fathers as often as once a week. Wallerstein and Kelly found that 60 percent of the fathers studied visited less than once a week following separation; 25 percent visited erratically and infrequently (less than once a month). Nine- to twelve-year-olds were particularly deprived: one-half of the fathers of children in this age group visited infrequently. A child who is used to seeing a parent every day experiences a deep sense of loss when forced to wait weeks between visits. For most children, and particularly for boys, infrequent and erratic visits deepen the anger and sense of rejection they feel.

In addition to parents' increased remoteness and unavailability, children are often forced to contend with frightening displays of rage and blaming. Badmouthing and backbiting were common for approximately half of the mothers and fathers in the Wallerstein and Kelly study. In most cases, embittered parents simply failed to shield their children from the emotional chaos surrounding the separation. Children heard their fathers attacked as "liars, bastards, terrible parents, unreliable, disgusting, and crazy." They heard their mothers dismissed as "whores, unfit, drunken bitches, greedy, sexually inadequate, and crazy."

Aside from the trauma of the actual breakup, children are most seriously distressed by the bitterness they are forced to witness and encouraged to join. Children of parents who rage and backbite tend to be extremely anxious. They obsess about the content of the fights, worry about the future, and are torn by their loyalties to both parents.

Major Themes

Wallerstein and Kelly identified six major themes in the responses of the children they studied:

1. *A pervasive sense of loss.* One-half of the children were tearful and moody. One-third showed depressive symptoms such as sleeplessness, restlessness, and difficulty concentrating.

2. *Anxiety.* Three-quarters of the children worried that their basic needs would not be attended to. One-third feared that their mothers would abandon them. Most felt that the world had become uncertain and unpredictable. They feared being left alone. They worried about money and about their parents' emotional and physical health.

3. *Feeling rejected.* Half of the children reported feeling rejected by one or both parents.

4. *Loneliness.* Two-thirds of the children longed for the absent father, and many were preoccupied with fantasies of reconciliation. In general, children received less attention from both parents.

5. *Anger.* One-quarter of the children studied showed symptoms of explosive rage. One-third of all children reported feeling extremely angry. For the majority, the anger was directed at the absent father.

6. *Conflicted loyalties.* Two-thirds of the parents studied competed for their children's affection and allegiance. The children walked a tightrope, afraid that enjoyment and intimacy with one parent might seem a betrayal of the other.

Age Differences

Wallerstein and Kelly found that children of different ages had very different responses to divorce. Four age groups were studied: preschoolers, six- to eight-year-olds, nine- to twelve-year-olds, and teenagers. Preschoolers (three- to five-year-olds) were fearful of being abandoned. They often became anxious at bedtime and exhibited disturbed sleep. During the day they were clinging and cranky and showed increased irritability and aggressiveness toward other children. Preschoolers often regressed to earlier habits such as bedwetting, thumb sucking, or carrying security blankets. Masturbatory activity increased. Some children denied that a parent had left, while others spent hours fantasizing of a father's return. Many of the preschoolers blamed themselves for the breakup. One child felt that her play had been too noisy, while another thought that daddy didn't like her dog.

The six- to eight-year-olds felt the most intense sadness of any age group. Unlike younger children, who used denial and fantasy as a defense, these children were often on the brink of tears. A great yearning for the departed parent accompanied their sadness. Half of the children missed their fathers intensely. Many felt abandoned and grieved openly. Although one-quarter of the children were under pressure from mothers to reject their dads, few criticized or expressed anger to their fathers.

Many of the children in this group worried about being left without a family or deprived of food and toys. Half slipped significantly in school performance. In contrast to the younger group, most of these children denied feeling any responsibility for the divorce. But most continued to wish for a reconciliation and clung to such fantasies even after the remarriage of one or both parents.

The reaction of the nine- to twelve-year-olds was predominantly anger. This anger was usually directed toward the parent who appeared responsible for the divorce. One-fifth of the children in this age group were seduced into a strong alliance with one parent against the other. Alignments with the mother occurred in twice as many cases as alignments with the father. Particularly susceptible to being caught up in one parent's anger and rage, this age group became faithful allies and agents in parental wars. The nine- to twelve-year-olds also grieved and felt anxious and lonely, but these feelings were less marked than their anger.

Teenagers (thirteen- to eighteen-year-olds) expressed anger about their parents' dating, which they experienced as competition with their own emerging sexuality. They also felt anxiety about whether the breakup foreshadowed failure in their own relationships. Like the youngest children, many adolescents experienced a deep sense of loss. They reported feelings of emptiness, troubled dreams, difficulty concentrating, and chronic fatigue. These symptoms of mourning reflect a grief for the lost family of childhood.

Approximately one-third of the teenagers used the divorce as a catalyst for growing up. They took on more household responsibilities and helped in the care of younger children. They showed increased sensitivity and maturity in their relationships. Another third reacted by pulling away and distancing themselves from the family crisis. They displayed a marked increase in both social and sexual activities, often as a way of acting out anger toward their parents.

Sex Differences

Boys tend to respond to separation with more grief and sadness than girls of the same age. The impact of divorce is also more pervasive and lasting for boys. This may be so because boys tend to feel very rejected by their fathers. Many see themselves stuck with mom because dad doesn't want them anymore. As one boy put it, "I'm here because he wouldn't get an extra room for me."

A second reason for the heavier toll on boys is that divorce often disrupts the process of identification that a boy experiences with his dad. His father, whom he once idealized, has abandoned him and may now be condemned by his mother. To "be like dad" suddenly means being the one who betrayed the family, the one who failed, and continued identification may threaten the boy's relationship with the primary parent.

A third reason noted by Wallerstein and Kelly is that girls were found to be treated with better consideration by their mothers. High levels of bitterness and anger may lead some mothers to perceive male children as similar to the rejected spouse. This finding was corroborated by a study conducted in the San Francisco Bay Area by Eleanor Beth Karp. She found that boys in single custody perceived more negative feelings directed toward them from their mothers than girls did. She also found that girls in joint custody had higher self-esteem than boys had and also felt more positive parental involvement.

In the eighteen-month follow-up to the Wallerstein and Kelly study, girls were clearly the better adjusted. Nearly twice as many girls as boys had improved in overall functioning since the initial assessment. Boys were significantly more stressed in the postdivorce families, more depressed, and more focused on hopes of reconciliation. The girls had more friends and used them as a support system.

Five Years Later

Thirty-four percent of the children were doing exceptionally well in the five-year follow-up to the Wallerstein and Kelly study. Twenty-nine percent were thought to be adjusting adequately. Thirty-seven percent, however, were found to be in poor psychological health. All of the children in this group were moderately to severely depressed.

Anger played a major part in the emotional life of 23 percent of the children—anger linked to school failure, delinquency, and sexual acting-out. In most cases the anger was directed at the father, who was blamed for deteriorated parent-child relationships.

While 17 percent of the children felt rejected and uncared for by their mothers, the majority felt comfortable with the primary parent. Children who were doing well after five years had a nurturing, dependable relationship with their primary parent (usually the mother). She was psychologically stable and had not displayed chronic depression or unremitting bitterness. The child had not been forced into a pathological alliance against the father.

Thirty percent of the children felt rejected and uncared for by their fathers. Twenty percent still yearned for the absent father, and 25 percent were "very disappointed with the visiting relationship." Good father/child relationships were linked to high self-esteem and absence of depression in both sexes. Above the age of nine, however, the boys' adjustment was more correlated with the father/son relationship and the girls' with the mother/daughter relationship. Children who were rarely visited or were left unvisited by the father often felt unloved and unlovable.

Parenting Problems Immediately After Divorce

The emotional extremes that follow separation confront parents with special problems and challenges. There may be no other time in your relationship with your child when the stakes will be so high and your emotional resources so depleted. The following are some of these special challenges, with suggestions for coping with them.

1. The angry child. Most children, and particularly nine- to twelve-year-olds, experience an upsurge of anger and aggression following separation. Much of this anger is directed toward the primary parent, rather than the visiting one. A primary parent can easily feel victimized by this unfairly distributed hostility.

It's true, the situation *is* unfair. As the primary parent, you carry most of the burden and also take most of the flak. Younger children are generally afraid to confront the visiting parent (usually dad) because of the very real possibility that their anger may drive him away. It's also obviously true that you're around to take the heat and the visiting parent isn't. How can you cope?

The first step is to recognize that this process is normal and necessary and an experience that many parents endure following separation. The second step is to encourage your children to *talk* about their feelings, rather than *dump* them. Set aside a time that is just for them to share their feelings with you—not only their frustrations and fears about the things that have changed, but in particular their feelings about you. It isn't always easy to find regular intervals for these "check-ins," but a consistent effort will reduce the frequency of fights and blowups. As one woman explained, "The tension between us would get so thick you could cut it with a knife. And then we'd have a socko, knockdown fight. Now I sit down with the kids every few days and find out what's bugging them."

2. The parent's aggravation cycle. A primary parent is under enormous stress following separation. He or she is on an emotional rollercoaster, and also must somehow keep the house running, keep food on the table, and continue attending to each child. Irritations may accumulate and then suddenly spill out in angry attacks on the kids. As the rage dissipates, you feel waves of panic ("Am I doing them harm?") and remorse. The irritation-anger-remorse cycle may continue for months as you adjust to all the new stresses.

This aggravation cycle can be short-circuited in two ways. First, keep track of your level of irritation and stress. Don't let it build up to the point that you become a ticking time bomb. Scan your body for tension and take notice when you are feeling emotionally fragile. These are cues to take time off, to decompress in front of the TV or go play raquetball. Give yourself a special treat. One woman described how she would start hunching her shoulders as a symptom of stress. "So I'd put him in the playpen, open a soda, and put on the earphones for awhile. A pleasure break really helped." Second, try relieving your stress with some adult contact. The nonstop demands and natural egocentricity of children can be frazzling. Even if you do no more than make a brief phone call, time with your adult friends can be renewing.

3. The overburdened parent. Kids, work, kids. This routine is hard enough when you have a partner to help. Alone, it's exhausting. The answer is to get as much help as you can. The more emotionally and physically exhausted you become, the poorer you will be at parenting. You have a responsibility to your children and to yourself to arrange your life so you don't go into emotional bankruptcy.

If you can afford child care, arrange for it. If the second parent is willing to take your children for overnights, set up a regular and predictable schedule that lets you look forward to time off. Join a childcare collective, or share childcare responsibilities with a neighbor who has children near in age to your kids.

Many parents also find that their children can be an important resource. Kids can often take over certain household responsibilities that were once exclusively handled by grown-ups. Don't be afraid to assign shopping, cooking, and cleaning tasks to the older ones.

Being overburdened means being less available. Wallerstein and Kelly found that 25 percent of mothers spent substantially less time with children six months after separation. One way to avoid losing contact with the children is to do many of the household tasks together. Mom washes and Jimmy dries, Susan cleans the tub and mom does the sink, Ed makes the salad and dad makes the hamburgers.

4. Children who won't behave. An upsurge in mischief, talking back, and problems at school are common following separation. Since it was often the children's father who provided the real discipline at home, mothers may feel uncertain how to establish control. As one woman put it, "They won't mind because they know I can't really hurt them. I yell, and they yell back at me."

The answer is to make clear rules with definite sanctions, and then stick to them. If you've decreed that the children lose their allowance when they yell at you, then you *must* take away the allowance when there is an infraction. Giving the children a second chance or letting them ignore your rules teaches them not to take you seriously. Everyone has known a mother who had to call her kids twenty times before they came in. She waited at the front door, hoarse with screaming. If she had understood the principle of consistent reinforcement, she would have had to call only once. Children who didn't come when they were called would lose a valuable privilege. If they did come, they'd get praise and a hug.

Many parents get better cooperation when they encourage the children to participate in making up house rules. By developing rules through compromise and consensus, each child feels a part of the decision making. As one mother said, "When the boys have a role in the cleanup decisions, they get the work done without much fuss. When I just lay down the law, they take a month of Sundays to scrub the sink."

Problems at school or delinquent behavior should be addressed by both parents. It's hard to face an irate principal alone, and the children's father can be an important support. He can also help reestablish limits when the child has gone temporarily out of control. See the chapters on coparenting for help in establishing a cooperative relationship with the second parent.

5. Visit anxiety. Fathers who are no longer part of the daily lives of their children often feel depressed after a visit. They have lost their role of protector and provider and the power of decision making. Dads also go through torture trying to invent fun outings each week. They are reduced to playing the good-time parent who never confronts or disciplines the children.

If you are a second parent, it is recommended that you bring the children to your new apartment as soon as possible. In this way they will learn that you have a real place in the universe. They'll know where you live and what it's like there. Overnights are especially helpful, because they give you a chance to do some real parenting. The visit becomes more than a frenetic trip to Marine World and instead offers a chance for quiet talks and bedtime stories. One father explained it this way: "I was always planning something special. I didn't think they'd want to just *be* with me. But when I started doing overnights, everything slowed down. We talked quietly instead of screaming over the roar at a baseball game. We could do ordinary things. I felt I could still teach them things."

Introduce the children to your neighborhood. Encourage them to make friends with kids in the area. When your children can play happily in the local park and have made some friends on your block, much of the pressure will be off. You will feel significantly less visit anxiety.

Recommendations

Here are some guidelines to help you protect your children during the first crucial months following separation.

- Maintain a consistent pattern of frequent visits. Losing contact with a parent can be a crushing experience for a child, whose immediate response is to feel rejected and unloved. The long-term result is often a lowering of self-esteem. Although children need both parents, a large majority of fathers choose to visit infrequently. Consistency is as important as frequency. A visiting parent must keep his promises. Don't fail to show up; try not to cancel.

- Consult your child about the visitation schedule. Many children complain that they are forced into a pattern designed only for their parents' convenience. The kids resent it and eventually begin finding excuses to avoid the visits. Take the needs of your children into consideration when arranging visitation. Keep the schedule adaptable and flexible.

- Keep up any child support payments. Only 35 percent of women who are eligible for child support receive it (Bureau of the Census Survey, 1979). The obvious result is a greater or lesser degree of economic hardship for the children. The less obvious result is loss of contact with dad. Fathers who stop making child support payments tend to see their children infrequently. As they fall behind, they are criticized by their ex-wives and may be denied visitation privileges. Furstenberg and Nord found that only 8 percent of the children whose fathers were not making payments saw their dads once a week or more. Thirty-five percent had had no contact with their fathers in more than five years.

- Subject children to as few changes as possible. In the year following separation, children experience less stress if they can remain in the same home, neighborhood, and school. Explain concretely where, when, how, and with whom a new experience will take place.

- Don't use the children as messengers or spies. Try not to ask your kids about the other parent's life. Avoid reporting to your child how angry, lonely, or economically strapped you are, in the hope that he will carry this information to your ex-spouse. Communicate directly with the other parent. When you need information, ask for it. If you want to give information, make sure the other parent gets it directly from you.

- Avoid using children as allies in parental battles. No child should be forced to choose one parent over another. No matter how much you may hate your ex-spouse, don't let your feelings interfere in any way in your parent-child relationship. Don't encourage a child to share your resentments toward the other parent; don't block visits.

- Avoid joining in your child's anger toward the other parent. This kind of rapport is just another way of forming alliances. Encourage your child to talk the problem over with the other parent; let them work it out.

- Keep kids out of the middle. Marla Isaacs studied 96 divorcing families in Pennsylvania and New Jersey. She found that children who had become involved in parental conflicts during the first year after separation displayed more behavioral problems than children who were not pulled into the fighting. Do *not* denigrate, malign, or badmouth the other parent. Attacking or blaming the other puts children in an untenable position. They must either lie about their feelings in order to agree with you, or bring their feelings into line with yours and basically lose a parent.

- Stay out of custody battles. Approximately 10 to 15 percent of divorcing families struggle over their children in court. The only people who win such battles are the lawyers. The underlying motive is often to take revenge on an offending spouse, and the usual result is that the children become pawns in a shattering legal war. If at all possible, enlist the services of a mediator to help with custody conflicts. Examine coparenting and joint-custody options as ways of sharing the parenting role.

- Avoid frightening the children with threats or with your worries about eventualities. Many children have been severely disturbed by parents who threaten suicide or promise that they'll move away or block visitation if a child doesn't behave. Don't share your fears about money until the squeeze brings a concrete change in the child's life. At all costs, give your child the feeling that there will always be enough to eat, that he will always have a place to live, and that he will always have you.

- Stay in the role of parent. Be honest with your children and let them know when you feel bad, but don't turn them into emotional props or force them into the grown-up roles of confidant and decision maker. Children need to mature at their own pace. It's natural for them to accept more responsibility following a separation, but those responsibilities should not include being your therapist or soul mate. Reassure the children that *you know what you are doing and can take care of them.*

- If you are severely depressed (can't work, can't get out of bed) or dysfunctional (paralyzed by anxiety or bitterness) you should seek professional help. A child needs a functional mother and father. You owe it to your child to get whatever help you need to recover your parenting effectiveness.

- If children fail to resume normal development after the first year, they too should receive professional attention. Signals that help is needed are persistent anger or depression or the presence of serious behavior problems. Any professional help you seek should include family therapy. Children's problems usually develop in response to the family milieu as a whole and are rarely treated effectively without involving at least the primary parent and siblings. Many family therapists also prefer to include the second parent as well.

14

Single Parenting

Single parenting (also called "sole" or "exclusive" custody) describes the traditional postdivorce situation where one parent has the children in his or her care most of the time. Nine out of ten single parents are women. Usually the other parent has visitation rights, typically on weekends, but sometimes for a month or more during the summer. Although in the past fathers have usually paid child support to custodial mothers, this situation is changing. As the number of working mothers increases, fewer fathers are left to carry the entire financial responsibility, and a small number of mothers now pay child support to their former husbands. Many coparenting arrangements have unique child support schemes whereby each parent pays a percentage of the children's monthly expenses.

While some people have single parenting thrust on them, many others are now actively choosing this alternative to the traditional nuclear family. Many fathers are also asking for physical as well as legal custody of their children, as was depicted in the recent film, *Kramer vs. Kramer.*

Having sole responsibility for your children can be a heavy burden. As one woman put it, "There is nothing, nothing in my life that even begins to compare with the difficulty of raising these kids alone. It's the hardest thing I've ever had to do." A single parent has to "do it all." Here's a partial list of the many single parent roles:

- *Sergeant-at-arms:* The responsibility for all discipline now rests with you. You can't ask the other parent to back you up or threaten the kids with "Wait 'til daddy gets home." You have to make the rules and establish consistent consequences when they are broken.
- *Short-order cook:* You have to organize some kind of breakfast during the hectic morning rush. At the same time you may also have to throw lunch together. Dinner requires planning in order to come up with something more nutritional than a nightly diet of franks and beans.

- *Teacher:* You teach basic life skills. How to tell time, cross the street, finish a task, straighten up a room. How to take care of hygiene and homework; how to handle money, relatives, disappointments, boredom, and sexual attraction. How to be caring and considerate of others.
- *Nurse:* You are the one who treats scrapes, splinters, and colds; the one who pulls a loose tooth and gives a sponge bath for a fever. You might have to stay home from work when your child is ill.
- *Handy person:* Sewing buttons, getting the iron to work, propping up a broken bed, building shelves, unplugging the sink, getting the stove to light, changing fuses. You do as much of it as you can and then call for help.
- *Manager:* You have contingency plans for getting a sick child home from school. You plan vacations, weekends, entertainment, and child care. You plan meals, cope with the budget, decide which school clothes to buy.
- *Maid:* Laundry, cleaning, dishes, pick-up, making beds, vacuuming, etc., etc.
- *Liaison:* You endure the parent/teacher conferences. You talk to doctors, orthodontists, piano teachers, and other parents. Sometimes it's necessary to deal with police, courts, and juvenile authorities.
- *Confidante:* You are the one your children talk to and trust. You hear about triumphs at school, rejections, hurts, new friends, bullies, fears of the dark. And you get the anger, the murderous looks. They trust you with those too.
- *Nurturer:* You hold and hug. You read bedtime stories, you kiss away the cuts and bruises. You're there—week after week, year after year.

Should You Be a Single Parent?

If you are considering becoming a single parent, please think through your answers to the following questions.

1. Are you and your divorcing partner willing and able to cooperate? If hurt and anger have made you bitter enemies, then joint or shared parenting would probably be extremely difficult, and single parenting is the preferred alternative.
2. Do you believe honestly that you are the better parent—more loving, more responsible, more interested—and that you should therefore assume exclusive custody? This is not a time to be selfish, but rather a time to keep in mind the best interests of the children.
3. Have you gotten feedback from the children about their needs? If children are ten years old or older, consulting them is recommended. Younger children can also be asked for their feelings. How much time do they need to be with the other parent? Are they comfortable with visits, or would they like to live part-time with each parent? Bear

in mind that the children's opinions should not be the controlling factor. In fact, putting the whole burden on them would be a real surrender of parenting responsibilities.

Before making the decision to become a single parent, it will be useful for you to determine how much time you should spend with your children and how much support you will need as a parent.

1. Do you like being with children? Not just your own kids, but their friends as well? How much does it cost you—physically and emotionally—to feed and clean up after the kids?
2. Do you believe that your children are "special," or in Tillie Olsen's words "no miracle at all?" Is having them with you worth making the inevitable sacrifices?
3. Can you let your children act childish (cry, fight over sibling rivalries, wake you with a bad dream at 3:00 a.m., throw a temper tantrum) without feeling burdened to the point of intolerance?
4. Do you enjoy being affectionate and "physical" with your children?
5. Are you prepared to take on whatever emotional problems (guilt slinging, blame, tantrums) your children may have in reaction to the separation?
6. Are you willing to handle the household chores—shopping, washing clothes, cleaning kitchens and bathrooms?
7. How do you feel about having to restrict your personal life because of your responsibilities as a parent? About having less time for dating and socializing? A sick child may cause a last minute change in plans; your sex life may be limited.
8. Are you prepared to feel that there's never enough time to do all you need (much less want) to do? To feel there's never enough money or adult companionship or just plain quiet?

Your answers to some of these questions may be no. That doesn't mean you have to give up being a parent. But it does mean that you'll need to do some careful planning and develop special supports for your parenting.

Many parents, after much thought and self-examination, conclude that they don't want or can't handle the responsibility of children. This is often a healthy decision, both for the parent and the child. The child gets a concerned, loving parent who visits, rather than a harried or depressed custodial parent. The important thing is to realize that you have a whole range of parenting choices. You aren't limited to the choice of being either a full-time single parent or no parent at all.

Rewards of Single Parenting

"Single parenting has given me self-esteem," Pauline said. "Women tend to let men do all the hard things, but I've had to learn to do them myself. Another thing is that relationships like marriage take a lot of time and work. As a single parent, I have all my energy available for the parenting role. It's the best way I know to be truly intimate with my children."

"I've always been a single parent," said Carla with a cynical smile. She had divorced after ten years of marriage. "Now it's such a relief not to have to consult with anyone. I get to make the final decisions and I take all the responsibility."

While single parenting does take a great deal of work, many experts believe that it offers children what they need most: a consistent, predictable homelife with a parent they can feel close to. Harry, a single parent working full-time, believes that having a routine is as helpful to the adult as it is to the child. "My son feels more secure when he knows who's going to pick him up from school, what's for dinner, and when it's time for bed. It also gives me a sense of being in control, that I know what I'm doing."

Children who are seen as partners in the single parent household where they are raised tend to be more capable and self-reliant. In times of crisis they rise to the occasion, because they believe in their ability to handle things. Pauline has a lot of confidence in her daughters (ages 14 and 16). She even sent them ahead to California to research homes to buy, while she stayed behind on the East Coast to close the old house. She says, "There's not a thing my kids can't do, because they've seen me struggle and accomplish things I thought impossible."

Perhaps the most gratifying aspect of single parenting is the closeness that develops between parent and child. You are a privileged companion as the children move from crawling, to walking, to walking away. You share the ups and downs: staying up all night with a teething baby, the first day of nursery school, waiting up at home after your child's first date.

Another benefit of single parenting is that it encourages deeper communication between parent and child. The single parent can no longer remain locked in a "super mom" or "macho man" role. Single parents often find that they are freer to express and acknowledge feelings to their children than they were when two parents were on the scene. One mother said, "When I let myself cry in front of the children, everyone benefited. I felt much better afterward, and the children got to see that their mom was human too."

The Principle of Responsible Selfishness

Single parents who martyr themselves, sacrificing everything for their children, usually end up feeling resentful and unfulfilled. Kids who are excessively catered to experience the world as revolving around them.

This unrealistic world view fails to prepare children for the harsh realities of grown-up life.

Bryan Knight, author of *Enjoying Single Parenthood,* has pointed out this paradox: single parents serve their children best by putting themselves first. He has termed this phenomenon *responsible selfishness.*

The most frequent complaint of divorced mothers is lack of time, especially time to be alone and "just do nothing." Time alone is essential for the mental health of the single parent. One single mother of two small children resolved this problem by scheduling two hours of private time for herself after the children were asleep. She would unplug the telephone, take a bubble bath, or "read an old Perry Mason novel."

Adults need time to play too. Whether attending a concert or hitting a tennis ball, it's essential to give yourself the chance to relax. It's important to make time in your life for things that give you pleasure away from your children. This will benefit both you and the kids. One adventurous single mother took to skydiving. While this is a riskier activity than most people want to try, it gave her the feeling of freedom and excitement which she said "helped balance the weight of responsibility" typical of the rest of her life.

Time and Management Problems

"The hardest part for me," said Mary, "is trying to be mother *and* father. The children feel hurt and angry about their father deserting them, and look to me for support and comfort." Most single parents with more than one child find the physical burden of *trying to be everywhere* a frustrating task. This is especially true when it involves chauffering children to and from school, after-school activities, lessons, dental appointments, and so on. You may have friends you can call on to help you out, but can't do it too often for fear of wearing out your welcome.

"Getting things organized was probably my biggest problem," said Dorothy, who works a full-time job. "Making breakfast and packing lunches while getting ready to go to work myself, then shopping, cooking, cleaning, and keeping up with the children's social activities really had me going for awhile." Harry had shared in the chores during his marriage, but he still wasn't prepared to do it all alone. "I was overwhelmed at first, I'd never had to do all the cooking and cleaning before *and* hem my daughter's skirt as well. What's more, I'd never had to do all these things *all* the time. The only way to survive was to get into a routine."

Most single parents have to work, and this inevitably puts a considerable strain on their parenting time. If you work, it means you will need to do some careful planning so you and your children spend a good amount of quality time together each week. It also means you need plans for emergencies, after-school supervising, quick nutritious meals, and so on. There are a number of resources you can turn to for help in coping with the strain.

Baby-sitters. Finding a sitter for your "baby" is no simple matter. Ask other parents for recommendations—and ask your potential sitter for references. You should prepare a list of "do's and don'ts, and it's also a good idea to have a list of telephone numbers the sitter can call for a backup. A release form for emergency treatment and hospital I.D. numbers should be prominently posted.

Single fathers have special problems with credibility. It often helps to reassure your sitter's parents if you meet with them or provide references from previous sitters who can vouch for you.

Day care. Adequate daycare centers are essential for the single working parent, yet they have consistently lacked federal support. In 1971, Congress approved a fifteen billion dollar appropriation to provide large scale "quality child care." President Nixon vetoed the bill, claiming that government interference would "threaten family life."

Ideally, day care should be a community service, dedicated to the well-being of the child. The only criteria for admittance should be the child's readiness. Until that day, parents will have to continue to struggle, seeking out viable alternatives to expensive private facilities.

The Parents Nursery School, in Palo Alto, California, offers an innovative solution: ostensibly an extension course for parents, in reality it operates as a cooperative daycare center with parent volunteers. Two paid teachers serve to educate the parents and supervise the operation of the center.

Parents have also joined together to form "co-op" nurseries or "play groups." The members of these groups take turns watching children either in their own homes or in a rented space.

Living cooperatively. Some single parents are now experimenting with intentional extended families. These groups are usually not made up of relatives, but rather of peers and friends who have built up trusting relationships and made a mutual commitment to raising children who are not "their own." The children raised in these collectives appear to thrive and are capable of accepting support from many different adults. The cost for a mother who joins such a group is that her relationship with "her baby" is no longer an exclusive one, but the benefits for the child may make the sacrifice worthwhile.

Other shared living arrangements. One option involves taking on a boarder, often a college student, who can contribute money toward the rent or barter for it with child care and housework. Another option is for two single-parent families to share a house, trading off cooking and child care. Both options provide an extra measure of much-needed adult energy.

Planning. Organizing your time is essential for the single parent. As a single working mother of three children, Kathy has had to learn to be efficient. Everybody helps out. The older children help with the cooking, shopping, cleaning, and dishes. Even the youngest brings his dishes into the kitchen and puts his dirty clothes in the hamper.

Arthur, single father of two boys, uses a time log. He checks off each activity or task on a daily timesheet, and the results are discussed at a family meeting on Sunday. Priorities are reassessed and new decisions are made by the entire group.

Food. Most single parents are forced to relax their standards about mealtime niceties. Proper nutrition is the important issue, and untraditional methods may work best for you. Leftover cold chicken and an orange for breakfast will provide more protein than packaged cereals loaded with useless sugar. Avoid the easy trap of serving junk food, as these are not only potentially hazardous to your health, but also more expensive than nutritionally sounder food. A crockpot (or slow-cooker) will allow you to put some things together in the morning and come home to a hot supper. One single parent prepares a whole turkey once every six weeks. This is cut up and frozen in small packages to be defrosted for individual servings as desired. The same idea works well for large casseroles or a roast.

Reserved time for your kids. Make a shared evening meal a priority. This is an opportunity for a lot of talking and catching up after a day apart. It's a time for real family contact. In addition to conversation at supper, many single parents make a conscious effort to check in with each child individually some time during the evening. This facilitates some "private sharing" and nurturing. The principle of responsible selfishness suggests that you reserve some of the weekend time for yourself. You can also reserve some time for your children: make specific arrangements for shared activities and special day trips.

Emotional Problems of Single Parenting

A major problem inherent in single parenting is *depression*. With all that energy going out, it's easy to feel drained. Many single parents get immobilized to the point of withdrawing and rarely leaving home. This social isolation can become infectious, and the children may become seriously depressed as well.

Failure to do something about those depressed feelings may lead to a second problem of relying too heavily on your children for support. To a degree this is fine, since single parents and their children must expect more from each other than in traditional families. Problems may arise if the parent begins to sleep in the same room with the children and starts to use them as confidants. This can lead to the "parentified child" syndrome, where the usual roles are reversed and children are prematurely forced into taking adult responsibilities that they are not yet ready to handle.

A third problem results when custodial parents hold on to the hurt and anger they feel toward their former spouse. This often has the effect of poisoning the child's relationship with the other parent. A child who constantly hears his father being blamed and criticized may find it difficult to maintain a normal relationship with him. Children caught in the middle often end up feeling helpless and guilty.

Getting support. It's OK to get professional help to get over the rough spots. Talking with psychiatrists, psychologists, family counselors, or clergymen experienced in family problems can be very helpful. In many ways, divorce and separation require going through the same kind of process as mourning or grieving for the loss of a loved one. If the children's school work is affected, use the services of the school psychologist.

Another way to go is to find a *peer support group*. The primary group of this kind is Parents Without Partners. Here you can meet and be with other adults who are in a situation similar to your own. These groups usually have weekend activities for the whole family, providing your children the opportunity for contact with other-gender role models. Individual chapters vary, and you may have to try several before finding the most congenial group for you to join.

Relating to Your Children

After divorce, most people find that all the old rules for relationships are open to reexamination. You will definitely see differences in the ways you relate to your children and they relate to you.

Dealing with the children's feelings after divorce. Children need time and permission to ventilate their feelings about the separation. They will naturally feel hurt and angry. As a single parent, you can help by speaking honestly to your child. Explain that even though you and your ex-spouse are no longer together, you both still love the children. It's particularly important to reassure your children that the separation was not caused by them.

Being open. It's also helpful if you express your feelings. Many parents believe that their concerns about living alone with the children, the burden of work, and other problems have to go unexpressed. If you've been holding back and swallowing your feelings, you may begin to feel resentment toward your children. Or they may develop an unrealistic perception of you as a person devoid of emotions. Naturally, as an adult you don't want to overload your children with adult worries. But teaching your children how to handle negative feelings is an important part of your parental role. Finding a balance between openness and reassurance is the key.

Listening. Kids have strong feelings. It helps to encourage them to express their feelings about being a member of a single parent household. You don't have to react by feeling guilty or defensive or trying to make everything "all right." Sometimes it helps just to listen.

Tracy and her son Todd were always at each other. Petty bickering led to major fights. After a few sessions with a counselor, they learned the trick of taking turns talking and listening. Now that they can hear each other's feelings, escalation has become less frequent—and hugs have become more common.

Quality time. Many single parents are seriously concerned about the lack of time available to them to spend with their children. This is especially true of working parents. The real problem is not the *amount* of time spent, but the *quality* of that time. Fifteen minutes of giving your child your undivided attention is worth more than a whole evening of being in the house together doing chores or watching TV.

Some single parents solve this problem by setting aside a certain time of the day to spend with their children. One father cleared his morning schedule so that he could always make breakfast for his daughter and drive her to school, even though it meant that he arrived at work at ten a.m. Another working mother keeps the six to eight dinner time inviolate. She even unplugs the telephone.

Discipline. Children learn self-discipline from being in an orderly environment. Having clear rules and clear consequences for breaking them is the first step. It's important to follow through. If you tell your child that she'll be grounded for a week if she gets home more than half an hour late, do it—even if she was only 35 minutes overdue. If the dishes aren't done when they're supposed to be, withhold some allowance. Whatever the agreement is, stick to it.

Having fun with your child. Luckily, all the hard work and trying times are more than compensated for by the good times: being there when she scores her first soccer goal, the surprise pancakes on father's day morning, or just walking together in the woods and listening to the trees. "I'll never forget my daughter's first visit to the zoo," Paul said. "She kept pulling me this way and that. 'What's that big bird? Look at the monkeys! Ooh! The baby lions are cute!'" Whether it's spending a rainy day making ornaments for the Christmas tree or getting each other wet while washing the car, time spent with your children can be a treasure and a joy. As Dr. Seuss says, "If you have not done these things, you should. These things are fun, *and fun is good!*"

Single parenting can be a joy or a curse. Whether you actively choose it, or accept it as "the only way out," it requires a lot of work and is demanding on both parent and children. Yet the majority of divorced parents still find single parenting to be the most workable arrangement. The important thing to remember is that *you are not alone*. Others have traveled this path before, and there are helpful resources available and more options than you might have thought possible.

15

The Second Parent

Of all the losses associated with divorce, often the most grievous is the loss of your children. During the postdivorce years, a large majority of father-child relationships decline in both consistency and depth. Wallerstein and Kelly found in their California study that only 30 percent of children and their fathers were able to create and sustain a rewarding, nurturing relationship. The remaining 70 percent of relationships were too limited to be really satisfying for either father or child. This chapter is about how to be a visiting parent, about how to sustain, support, and *keep* your children.

The most important thing to realize is that your children love and need you. They may rely more on your ex-spouse, but you are still critical to their happiness. After a divorce it is vital that you assure your children of three things.

1. *They were not the cause of the divorce.* Many children conclude that you moved out because of them. They drove you away because they were rotten children. Make it clear to them that your divorce was due to an inability to get along with your ex-spouse, not to any feeling on their part.

2. *You still love them.* No matter how often you demonstrated this in the past, they will still doubt your love after you move out. Show your love, don't make them guess. Say "I love you" and express it through physical contact: an arm around the shoulder, holding hands, hugging, and kissing will all effectively communicate the message.

3. *You are still their parent.* Let them know that even though you won't be around as often as before, you will still be there when they need you. You'll continue to play an active role in their lives.

The Mother as Second Parent

While more than 80 percent of second parents are fathers, an increasing number of women are choosing to be noncustodial parents after divorce. Because of the cultural expectation that mothers should keep their children, noncustodial mothers must be prepared for some flak from relatives, friends, and acquaintances. Women who choose not to live with their children often experience guilt as well as disapproval. By violating the old values that charge women with ultimate responsibility for their children, noncustodial mothers are often left to feel that something's wrong with them, that they don't love their children enough. The truth is that many women choose to be second parents precisely because they *do* love their children. They know that the kids, for whatever reason, will fare better with their father. A woman's choice to be a second parent is more likely to be an act of courage rather than an abdication of responsibility.

Many women unfortunately feel the need to insist on custody despite the fact that everyone would be happier if dad took the kids. There are many legitimate reasons for being a noncustodial mother.

1. The children may feel closer to their father.
2. Their father may be more suited for the role of single parent. He may have more time, patience, or interest in the day-to-day tasks of childrearing.
3. The mother may have time commitments to career or educational goals.
4. The mother may have psychological needs: she may need the freedom to pursue areas of growth or time to recover from the trauma of divorce.

The decision to be a noncustodial mother is a difficult one. But don't let this prevent you from making a choice that is crucial for your happiness and that of your family.

Visitation Rights

Once you move out of the family home, it's essential that you insist on frequent visitation rights. When negotiating with the custodial parent, avoid emphasizing *your* need to be with the children. Your ex-spouse may feel quite bitter and use this opportunity to hurt you, using the children as a weapon. Stress the fact that the children need two parents, not one, and that it is essential for *their* welfare, not yours, that you receive liberal visitation rights. Make it clear that hard feelings between divorcing parents must not be allowed to interfere with the needs of the children.

Of course, the best way to safeguard your visitation rights is to maintain a good relationship with your ex-spouse. If negotiations break down, you should be prepared to fight for your rights in court, if necessary. But no matter what the court requires, the custodial parent can erect roadblocks to your seeing the children. Wallerstein and Kelly found that one-fifth of ex-spouses actively tried to sabotage the second parent's visits. A number of very frustrating strategies were used. Some children were sent away just before their father's arrival. Many fathers arrived at the appointed time, only to be told that the child was ill or had mountains of homework. Some fathers were discouraged from visiting because at each encounter the ex-wife made a scene.

Be sure to fulfill your financial obligations to your children. If you fall behind in child-support checks, your ex-spouse will have an excuse for cutting your visitation rights. Additionally, you may experience so much guilt about missed payments that you won't feel you have the right to see the children.

Visiting is usually a mixed bag. The pleasure of seeing your children can be tempered by a variety of very negative experiences.

1. Seeing your ex-spouse or former home can often be painful, particularly if the divorce was initiated by your ex-spouse and you still want a reconciliation. Seeing the person or home you love is sometimes traumatic. One way to avoid this pain is to pick up the children at a neutral site such as the school, baby-sitter's, or grandparent's house.

2. Lack of spontaneity. When you were living with your children, you could see them on the spur of the moment. Now you have to make an appointment. If you maintain good rapport with your ex-spouse, you may be able to "drop in" without previous notice. A word of caution: If you can't handle your ex-spouse dating others, be sure to call first to avoid embarrassing encounters.

3. Feeling like a baby-sitter. Many fathers resent the feeling that the kids are just "dumped" on them. "She calls me up at *her* convenience, when *she* has something to do. The point isn't for me to see my kids, the point is for me to be a free baby-sitter." *(37-year-old dentist, father of three)*

4. The children's anger. Wallerstein and Kelly found that half of the men studied feared rejection by their children. Older children are very often quite angry at dad and are likely to express their feelings. Dad may be blamed for abandoning them or for not working hard enough to save the marriage. They may also have been drawn into an alliance with mom, who is also angry and wants to punish her ex-spouse. In addition, fathers must frequently endure the natural fluctuations in their children's interests. It hurts when the kids are suddenly quite bored with the idea of seeing you. They may try to postpone visits, or develop new activities that fall on your traditional day with them.

5. Uncertainty about how to structure your time with the children. The act of visiting your own children often feels unnatural at first. There's a feeling that you have to do something special. Conversation runs dry after the first twenty minutes. At this point, many fathers report feeling an uncomfortable nervousness, almost a depression. "What do I do after I've asked about school, their friends, their new record album? I feel like it's not enough for them to just *be* with me. I've got to do the old soft-shoe, I've got to entertain them. Then I think, 'How did it happen that I can't be with my kids without stuffing them full of ice cream or spending hours at the video game parlors?'" *(32-year-old bartender)*

Why Many Second Parents Fail

There are a number of important factors that can make second parenting difficult. Perhaps the foremost is depression. Depressed fathers simply feel too tired and too unhappy to deal with the demands of the children. As one father put it, "I'm a basket case, and having a bunch of squabbling kids with their skinned knees and insatiable appetites drives me crazy. I just barely make it to work. A Saturday alone with the kids is too much to ask."

Guilt is equally debilitating. Men who feel guilty about having ended the marriage have much difficulty initiating and sustaining a pattern of frequent visits. They expect to be rejected by their children and feel unable to face their anger. Some fathers create unbelievable excuses to justify their fear of visiting. "I can't have my daughter to my place. She wrecks it. Besides, I live in a singles complex and there's no lifeguard at the pool." *(44-year-old draftsman)*

It's normal to have the guilty feeling that you are "abandoning your children." The best way to deal with this guilt is to resolve to be the best noncustodial parent you can possibly be. Just because you no longer live with your children doesn't mean you can't be a good parent. Many "off-site" parents are just as loving and supportive as the custodial parent is.

One major cause of guilt is the belief that you won't be able to spend enough time with your children. This isn't necessarily so. Ironically, many parents, particularly fathers, interact more with their children after the divorce. Before their marriages broke up, these fathers often took their children for granted and put their time and energy into careers. Interactions with the children were often limited to breakfast, dinner, and a couple of hours of TV watching each night. After a divorce, you may find yourself treasuring the time you have with your children and actually spending more "quality" time with them.

An important reason why second parents may fail is the "frozen relationship." Because they see their children infrequently, dads often fail to recognize changing needs and developing skills. The relationship remains frozen at the child's developmental level at the time of the divorce. Wallerstein and Kelly found that almost half of the father-child relationships they studied operated as if the child were significantly younger. The way to unfreeze your relationship is to visit frequently, sharing a wide variety of activities and tasks. "I used to take Jim swimming or to the park every Saturday. Now I have overnights. We cook and shop together. I have his friends stay over, and I've gotten involved in his scout troop. I can see him growing before my very eyes." *(38-year-old computer programmer)*

Men who are naturally shy and non-assertive often have special difficulties as a second parent. They fear their children's anger. They are easily discouraged by confrontations with the ex-spouse. Unless actively encouraged to participate, these men soon drop out of the picture. Each problem, each irritation, each small conflict pushes them further away.

When ex-spouses have a feuding relationship, the parent-child bond is often damaged. Wallerstein and Kelly found that one-third of ex-spouses openly competed for their children's loyalty and affection. Second parents who play this game are asking for trouble. In the end, children usually side with the custodial parent. They need the day-to-day support of the primary parent, and the second parent becomes expendable.

A significant percentage of second parents do well while they remain single but fail to safely navigate the troubled waters of a second marriage and family. The new wife and children need attention. It's common for the children from the first marriage to feel neglected.

KEYS TO SUCCESS FOR THE SECOND PARENT

Noncustodial parents who maintain a successful, nurturing relationship with their children have consistently made their kids a high priority. The incursions and demands of a busy life are not allowed to weaken the commitment to frequent visits. Nothing gets in the way—not promotions, girlfriends, wives, or children by a second marriage. As one man put it, "Those kids don't need me any less just because I got married again. They need me more. I have to keep showing them that my love won't fade."

Successful second parents get to know their children as individuals. They know each child's strengths, foibles, and idiosyncracies. They know the names of their teachers and friends, what frightens and fascinates them. This awareness makes it possible to keep up with a child's growth and development. As a child's needs change, as his style of relating matures, the second parent adapts and grows right along with the child. "I notice how our conversation changes. It used to be about his acrobatics on the skateboard. Now it's about the loneliness of high school and his fears about dating." *(Father of a 16-year-old)*

Wallerstein and Kelly found that dads who maintained a good visiting relationship showed a flexibility and maturity not present in less successful fathers. They could tolerate oscillations in their children's interest and affection. They could endure disappointments ("Aw, dad, not tonight") and anger ("Leave me alone, goodbye"), yet not withdraw into hurt and counter-reject their children. If kids resisted visiting, these dads persisted in making contact. They could not be discouraged.

Fathers must adapt not only to the capriciousness of children but also to that of ex-wives. The indignity of being forced to wait outside or being told that the children are not available is not uncommon for the second parent. Fathers who persevere are clear that the relationship with the children is their highest concern. They have the maturity to accept problems, even attacks, and keep coming back to see their kids. "She wanted me out of her life, so of course she made it difficult to see Al. I had to make appointments to visit weeks in advance. I couldn't see him on school nights, I couldn't take him to my house. I couldn't even come to the door to pick him up; I was supposed to honk my horn outside. Shit, I didn't care. Nothing was going to stop me seeing my son." *(29-year-old seaman)*

Second parents who succeed accept the limits of their role. They don't interfere with or fight against routines in the custodial parent's household. Wallerstein and Kelly found that the father-child relationship was stronger when dad refrained from criticizing the custodial mother. Attempts to polarize the children often backfired. One father described how he evolved in this respect: "I didn't like her ideas of rigid discipline. It was unbelievably frustrating having to stand by and watch a semi-incompetent job of child rearing. I thought the kids would agree with me. But when I complained to them about what kind of mother they had, they withdrew and defended her. Every time. I learned in a hurry that they didn't want to hear her bad-mouthed." *(31-year-old teacher)*

Maximizing Your Time With Your Children

Many noncustodial parents make a mistake in buying or renting a home far away from the children. There are many reasons for doing this: closeness to work, job transfers, getting away from bad memories, getting a fresh start in a new community. All of these are good reasons, but they place a strain on an already strained relationship. When the opportunity for promotion comes and you are asked to move away, carefully weigh the consequences for both you and your kids. Balance your needs for career development against the impact of diminished contact with your children.

If you do decide to move far away, commit yourself to maintaining the greatest possible contact with your kids.

1. Call them on the phone frequently. You can keep the expense of long distance calls down and also ensure that your children are home when you call by setting aside a specific time each week to call them (such as Sunday mornings, when the rates are low).
2. Send photographs of yourself and request that they do the same.
3. Send a cassette tape of yourself talking about your new job, neighborhood, softball team, and so on.
4. Write to your children frequently and ask them to do the same. Request that they mail you some of their school essays, drawings, and so on.
5. When you travel, be sure to mail them postcards.
6. Make a point of visiting your children (or having them visit you) *at least* once a year. This can be very expensive, but the alternative is running the risk of becoming a faint memory in your children's lives.

If you live close by to your children, the telephone is an excellent means for keeping in frequent contact. Be aware, however, that there is no substitute for seeing your children in person. Weekly overnights are good, particularly for younger children. But whether they stay overnight or not, frequency is the key. Frequent short visits are far more valuable than infrequent long ones. This is particularly true with young children, who have a short time-sense. For them even a week is quite a gap. They need to be reassured that you still love them and haven't disappeared from their lives.

Infrequent visits can have a demoralizing effect on your children. Children who are not visited or are visited rarely have a high probability of suffering chronic depression. They miss you and don't know why you've faded from their lives. Infrequent visits are uncomfortable visits—for both you and your child. You may have to play "catch-up" and reestablish your relationship with each visit. You have to learn about the important events that have happened since you last saw each other and new problems that have arisen. You will also find yourself trying to squeeze too much of a good time into a short interval to make up for being apart for so long. You may feel the pressure to make every minute count, to stretch three hours into a month's relationship. In addition, if your children suspect they won't see you again for a long time, there will be a painful parting.

How Much Time Is Enough?

The optimum amount of time to spend with your children varies from family to family. The simplest and safest answer is to spend as much time as possible with your kids. The obligatory Saturday afternoon visit usually isn't enough. Overnight visits or weekend stays are better. Some noncustodial parents pick the children up at school Friday afternoons and return them to school Monday mornings. In addition to weekends, many noncustodial parents have the kids over one or two weeknights as well. Spending long spans of time like this will transform your house or apartment into a second home for your children. See the chapters on co-parenting for detailed information about creating a two-home life style for your kids.

Children need differing amounts of contact, depending on their ages. Younger kids have less developed verbal skills and need lots of time, attention, and hugs to be secure in your love. Teenagers are more sophisticated verbally and can quickly reach a satisfying level of intimacy through words. They often prefer shorter visits, and may get all the contact they need in an hour or two.

Be prepared to make arrangements for child care. If your children are with you for long stretches of time, there's no rule that says you have to be with them continuously. Hire a baby-sitter so you can go out on a date on a Saturday night. On the other hand, if you are a second parent who rarely sees the children, don't drop them off at grandma's house after they've only been with you for half an hour and pick them up five hours later in order to drive them back home.

If the children stay overnight, you may discover a need to develop some housekeeping skills. Tom is a 34-year-old noncustodial parent of three. "When I got divorced, I couldn't even fry an egg. My ex-wife, Sally, laughed when I suggested I take the kids overnight. So I decided to shop, cook, and put the place into some semblance of order. Then I invited Sally and the kids over for a three-course dinner in my immaculate apartment. After that I got no argument when I asked for the kids."

One way to maximize the time you spend with your children is to schedule their visits even during busy times in your week. There's nothing wrong with having the kids over when you have certain jobs or commitments. Bring them along to the office or have them play in the next room while you work at home. Being with the kids doesn't have to be a prison. You are still free to have a normal life and get your needs met.

Enjoying Your Children

Charlie is a 43-year-old parent of a 13-year-old boy. "When I first started visiting Ron after the divorce, I felt I had to wine and dine him. I spent a lot of money on movies, rock concerts, restaurants, and amusement parks. After a while I started resenting the amount of money I was spending just to see my son. It was like I had to buy his company."

It's important to realize that spending money isn't the key to a good relationship with your kids. You don't have to be Santa Claus. Your children want and need to be with you. Expensive gifts may help alleviate your guilt, but they don't cement the relationship with your children. The most important gifts are free: your love and your time.

Bill is a 28-year-old father of a 5-year-old. "I was always on my best behavior whenever Ricky came over. I never got mad, never raised my voice. I had infinite patience. I know it sounds stupid, but I was afraid that if Ricky saw me in one of my rotten moods he wouldn't love me the next time I saw him. It got to the point where I was so 'perfect' that I couldn't enjoy myself with Ricky. Now I'm more natural with him. Sometimes we fight and sometimes I'm unpleasant to be around, but I know that Ricky still loves me and will look forward to seeing me next time."

Everybody has the right to be human. Intimacy with your children means that you reveal both sides of yourself—good and bad. By limiting yourself to positive emotions, you deprive your children of the total you. Deep down they will sense that you are hiding part of yourself and will feel the loss.

What kinds of things should you do with your children? Brian, a father of three, used to take the kids out to Disney films or an amusement park. The kids had a great time. But Brian hates any film rated G and hasn't enjoyed amusement parks since he was twelve.

Choose an activity that both you and the children will enjoy. You may like to play cards, go on picnics, hike, sunbathe, or go to concerts. Perhaps you enjoy sports, either as a spectator or as a participant. The time spent with your children should be motivated by enjoyment, not a sense of obligation.

Encourage your kids to bring toys from home to play with. Have some toys at your home waiting for them that are meant to stay at your home permanently. That way there will be something there that belongs to them and is associated with your home rather than that of your ex-spouse. Choose toys that you will have fun playing with and sharing with your children.

Becoming Involved in Your Child's World

A considerable part of your children's lives will be spent at school. If you wish to be a complete parent, involve yourself in this vital part of their lives.

1. Go to the school early each school year and introduce yourself to the teacher(s), principal, and secretarial staff. Let them know your marital situation and ask to be involved in major decisions concerning the child's education.
2. Ask for a copy of the school calendar so you always know when the children are at school and when they are free to be with you.
3. Ask to be put on the school mailing list. That way you will be advised about parent-teacher conferences, school plays, sporting events, spelling bees, parties, and so on. Attend these events as often as possible.

4. Maintain good lines of communication with your ex-spouse so that she will keep you informed of school-related news.
5. Volunteer at the school. You can be a lecturer during "Career Week," coach a team, help with fund raising, and so on.

Another way to involve yourself in your children's world is by meeting their friends. Encourage your kids to invite their friends to visit at your home, have dinner, and even spend the night. Offer your home as a site for parties for your children and their friends. Be sure to introduce your children to your friends as well.

What about your romantic friends? Many noncustodial parents avoid introducing new lovers for fear of the child's response. Your children may have a fantasy of mommy and daddy getting back together, so you may encounter some resentment. The best policy is openness. If there is someone new in your life, share her with your children. Make the first meeting at a neutral place: a picnic or a day at the beach. Then gradually integrate her into your children's days with you.

It's important to give yourself and your children time to adjust to the divorce. You may not hit it off right away. Especially if they're young, your children may feel insecure visiting your home. They may be frightened staying overnight. They may feel hostile toward you, either because they feel abandoned or because your ex-spouse has been criticizing you. Be patient and allow these problems to work themselves out. Remember the last time you started a new job. Think of all the problems you initially encountered. The same holds true for taking on your new role of noncustodial parent. In time you and your children will learn to accept the new circumstances.

Keep in mind that this is a brand new relationship. Wallerstein and Kelly found that there is no correlation between the quality of a dad's preseparation relationship to his kids and postseparation visiting patterns. Some previously close fathers withdraw from their children after a divorce. Some fathers who've never been close or had much time for their kids suddenly blossom into deeply committed parents. It's never too late to start being a father. Your children *do* need you.

16

Should You Coparent?

Traditional custody arrangements have awarded children to the mother while allowing the father visitation rights. The judicial preference for custody with the mother is based on the "tender years doctrine," which holds that the mother is best suited for protecting and nurturing pre-adolescent children. The father in this arrangement becomes a weekend visitor who often has no role in the decision making. The mother is left with the full burden of child care, a responsibility that assumes enormous weight as she tries to juggle work and parenting with her own personal needs.

Although two people divorce as lovers and mates, they needn't also divorce as parents. Coparenting is an alternative to the traditional model of sole custody. It provides a structure in which both parents share the responsibility and work of raising a child. It is a commitment to maintaining a cooperative parenting relationship that places the welfare of the children as its highest priority.

COPARENTING: A DEFINITION

Coparenting means that the children spend a significant amount of unbroken time with each parent. This can be fifty/fifty, one-third/two-thirds, two-sevenths/five-sevenths, or whatever ratio makes sense to the particular parents. Coparenting also means that the tasks of child rearing, not just the costs, are shared by both parents. All major decisions concerning school, health, and related issues are made jointly. Each parent drops the kids at school, packs lunches, drives to guitar lessons, and picks the kids up after softball. Both parents talk to teachers and doctors and get prescriptions filled. Both may buy clothes, blankets, toothbrushes, and toys.

"What is important in coparenting," writes Miriam Galper in her book, *Co-parenting*, "is that both parents assume a responsibility for meeting a share of all the physical needs, as well as the financial and emotional needs of their children."

THE LANGUAGE OF COPARENTING

Since coparenting is a departure from the tradition of sole custody, it requires a new vocabulary to describe the family relationships. Coparenting is easier when you think of your former spouse as "Johnny's mother or father." Terms such as "ex" or "ex-husband" describe a previous relationship. Your *current* relationship is as parents. Stick with being parents and call your former spouse "my son's dad."

Children do not *visit* mom or dad, they *live with* one parent at a time. Even if you only have your children on weekends, you say, "My children *live* with me two days a week." The words *live with* are extremely important because they imply a home and family. When your children sleep overnight in your house, when they spend a period of unbroken time in your care, they are living with you. The ratio of time spent with each parent is far less important than the understanding that a child has two homes, two parents, and a schedule whereby he lives with each parent some of the time.

The language of coparenting does not include the term *custody agreement*. A contract that stipulates where the children live and who has responsibility for them is called a *parenting agreement*. This new term presupposes that there are two parents involved and that they both have a voice in decisions relating to the child.

Terms such as *sole custody, parent with custody,* or *parent without custody* should be replaced with *primary residence, primary-home parent,* and *second-home parent.* These new terms suggest that the child has two homes, even though he may spend more time in one than in the other.

When both parents share the day-to-day responsibilities of raising a child, the money spent should not be called *child support.* The legal concept of *child support* has been the focus of many acrimonious divorce battles. Coparents make *contributions* to the expense of rearing a child. These contributions are determined by an agreement that takes into account the relative income and ratio of time spent with each parent.

It's amazing but true that something as small as changing a few words can have a major impact on your roles and attitudes. After two months of coparenting, a thirty-two-year-old mother described her experience as follows: "Jim has our daughter Thursday, Friday, and Saturday nights. As soon as I began thinking of Sandy as *living with* him half the week, I changed my whole perspective. I realized that Sandy really did have two homes, and I had to include Jim a lot more in decision making. Jim has also changed because Sandy lives with him. He's taken a far more active role with her than he ever did in our marriage."

ADVANTAGES OF COPARENTING

The first and biggest advantage of developing a coparenting relationship, is that children don't have to lose a father or a mother. The traditional custody arrangement, with its emphasis on visitation rights, tended to make fathers into weekend playmates. On Saturdays, dad took the kids to the ball park or skating rink. Many men, fearing rejection, tried to win affection with lavish gifts and promises. The visiting parent, in the end, became a person whose only function was to provide recreation or money. It's no wonder that many fathers found postdivorce relationships with their children unfulfilling and began to drift away.

In cases where the father has been granted sole custody, it is the mother who often gets left out. Many women, for emotional, financial, or career reasons, feel unable to be full-time parents. With the traditional custody model, their role is eventually limited to that of an occasional support figure or an old friend.

When a child lives with *both* parents, each parent maintains a strong, independent bond to the child. On their respective nights, mom and dad prepare dinner, help with schoolwork, and share household chores with the child. The child observes each parent doing the work of parenting. The message is very clear: mom and dad still care, they still drive me places, still feed me, still tuck me into bed.

A second major advantage of coparenting is that each parent gets time off. In old style custody arrangements, dad paid and mom was stuck with the kids. In a coparenting arrangement, when the children are at dad's house mom is free to do other things. Often the time off is just spent relaxing and recuperating from the fatigue of constant caring for children. Precious time alone can also be spent developing new interests, new friends, or intimate relationships. One forty-year-old father of three described time off in this way: "By the end of the week, I'm a basket case. I can't wait for Estelle to take them. I'm looking forward to socializing and relaxing during my week off. There's a lovely quiet in the house. Within a few days, though, I miss them, and by Sunday, when I pick them up, I can't wait to see them again."

A third advantage of coparenting is that you get support in the child-rearing process. The other parent can deal with the orthodontist, chauffeur the kids to soccer practice, help with clothes shopping, and be there during medical and emotional emergencies. Raising children can be a lonely process for the single parent. The best way to get the support you need is to have a fully participating second parent who cares as much about the kids as you do. One thirty-eight-year-old lawyer explained: "I couldn't do it alone. If my choice had been sole custody versus no custody, I would have had to give the children to Frank. I don't have the time or energy to be a full-time parent. But we now have it arranged that I take the children Friday, Saturday, and Sunday, and bring the children to school

Monday morning. I've got no social life on the weekend, but at least I can hold down a job."

The fourth advantage of coparenting is the opportunity it affords to have a deeper relationship with your children. Because you have time off, you will also have more energy during your time on. It's true that absence makes the heart grow fonder, and the first night back with the kids is often marked by intense contact. Some fathers, who never before spent time alone with their children, develop a new level of sharing and intimacy.

Parents who have two or more children have an option to spend time alone with just one child. "Sometimes instead of taking both kids, I'll just take either John or Nancy alone. It was scary at first, but it's really given me the chance to know each of them. In fact, I've gotten much closer to both my children since the divorce. I couldn't have told you their friends' names before. Now I can tell you who they like and who's on their shit list in any given week." *(Forty-year-old jeweler, father of twins)*

Over the years, a number of books and professional papers have appeared which argue the case for sole custody. It has been suggested that attempts to have two homes and two families undermine a child's stability at a time when he has the greatest need to feel secure. Some professionals have argued that children become confused as they move back and forth between two homes. Others have theorized that joint cutody (coparenting) produces a sense of rootlessness in children that later shows up as an inability to develop intimate relationships. These objections to coparenting have frightened many people into strict adherence to the single parent, single home model. The truth is that the professionals who condemn coparenting have never bothered to study successful coparenting arrangements. They are like travel agents who advise against a trip to Spain, but who have never been there themselves or talked to anyone who has.

Far from undermining stability, coparenting enhances stability following a divorce. A child is spared the trauma of losing one of his parents. Instead of having an ineffectual "visiting" parent, he has a fully functioning second parent with whom he lives part of the time.

Some children do experience confusion during the first few months of a coparenting arrangement. But the confusion is usually short-lived, and dissipates quickly when parents post and adhere to a definite schedule. Even the youngest children have an amazing capacity to remember which nights they are at mom's house and which nights they are at dad's. The confusion clears as the children settle into a regular and predictable schedule.

The picture of children shuttling back and forth from one house to another sometimes carries the impression of rootlessness and disrupted relationships. Most people who coparent, however, attempt to keep their children in the same school and same neighborhood as long as possible. One of the parents will quite often remain in the house where the children lived prior to divorce. Rather than a sense of rootlessness, children have the security of two homes. As parents develop new relationships and perhaps remarry, children have new opportunities to meet caring adults. Coparenting can increase a child's capacity for intimacy by providing new people to be close to.

PRINCIPLES OF COPARENTING

The basic rule of coparenting is that each parent's primary commitment is to the welfare of the child. This means that the child's needs come first. The following seven principles are a blueprint for developing the kind of relationship that establishes your child's welfare as the highest priority.

Autonomy

Most people assume that parents should agree about basic principles of child raising. This is not true in the coparenting situation. The children's mother and father are free to develop their own unique style of parenting. This means that there may be a different bedtime at dad's house, a different system of allocating chores at mom's. It means that a mother who values music can arrange for her daughter's violin lessons. And a father who's into fitness can enroll the same child in a gymnastics class.

As a coparent, you have a right to real independence when the children are living with you. The development of your own parenting style helps free you of the values and standards of your ex-spouse. You no longer have to present a "united front" with the other parent. The children begin to see you as two very different people, living in different environments.

Children are not confused by different rules, different bedtimes, and different expectations in their two homes. They are extremely adaptable. They live by one set of rules at school, another at grandma's house, and still other rules in the homes of friends. They are used to coping with different structures and institutions.

Respect

The first component of respect is *noninterference*. Since you have developed your own coparenting style, you no longer have the right to evaluate how the other parent is functioning. A coparent has the same right to autonomy that you do. Unless the other parent is guilty of the grossest kind of neglect or child abuse, he or she must be given the benefit of the doubt. If a coparent sends the children to school in not-so-clean clothes, it's none of your business. If the other parent is permissive while you are trying to teach the children responsibility, that too is not your affair.

A real estate broker, who lives two weeks on and two weeks off with his children, described noninterference in this way: "Personally I think the kids should be in bed by 8:30, but Sheila will let them stay up past 9:00. I don't like them eating sweets, but she's very permissive about ice cream and candy bars. Every Saturday morning we all work together to clean up the house, but Sheila thinks they're too young to vacuum and scrub sinks. We've discussed all this, but we each want to do it our own way. I let her be her because then she lets me be me."

A corollary of noninterference is *nonjudgment*. Coparents assume that they are each doing their best. The other parent isn't labeled an idiot for forgetting the kids' galoshes when it rains. When one parent is late with the children, it isn't taken as a deliberate ploy to create irritation. Assuming hostile motivations or mind-reading angry and judgmental thoughts can only lead to a breakdown in necessary cooperation.

The secret to not judging is *not expecting*. If you expect praise, appreciation, or support and none is forthcoming, you can become awfully angry. If you expect a certain philosophy or attitude toward child rearing that the other parent doesn't share, you are headed for a serious conflict. If you expect to maintain a high level of closeness and intimacy, you may end up feeling abandoned or betrayed. Ending a marriage is hard, and emotions change with rollercoaster speed. The only thing you can really expect during this time is for the other parent to keep his or her agreements. And even then, you should allow a certain quota for failure. Assume that the other parent will be late sometimes, forget some of the toys, neglect to drive a kid to the dentist. Try if possible to give a coparent the benefit of the doubt.

A basic component of respect is *courtesy*. Courtesy demands that you call first before coming over. It means that you make appointments rather than expecting to be seen on demand. A courteous person asks to come in, and acts like a guest in the other parent's home. Even though it is a home you may have lived in, even though you remember every crack in the bedroom ceiling, this is now someone else's territory. When you respect his or her autonomy and separateness, it will be easier to demand respect for your own.

A medical secretary described how she struggled to gain a basic level of respect from her son's father. "I do a lot of transcribing at home and he kept barging in—he still had a key—when I was in the middle of something. I hadn't been going out, but I thought, 'What if he did this when I had a man here?' I assumed he was checking up on me. When I finally got the courage to ask for the key back and suggested he call first before dropping by, I felt this huge sense of relief. It's funny, but up to that time I kept feeling very angry and suspicious that he was doing a lousy job on his days with the kids. But after I got my key back I felt a lot easier about how he was doing things."

Shared Responsibility

Coparenting requires shared decision making about school, health care, recreation, child care, vacations, and a host of other issues. You need to have prior agreements with the other parent on how to handle medical emergencies, who will pick out the new school clothes, and who will buy Johnny a skateboard.

Some parents share responsibility by dividing everything right down the middle. Each pays for half the child care, each one handles about half the transportation, each buys half the clothes, each takes a turn with the orthodontist appointments. Other parents allocate areas of responsibility. A father will take his daughter to her music lessons, while mom takes her for the weekly allergy shot. One parent will handle all the transportation between the two homes, while the other will do all the laundry. One parent will shop for all the clothes if the other will mend them.

Some parents divide the responsibility based on where the child is living at any particular time. "When Margie's at her dad's house, he's got to handle it all. He's got two weeks of laundry, dentists, ballet lessons, back and forth to school. I take a real break. When Margie's with me I rarely ask him for help. About the only things we do together are visit her teachers and go to her ballet performances." *(Thirty-three-year-old loan officer)*

The following are some of the areas of shared responsibilities that require agreement in a coparenting relationship:

1. Ratio of time spent with each parent
2. Education: tuition, supplies, supervision of homework, conferences with teachers
3. Medical/Dental: insurance payments, costs, transportation, treatment decisions
4. Recreation: sports, after school activities, lessons, transportation, costs
5. Holidays: which parent has the children for a given holiday, trade-offs
6. Child care: choice of sitters, day care, transportation, costs
7. Vacations: who takes the child, for how long
8. Transportation between homes
9. Contributions: direct payment as expenses occur or flat monthly payments

This list, adapted from Isolina Ricci's *Mom's House, Dad's House,* may appear rather formidable. But these are all areas that must be resolved in order to successfully coparent. Decisions must be made and responsibility taken in order to divide the parenting load equitably.

Cooperation

The key word for cooperation is compromise. Whenever disagreements arise, look for a way to share the problem, divide the problem, or delay the problem. One couple who had a son with dyslexia decided to share the cost of his special reading program. Sometimes its easier to divide responsibility in a problem area. The parents of a six-year-old boy and a four-year-old girl found themselves bickering over the children's clothes. They decided that dad would be responsible for his daughter's clothes, while mom would be responsible for her son's. Responsibility in this case meant shopping, laundering, and mending. There are also many difficult decisions that are best dealt with by delay. A woman who wanted to move from a San Francisco suburb back into town chose to delay moving at least until the youngest child was eight.

The enemy of compromise and cooperation is the hidden agenda. When your true intention is to pay back old hurts rather than solve a particular problem, the resulting impasse threatens the coparenting relationship. When your main agenda is proving the other parent bad or wrong, cooperation may soon become impossible. When you pick a fight in order to let the anger bring you closer, you are risking your relationship for a moment's relief.

Some anger, hurt, and distrust are always present following a divorce. But even people who hate each other can coparent. They achieve this by putting the welfare of the children first and keeping their contacts to a bare minimum. Big decisions and important issues are discussed every few months, but each parent takes full responsibility for day-to-day problems while the children live in his or her house. Parents who have had friendlier divorces may be in contact every day and have a large number of shared parenting tasks. A whole range of coparenting options lie between these poles. You can adjust the degree of contact and sharing to meet your particular needs.

Privacy

A basic principle of coparenting is that you have a right to your private life. Working closely to raise children does not oblige you to reveal feelings and experiences that are unrelated to the children or their welfare. You can tell as much or as little about yourself as you wish to the other parent. There is no obligation to invite the other parent into your home. You can meet in neutral environments such as coffee shops, parks, or even parking lots.

Many recently divorced parents do use contacts around the children as an opportunity to deal with other emotional issues. They do review work together to explore what went wrong in the marriage, they seek support during the trauma of separation, or they explore their current relationship. This is fine as long as it feels comfortable for both of you.

If you find that you need more privacy or distance in the relationship, try meeting or calling less often. Also try making a clear agenda for each meeting that focuses on the children and not on you.

Divorce and separation entitle you to psychological autonomy. That means that you can adjust the level of intimacy to meet your needs. The other parent has no emotional claims on you; only the children are your shared concern.

Direct Communication

There are two components of direct communication. Say what you mean; say it to the person you mean.

Saying what you mean takes awareness on your part. You have to *know* what you think, feel, and want before you can express it in a clear way. This may take some thought and preparation. Without thinking through in advance, you may blurt out something that's too hurtful, vague or inaccurate to be useful.

People who say what they mean don't have to hint, nor do they have to soften up the listener with a mutilating salvo of complaints. They are prepared to present what they *think, feel,* and *want* directly and supportively.

Direct communcation also requires that you "talk to the person you mean." It's dangerous to communicate your feelings and needs to the other parent via the children or third parties. Such messages can be easily distorted or lost. Children are especially unrealiable as message carriers. One woman kept telling her four-year-old son that "daddy was bringing him home too late." The boy's father finally called to ask why "daddy should keep him home late." Third-party communication can be especially dangerous when you express your irritation through friends, hoping it will get back to the other parent. The result quite often is a further erosion of trust and openness.

For more specific help in direct expression see Chapter 6, "Healthy Conflict."

Explicit Agreements

Your coparenting agreement should be written out and signed by both parents. It should detail when the children will be with each parent, how contributions will be handled, how the parents will deal with holidays and vacations, and who will be responsible for medical and educational decisions and costs. Some parents include a clause stipulating the maximum number of miles they will live from each other. Other clauses may cover the contingency of one parent moving out of town, a parent losing his or her job, or when to renegotiate the agreement.

Since your coparenting agreement is constantly evolving, and you will make dozens of large and small decisions in the course of any given year, it is often a good idea to write these decisions and agreements down. Isolina Ricci suggests that all agreements should be put in memo form and copies made for each parent. While many parents would find this too formal, you should be explicit and clear about your agreements whether or not you write them down. The more detailed and explicit you are, the less chance you have of a bitter misunderstanding. One thirty-five-year-old potter put it this way: "My motto used to be 'hang loose.' But we kept making arrangements that each of us would remember differently. I'd think Jenny was supposed to be back before dinner, and he'd think after. I'd say I was taking Jenny to L.A. for a week, and he'd plan something with her for the same time. Now I write everything down."

RETREAT FROM INTIMACY

As a marriage begins to dissolve, there may be a fair amount of negative intimacy. Blame and anger often replace the original trust, respect, and honesty with which the marriage began. For months and even years after separation, negative intimacy can disrupt your parenting relationship. Old patterns of hurt, withdrawal, or sudden rage can turn a discussion about the children's winter clothes into a huge tug-of-war.

A period of withdrawal from your ex-spouse is natural following a divorce. The withdrawal can seem cold and cutting, but it helps reestablish your separate identity. And it protects you from the hurts of negative intimacy.

It's OK to pull back, but if you do you'll need to find a new way of relating. One way is to take a business-like approach. The principles of autonomy, respect, privacy, and explicit agreements are your main guideposts in a business-style coparenting relationship. As time goes on, and the old patterns of negative intimacy abate, you may find new opportunities for friendship and mutual support with your children's other parent. Whether or not a new friendship emerges, coparenting can build on the love you still share for your children as you develop a working relationship devoted to their growth and well-being.

Sample Parenting Agreement

1. Jim Seligman and Marcia Seligman are the parents of Alan, Sandra, and Laura Seligman.

2. Jim and Marcia agree to contribute to the children's support in proportion to their incomes (currently 40 percent for Marcia and 60 percent for Jim). All outlays for the children will be added up at the end of the month and a payment or adjustment made so that each parent is contributing at the agreed percentage.

3. If the income of either Marcia or Jim falls below 25 percent of their total income, he or she will still be responsible to contribute 25 percent of the children's support.

4. The children will live with Jim Friday night through Monday morning and with Marcia Monday night through Friday morning. Schedule changes may be renegotiated at any time.

5. Jim will continue to pay the children's health and dental insurance.

6. Jim and Marcia will jointly make and be responsible for educational, health, and welfare decisions for their children.

7. Both parents will have access to all school, medical, and other records of the children.

8. All childcare arrangements and baby-sitters will be chosen jointly and paid at the same ratio given in the second paragraph above.

9. Either parent can have the children for a two-week vacation. Longer periods are to be negotiated.

10. The children will be with a particular parent on alternating holidays.

11. Marcia and Jim will live no farther than ten miles from each other for the next four years.

12. If either Marcia or Jim move away from the Chicago area, she or he will give up primary parenting responsibilities.

_____
Marcia Seligman

_____
Jim Seligman

17

How to Coparent

Developing a strategy for coparenting is like buying a suit. The style and fit have to be right for you. No one wants a floppy clown suit, and no one wants a corset. And like a suit, your style of coparenting may have to be changed or altered as your needs change. How you share child-rearing tasks, how much time you want to live with your children, how much time you wish to spend consulting with the other parent, and how you want to share costs will all become part of the mix that is your unique coparenting style.

Coparenting means trying things to see what works. The mechanics will take time to smooth out. But you should feel free to experiment with different schedules and task distributions to see what feels best. During their first few months of coparenting, Alan and Sandra arranged a trade: Sandra would do all the children's laundry if Alan would take care of all transportation between their homes. After six months, it dawned on Sandra that she was putting a lot more time into the laundry than Alan put into transportation. Since the children lived with each parent 50 percent of the time, Sandra suggested that laundry and transportation tasks be handled as they came up by the parent with whom the children were living at the time. This adjustment relieved a slowly growing resentment that might otherwise have weakened the coparenting relationship.

Some parents agree to renegotiate their coparenting contract every year. Sal and Pamela had agreed that the children were to live with Sal from Monday to Friday and with Pamela from Friday to Monday. This arrangement originally made sense because Pamela worked long hours except on the weekend. When her work schedule changed, Pamela realized that the coparenting agreement left her no time for weekend socializing. When the time came to renegotiate, Pamela suggested a schedule of alternating weekends.

MECHANICS

How Much Time in Each Home?

You don't have to divide your children fifty/fifty in order to be a fully participating coparent. What you do need is a period of unbroken time, a day and a night, and preferably several days in a row, to develop a sense of living with your child. Here are some of the many possible coparenting schedules:

- Every other week
- Every two weeks
- Every other month
- Monday afternoon through Thursday morning/Thursday afternoon through Monday morning
- Tuesday afternoon through Friday morning/Friday afternoon through Tuesday morning
- Wednesday afternoon through Saturday morning/Saturday afternoon through Wednesday morning
- Tuesday and Wednesday/Thursday through Monday
- Tuesday through Saturday/Sunday and Monday
- Every other year
- September through June/June through September

In addition to these options, there are very complex arrangements where the schedule changes weekly to accommodate work or social needs. Some parents switch residences themselves so that the children can always remain in a stable environment. This is accomplished by renting an apartment where each parent resides on the "off weeks" when he or she is not living with the children.

Any coparenting schedule can work, if you work at it. Remember, if problems develop, you can always renegotiate a new schedule.

Contributions

There are four basic ways to handle contributions for your children's support: (1) flat monthly payments, (2) pay your own way, (3) add up and divide, and (4) pay by item. The *flat payment* is the traditional way contributions have been made. One parent, usually the father, pays a certain amount each month for the support of his children. The flat payment is a more complicated arrangement for coparents because the amount paid should take into account the ratio of time that the children live with each parent as well as each parent's income.

Many counties have published charts that are used as guides to determine child support. These guides are all based on the assumption that the child lives with only one parent. Since there is no established formula for contributions in a coparenting agreement, the flat payment system can be a problem. If you use the flat payment, you will probably have to rely on a court-determined formula for contributions (based on the differential between each parent's income). You will then have to customize this guideline to your own situation by taking into account the percentage of time your children spend at each parent's home.

Pay your own way is the method of choice when parents have relatively equal incomes and share the children approximately fifty percent of the time. Major expenses such as summer camps, medical care, winter clothes, and costly toys may be shared.

The *add up and divide* method is simple and straightforward. Both parents add up all child-related expenses incurred during a given month. Each parent is responsible to pay an agreed percentage of the total. If the ratio of the two parents' salaries to their total income were 25/75, then one parent would be expected to pay a quarter and the other three-quarters of all expenses. If one parent spends less than the agreed percentage, an adjustment payment is made at the end of each month.

The *pay by item* method is for people who don't have to have things exactly even. In this system, dad might pay for child care and the piano teacher while mom pays for the orthodontist and the summer school tuition. It's clear that the dollar amounts are not going to be equal, but parents who prefer this method enjoy its sense of looseness and flexibility.

The way you deal with contributions should fit the unique relationship between you and the other parent. The method that's right for you will depend on your financial situation and the degree to which you can trust and cooperate with the coparent.

Geography

In the ideal arrangement, the two parents live close enough to each other that the children can walk or bicycle between mom's house and dad's house. To live farther than biking distance leaves all the responsibility for transportation with you, the parent. Living close also makes it easier to drop children off and pick them up at school, as well as share the same baby-sitter and childcare resources.

Following a divorce, some people feel a strong impulse to move as far away from the ex-spouse as possible. There is a natural desire to develop a new life and new identity. Any reminders of the old life are unwelcome. The desire for a new neighborhood, even a new city, must be tempered with the knowledge that every extra mile makes your job as a coparent that much harder. In the end, as is so often the case in coparenting, compromise may be the only answer. You might decide to live closer than you'd wished, running the risk of seeing your ex-partner in the laundromat or supermaket, but also making it easier to participate in your children's daily activities. A forty-year-old father of three described how he wrestled with the geography problem: "I had a chance to teach at Adelphi. Now it isn't far from Jersey City, but I saw myself having the kids only on weekends at best. The weekend dad is a cliche, I just didn't want to do it. I *wanted* to help with the homework, I *wanted* to bring them to school. If I wasn't there for the everyday stuff, I'd be just a visitor in their lives."

MOVING IN

Making a Home

Children do better in a fully functional home. This is a home where meals are prepared, where children participate in chores, where the laundry gets done. The functional home has rules: there are bedtimes, limits on the TV, health and safety rules, and neighbors to call in an emergency.

One of the great dangers of coparenting is that one home will be work and the other will be play; one parent will be seen as a taskmaster, and the other as a recreation director. But the home without chores or rules or limits isn't really a home. Going there is like going to the bowling alley or the movies. Everyone likes a good time, but a child needs more than good times to grow up. To avoid this polarity, each parent should develop a routine and structure that makes the home work. One of the best ways to do this is for parents and children to do chores together, prepare meals together, even shop together.

The Children's Things

It's important for children to feel that they have their own territory in each home. They need to have their own beds, their own toothbrushes, and their own dressers or at least their own drawers. Children should also have their own toys in each home and a space to put them. Some favorite toys, of course, will go back and forth between homes. But other toys remain a permanent part of the environment at dad's house or mom's house, and will be there waiting when the child returns.

Clothes are a special problem. Many parents find it financially impossible to buy two separate wardrobes for each child. Some clothes will probably go back and forth between each home, but the fewer the better. A child who lives out of a suitcase feels a sense of impermanence. A home is where you have your own things and your own space. If at all possible, children should have their own underthings, socks, and shirts or blouses at each home. Several trousers or skirts are also helpful. Winter clothes, dress clothes, and favorite garments can make the commute between the two houses.

The importance of providing children with their own territory cannot be over-emphasized. Without their own clothes, toys, bed, and storage area, the children may see their second home as a place to visit, not live. As time goes on, they may resist going to the second home because they lack a real sense of personal space there.

Another reason for children to keep some things in each home is that commuting is made easier. If you live close enough for your children to travel under their own power, anything they have to carry becomes a problem and increases their reliance on you as the chauffeur. Ideally, the trip to their other house should involve carrying no more than what fits comfortably in a knapsack.

Continuity

No matter how you cushion it, divorce is a trauma for children. A good rule of thumb following a separation is that you should make only one major change at a time. If possible, one of the parents should remain in the original home for at least the first year. This means that the children can stay in the same school, keep the same friends, and play in the same neighborhood. Your children will already have plenty to adjust to as they learn about their second home and neighborhood. One big change is enough.

A thirty-year-old preschool teacher described her conflicts over the continuity issue. "I hated the house. Those last months were so horrible that I wanted to hang up a 'for sale' sign and never come back. But we agreed that one of us had to stay there so the kids could finish Edgemont grammar school and wouldn't be up-rooted just now. Finally, Jim agreed to stay in the house, and I moved to Burlingame—ten miles away. It's a long commute on mornings when I have to bring them to school, but I knew they had to stay put for awhile."

The New Neighborhood

If you are the parent who moves, you and your child have an important task. You both have to orient to your new neighborhood. The best way is to take a walk, noticing as you go the parks and playing fields, the important landmarks, the busy streets where a child shouldn't play. This is the time to clearly delineate the boundaries your child may not roam beyond without an adult.

The process of learning about a new neighborhood can be an adventure for both of you. You can say hello to potential playmates, look into the local stores, and introduce yourselves to neighbors. Each orientation walk makes a very important statement to your child. You're saying, "This is our home and our neighborhood. As you parent, I'm showing you the limits and the potentials of this place we share."

Avoiding Confusion

It's natural for the children to have a period of confusion during the first few weeks of coparenting. They have a whole new environment to adjust to. There will be new rules and new customs as mom and dad develop their independent parenting styles.

Children are flexible and adaptive. What they need most are two fully-involved parents. As long as a child doesn't feel abandoned, he or she can tolerate a great deal of change.

Some of the initial two-home confusion is avoidable. Children who know where they will be on any given night are less confused than children who are given no information about the coparenting schedule. The best plan is to post a schedule in each home, and go over with your child exactly where he or she will be during the next few weeks.

Even three- and four-year-olds seem perfectly able to remember which days they "switch." The scheduled moves between each parent's home become part of the child's internal calendar. Just as he knows what days he has to get up for school and what days he goes to cub scouts, he also knows when he will next be at his other parent's home.

One mother described how she used a posted schedule to allay her child's anxiety during the first month of coparenting. Her schedule was a complicated one, so she layed it out over a four-week period.

	Monday	Tuesday	Wednesday	Thursday	Friday	Saturday	Sunday
Week 1	Mom's	Mom's	Dad's	Dad's	Dad's	Dad's	Dad's
Week 2	Mom's	Mom's	Dad's	Dad's	Mom's	Mom's	Mom's
Week 3	Mom's	Mom's	Dad's	Dad's	Dad's	Dad's	Dad's
Week 4	Mom's	Mom's	Dad's	Dad's	Mom's	Mom's	Mom's

"During the first month, Billy occasionally had to ask which week he was in. Since the chart was up in both houses, his father helped him keep track by marking the week that was about to begin. By the second month he had no trouble anticipating when he switched."

Children's Participation

Coparenting decisions should be made by the parents. A child's input is important, but he should never be burdened with the responsibility of choosing which parent he will live with or what schedule is best for him.

As children get older, they will give more spontaneous feedback about the coparenting arrangement. From a ten-year-old little league fanatic: "I want to be at dad's house on Saturdays 'cause that's when we have practice. Dad understands the game. He can tell whether I've hit a home run or a pop fly to center. It's just more fun when he's there." Children also give input about the toys and articles of clothing that they want to keep at each house. "We have this huge suitcase that we have to pack every Wednesday night when we go to dad's. It would be a lot easier if I had some school clothes at his house." *(Nine-year-old girl)* "The erector set should be at dad's. He's the only one who can work it." *(Seven-year-old boy)*

When children get to age 14 or 15, they may spontaneously decide that they prefer to live at one house or the other. Some parents go along with this, feeling that the middle teen years are a good time to share coparenting decisions with the children. Other parents keep control longer. It's a matter of preference and style. What's clear is that the input you allow your child should be age-appropriate. Younger children are frightened by too much responsibility and need you to be in firm control. As children get older, and begin struggling toward autonomy, their input should play an increasing role in your decision making.

HURDLES

Responsible Child Care

Here is one of the most fundamental parenting rules: *Every parent needs time off.* Parents who have the kids for stretches of a week or more *must* have time off, both for their own sake and for that of the children. You need the renewal you get from time alone and from contact with other adults. Without it you will become emotionally malnourished and short on the patience, energy, and creativity required for effective parenting. A good baby-sitter, someone you and your coparent trust, will give you the time you need for yourself so that you can spend higher-quality time with your children.

A 32-year-old mother of three, whose children ranged from 2 to 6, described her evolving attitude toward baby-sitters. "Partly from a philosophical position and partly because we haven't much money, I tried to handle all the child care myself. I thought, 'I just have the kids every other week, I can hack it.' But I found you can't have a social life every other week. Men don't want to be on hold that long. I was running myself into the ground."

Since most parents work, child care in the afternoon is often a major consideration. The ideal arrangement is for both parents to use the same childcare resource. When this isn't possible, parents are encouraged to jointly interview and select the childcare arrangements for each home.

The cost of child care is a major factor in many coparenting agreements. Some parents, who choose to share their children equally, simply agree that each will pay for his or her own child care. Where there is a serious disparity in income, the total childcare bill can be paid on a percentage basis (split 60/40, for example). One parent may elect to work fewer hours in order to take on more childcare duties. In such cases, the other parent may contribute more in order to compensate for the loss of income. "Dave and I both felt I should spend more time with the children while they're still preschoolers. So I cut down at work to 20 hours a week and he helps me make up the difference. We figure we'd have to pay for more child care if I worked full-time, so we're not losing that much." *(31-year-old respiratory therapist)*

Keeping Current

One of the hardest things to get used to as a coparent is that a significant part of your child's life is spent in another world. He's meeting people and having important experiences that you know nothing about. A six-year-old described this weekend at dad's house: "The nicest thing that happened, mom, was that Sally took me and Jeff to Marine World. . .Oh that's right, she's this woman who lives in the apartment next to dad, and Jeff is a year younger than me." And there are events you'll hear nothing about at all. Scrapes and bruises, minor health problems, and difficulties at school may never reach your ears.

The way to deal with this information gap is to stay current. That means regular conferences with the other parent and a check-in whenever the children change houses. This check-in should include a review of major systems: school, health, relationships, meaningful events. The check-in will keep you from feeling so cut off from your child's other life. It will also help you with continuity. If Johnny was being picked on at school while he was at your house, you can ask how Johnny's been coping with the bully during his stay with his dad.

Another way to stay current is to make sure you are privy to all school and health records. If you are a child's second parent (the one who moved to another home), you are going to need to take steps to establish your identity with the school. Call in your name, address, and phone number and request that copies of report cards be sent to you. Make sure that you are informed about any behavioral or academic problems. Your child's doctor should also have your address and number. He or she should get used to hearing from both parents when a medical problem arises. It's a good idea to give your number to den mothers, reading tutors, and parents of the kid's friends. In that way you are part of the network of people who have some relationship to your child.

Special Schedules

Some of the biggest conflicts for coparents arise from the scheduling of holidays and birthdays. "Stan always wanted Peter on his birthday. I went along with it for a few years and then I began to think, 'Why should I always miss out on my son's birthday?' Stan insisted that I had Peter with me more of the time and this was one way of compensating for that. I couldn't believe that he was being so pigheaded. We finally agreed to have him every other year. Don't ask about Christmas, that's still a mess."

The best way to avoid this hassle is to schedule vacations, holidays, and birthdays in advance. If there are conflicts, trade off holidays every other year.

It is extremely important that coparents make contingency plans in the event of illness or special problems. If a child is sick at school, make sure you know who picks him up, who takes the day off to care for him. "The first time Kim had a problem at school, we were both completely thrown. We had a fight on the phone about who would pick her up. It came down to whose job was more important, who could afford to miss work. When the crisis was over, we sat down and decided what we would do if Kim were sick again. I just couldn't go through another crazy phone conversation like that while she was lying ill in the nurse's office." *(Recently divorced father of seven-year-old Kim)*

New Relationships

Coparenting relationships often reach a critical point when a new lover or a mate comes into either parent's life. Your child suddenly has another father or mother figure. It's natural to feel concern about sharing your children with a stranger. Feelings of resentment and jealousy may surface, as well as real questions about the parenting abilities of the new person.

When a coparent finds a new mate, it's normal to feel some competitiveness. What if your child seems strongly attracted to this new person? What if he pulls away from you? This fear may cover a secret belief that you are unlovable, that your child would abandon you if he had anyone else to play your role. But you are irreplaceable. You've been there from the beginning, sharing sickness and joy, hurt and affection. Your bond runs deep. This fear of loss may also grow from an assumption that your child's love and affection is like a pie that must be divided in thinner and thinner slices as more parenting figures enter his life. The truth is that children have an unlimited capacity to love. Your child's love for you will not diminish because another caring adult has entered his life. One mother put it this way: "I could sense that Timmy was strongly drawn to his dad's girlfriend. She bought him things and generally doted on him. I was afraid she would be a good-time mommy and by comparison I'd look like the wicked witch of the west. But even though Timmy enjoys her and appreciates her, our relationship is about the same. If anything, he seems a little happier with me because he's also happier at his dad's house."

Here is another natural fear: that the new lover or.mate will try to take over and do an incompetent job of parenting. It's true that your child's environment in the other home may be very much determined by a new lover or mate. But you are still your child's parent. You are still the one who *knows* and *decides*. "I felt this wave of anger when Julie had Tom move in with her. Tom was nice enough, but I didn't want my daughter to have two fathers. To be honest, I guess I was scared that she'd like him better than me. I thought he was too easy-going with her. Finally I just realized I couldn't control what happened at Julie's house. I had my daughter three nights a week, and July and I made most of the decisions together, so there was no point in going crazy about the whole thing." *(Father of a three-year-old)*

Over a Lot of Objections

Friends, family, and lawyers will usually be puzzled, and sometimes disapproving, when you discuss your coparenting plans. A lot of people remain firm believers that children belong with one parent, in one home. Lawyers in particular will give you a hard time. They won't know how to write a coparenting agreement or work out a contribution system. They may immediately tell you that it can't work, or a court won't allow it, or that you are weakening your case. Don't listen. If your lawyer won't cooperate, find one who will. Or be a broken record: "Yes, I realize it's unusual, and there's quite a problem working out the details, but we each intend to have the children about fifty percent of the time . . . Yes, I know it's unusual, but I want you to write an agreement that assumes the children will live some of the time in each home."

Grandparents and relatives may be horrified, or at the very least uncomfortable, with a two-home arrangement. Argument won't get you anywhere. Their concerns are based on values and traditions that you are trying to change. Your family will come around when they see that the children stay happy and healthy despite their commute between two homes. The grandfather of a six-year-old described his changing viewpoint in this way: "I couldn't believe she wasn't going to be harmed by this setup. Three nights here and four nights there. It seemed like it would be too confusing and uprooting for a small child. But it's a year now and I can't see any sign of trouble. The divorce didn't seem to affect her like it does a lot of kids. She seems very close to my son and daughter-in-law."

IV

18

Surviving as a Single

The sudden plunge into single life following a divorce can be enormously unsettling. There's much to adjust to. Most people face a reduced standard of living and a change of life style. The responsibilities of single parenting may weigh heavily, while at the same time decisions must be made about returning to school or reentering the job market. Self-doubt and fear of the unknown mix with loneliness in a painful approach-avoidance conflict about dating and new relationships. A newly divorced single may want to reach out to the opposite sex, but many years may have passed since he or she last dated. The rules and mores have changed. Socializing with other single adults seems foreign, almost dangerous.

Returning to the single life is not something that happens overnight. It involves acquiring new skills and changing old attitudes. This chapter, and the two that follow, focus on specific skills you'll need to live comfortably and competently in the single world. They will also focus on attitudes and beliefs that inhibit and undermine your adjustment.

FINANCES

If you're newly separated or divorced, money is likely to be your most immediate problem. Cases where the financial status of the two ex-spouses makes it unnecessary for either to lower his or her standard of living are extremely rare. The old adage that two can live as cheaply as one may not be totally accurate, but two separate households are usually much more expensive to maintain than a single home.

Many newly divorced people have an unrealistic picture of how much it costs to survive as a single person or single parent. If your spouse handled all of the budgeting or did most of the shopping, you may not know how much income you need to survive as a single person. An indispensable first step is to establish a budget that lists your sources of income and your monthly expenses. (See the sample monthly budget.)

Very often, on the first time through a budget, you'll find that total expenses exceed your total income. So it's time to find ways to save. Here are some suggestions.

Food

- Don't shop with your children. They'll encourage you to buy expensive junk food and sugar-laden cereals.
- Buy generic or housename brands. When you purchase brand names, you're paying for the advertising.
- Buy fowl rather than red meat. Buy whole birds and cut them yourself.
- Take only the amount you can afford to spend to the store.
- Buy in bulk. Get hamburger in large, freezer lots, rewrap in aluminum, and freeze.
- Establish a budget for food and rigidly adhere to it. Bring a small calculator to the store and keep a running total as you shop.

Clothing

- Shop at thrift stores or factory outlets.
- Go to department stores only during special sales days.
- Flea markets or tag sales are a good source for young children's clothes.

Rent and Mortgage Payments

- Rent a room in your house to a college student or a person you'd be comfortable living with.
- Rent out your garage.
- Share an apartment with another single.

Insurance

- Research alternate plans. For example, health maintenance organizations such as Kaiser-Permanente are often cheaper than carriers such as Blue Cross.

Child Care

- Childcare co-ops where you donate your time are cheaper than hiring baby-sitters.
- Investigate publicly funded daycare programs in your area.

Utilities

- Don't heat rooms you're not currently using.
- At night, keep heat in by drawing the drapes.
- Consider the cost-effectiveness of insulating your house.

Transportation

- Join a car pool.
- Consider giving up your car for a bike or motor scooter.
- For out-of-town trips, use buses or trains.

MONTHLY BUDGET

Income		Expenses	
Salary	_____	Food	_____
Commissions	_____	Clothing	_____
Interest	_____	Rent or mortgage payments	_____
Dividends from stocks and bonds	_____	Insurance	_____
Other sources of income	_____	Child care	_____
Alimony	_____	Taxes	_____
Child support	_____	Education	_____
		Medical	_____
		Utilities	_____
		Transportation	_____
		Recreation and entertainment	_____
		Children's allowances	_____
		Other expenses	_____
		Alimony	_____
		Child support	_____
TOTAL INCOME	_____	TOTAL EXPENSES	_____

MONTHLY SURPLUS OR DEFICIT   _____

Miscellaneous

- Invest in electric clippers and do your hair-cutting at home.
- Allow your magazine subscriptions and book clubs to expire. These are often quite expensive and little-read.
- Do-it-yourself: painting, repairing, shelves, gardening.
- Don't use credit cards. If you do use plastic, be sure to pay the full bill at the end of each month to avoid interest charges.
- Make your own lunch and lunches for the children.
- Buy household items from garage sales.
- Buy from discount, wholesale, or factory outlets for big ticket items.

Having considered ways to save, review your budget with an eye to balancing it. If the totals still look bleak, turn to the income side of the ledger. You may need more money from child or spousal support, or you may need to generate additional earned income. A budget is something to be played with. While the figures can sometimes be gloomy reminders of a lowered standard of living, they can also be altered as you find new ways to economize or discover additional sources of income. A budget will help you know your limits. As you approach your monthly allocation for a particular item or category, you can begin to economize. You will probably discover as you go along that you have budgeted too much for some items, too little for others. These adjustments will help you make more realistic plans and keep you from living in the red.

JOBS

Newly divorced women face an important challenge when they attempt to reenter the job market. There are often pressures from ex-husbands, or even from the courts in the form of "rehabilitative alimony," to begin a frantic search for work. The inability to balance your budget without a drastic change in life style may also fuel your anxiety to find work. The first step is to determine the level of employment you need.

Many divorced women with children make extra money at home. Mary, who had always enjoyed amateur photography, built up a business from her knack of taking children's portraits. Clients came to her house, where she had set up a small studio. Perhaps the most common way to earn money at home is by baby-sitting. As one woman put it, "Adding a few more kids to the brood doesn't make much difference. I make a few hundred extra a month, and it's very little extra work." Other women make money through crafts such as macrame, jewelry, leather, and pottery. Some women silkscreen T-shirts or go in for clothes design.

The next level of employment is part-time work. This is again for women with small children who want to work while the children are at school or at day care. The most likely sources for such jobs are local shops, businesses that need part-time bookkeepers, and individuals looking for housekeepers, cooks, or gardeners.

The next higher level of employment is full-time, semi-skilled. Receptionists, secretaries, and waitresses fall into this category. These are jobs that women can walk into without huge amounts of training or experience. The disadvantages are that they often involve very hard work for relatively little pay. A secretary who never gets a moment's rest may make a quarter of her boss's salary.

The highest employment level is full-time, skilled. These jobs may take years of training. Nurses, computer programmers, managers, teachers, and physical therapists are examples. Choosing this level of employment may mean holding down a part- or full-time job while going to night school.

How you look for a job will very much depend on the level of employment you need. If you do arts and crafts at home, your task will be finding stores that are willing to sell your products on consignment. If you're looking for a part-time job in a neighborhood shop, your best bet is to canvas the stores by personally calling on the owners or managers. It takes courage to walk in cold and ask for a job, but this is probably the most effective method for getting hired as a salesperson, a waitress, or a service station attendant.

The first step in reentering the job market at the full-time, semi-skilled level is to determine what jobs are available in the areas where you are qualified. Checking the newspaper want-ads is a severely limited method, since so many people read them and competition for the jobs listed is stiff. Unless you have special skills, the want-ads may not work for you. If you can afford the initial expense, you might consider seeing one of the career consultants listed in your phone book. If not, go to the library or local bookstore and read one of the many books on the subject of careers and career training (*What Color Is Your Parachute?* is among the best). Local colleges and high schools also usually have low-cost or free classes and lectures on the subject of reentry into the job market.

One of the most important pieces of advice you'll hear is that word-of-mouth and personal contact are much more likely to provide job opportunities than ads in a newspaper. One 39-year-old nurse explained the process in this way. "There's a nursing glut right now, and there are a lot fewer openings than there used to be. I started out looking at ads, but there were 35 applicants for every opening. Then I realized that I had friends who were nurses at five local hospitals. I asked them to give me advance notice of any openings and to let me know what the specific job requirements would be. I got a job in three weeks that way."

Getting the job you want can take several steps. You may have to take a temporary, less-desirable position while you get trained in skills for a really good job. It took Sandra almost three years to reach her career goal. After years of raising children at home, she had to attend a local community college class to get her typing speed up to acceptable levels. After three months of daily classes, she was typing fast enough to get a job through a temporary employment agency. Six months later, one of the companies she worked for as a "temp" finally offered her a job. With the security of steady employment, Sandra enrolled in a school for computer programming. Two years of night classes got her a certificate and a job with a local bank.

What Fields Are Open?

According to a 1981 survey by the Bureau of Labor Statistics, these are the fields that offer the most promise in the 1980s:

- Paralegal services
- Computer technology and data processing
- Food preparation
- Employment interviewing
- Architecture
- Dentistry
- Physical Therapy
- Childcare services
- Veterinary science
- Travel agencies
- Health care

Each of these fields contains many specific job categories. Dentistry, for example, includes hygienists, surgical assistants, receptionists, and so on. Computer technology includes CRT operators, data processing, keypunchers, programmers, researchers, systems analysts, technicians, salespersons, repair personnel, and so on. Health care is a rapidly growing field, and there's a particularly high demand for nurses' aides and orderlies. There is also a demand for dieticians, electro-cardiograph technicians, emergency medical technicians, lab technicians, nurses, and physical, occupational, and respiratory therapists.

Finding Work

Ask a friend. Get the word out to all your relatives, friends, and neighbors. Any of them might have the lead you've been looking for. The more people you ask, the more opportunity you have of getting the most precious of commodities: the inside tip. Companies often give preference in hiring to individuals suggested by their own employees. If you can get a recommendation as well as a lead, it vastly improves your chances of being hired.

One of the best ways of reinforcing your seriousness about getting a job is to give your friends a copy of your resume. Go over it with them, describe your strong points, and tell them what you're looking for. Encourage them to pass it along to anyone who might be interested.

Private employment agencies. The nice thing about employment agencies is the possibility of "one-stop shopping." One agency can put you in touch with many potential employers and help you to search for jobs in several different employment categories. The usual course is for agencies to provide you with a description of job openings which fit your particular qualifications. You then make the choice of which of these opportunities to pursue.

Agencies charge fees that may be paid by the employer, the job-seeker, or both. When signing up with an agency, be sure you are clear who is paying the fee and how it will be paid. Choose an appropriate agency. The majority of private agencies specialize in certain fields and professions. You don't want to go to an agency which specializes in placing salesmen if you're looking for work as an editor.

Government employment agencies. Government agencies charge no fee. They tend to have a large number of listings, particularly in semi-skilled job categories. Counselors at these agencies are often willing to help with tips on interviewing techniques as well as to provide information about which fields have higher job availability.

Government jobs. Federal, state, and local governments combined employ nearly 15 million Americans. One out of six employed persons works for the government. Government employs people in every job classification imaginable and provides the added advantage of civil service protection.

Nearly all government jobs are filled by competitive examination. These tests may be written, oral, or require you to actually perform tasks that are typical of the job. If you pass the test, you are put on "the list." The highest scores are called first, and a list may exist for months or years before another round of testing.

Getting a job with the government requires research. You have to find out all the job classifications for which tests will be held in the near future. Unfortunately these efforts must be duplicated at the federal, state, and local levels.

Big companies. Make a list of the major corporations in your area. The chamber of commerce will help you research such a list if you need help. Big utilities in particular do a lot of hiring in many different job categories. A trip to the personnel department at these large firms may not yield a job on the first try, but if you keep calling and keep updating your application, you may eventually land something.

Temporary services. Temporary agencies are an ideal way to secure a full-time *permanent* job. The paradox of a temporary position turning into a permanent one is a simple matter of being at the right place at the right time. A good temporary worker is often the first one offered a job when an opening occurs for a permanent position. Hiring temporary employees for permanent positions is good economics. Why should a company run ads and go through an extensive interview process when they already have a worker who's proven that he or she can do the job?

A temporary position has other advantages. It allows you to sample a number of office and business environments. When Aretha was hired to do a temporary job with a publishing firm, she found that she liked an environment where people talked about books. She eventually got a permanent job as a proofreader and within two years was an assistant editor. Arthur worked as a temporary clerk at a local diabetes association. He became very interested in the organization's activities. When a funding increase enabled the association to hire an assistant to the director, no interviews were held. Arthur immediately stepped into the position.

Volunteer work. Surprisingly, volunteer work is one of the best ways to find a paid position. Like temporary work, it's a good way to establish a track record and prove that you can do a job well. Volunteering also provides an opportunity to learn or improve skills so you can be more competitive in the job market.

There are two primary ways you can parlay volunteer work into paid employment: (1) volunteer in a particular field so that you can show current job experience on your resume, or (2) volunteer at an agency where you'd like a job and then make yourself indispensable. Sandra hadn't worked in ten years, but her last job was for a company that put on conventions and industrial exhibits. In order to get current convention experience, she volunteered at the San Francisco Convention Center for six months. The experience increased her confidence and was an important plus on her resume. Janelle had gotten a master's degree in social welfare during her married years, but had never worked. Following her separation, she began volunteering at a treatment center for adolescent girls. Four months later she was offered a paid half-time position.

Help wanted ads. No one looking for work can ignore the classified ads. When looking through the classifieds, be sure you know all the terms and descriptions used for the particular job categories you seek. It's advisable to pursue as many opportunities as possible. Try for a lot of interviews: a job that seems even vaguely promising should be followed up with a resume or a phone call.

Situation wanted ads. This is a long shot, but it could pay off. Situation wanteds in local newspapers seem to be mostly used by baby-sitters, gardeners, and handymen. They probably won't land you a job as a computer programmer or industrial consultant. If you're looking for a job that's closer to consultant than baby-sitter, you might try a classified ad in a trade journal that's published specifically for your field. Trade journals are geared to the needs of specialists for particular businesses and industries. To find the names of trade journals in your field, ask a reference librarian for a copy of *Standard, Rates, and Data,* a directory listing names and descriptions of all major periodicals.

Direct mail campaigns. This approach can be an important part of job hunting. The first step is to compile a list of possible employers. Use the yellow pages or names provided by your local chamber of commerce. Remember that you'll have to write a cover letter to every employer on your list, so don't make it too long. Your cover letter should say what position you are applying for and include a short statement indicating your qualifications. Highlight any relevant experience from your resume. Your final paragraph should indicate that you'll call in a few days to arrange an interview. Three things are important in a cover letter: that it be short, individually typed, and addressed, if possible, to a particular person.

Your resume, sent along with a cover letter, should be a one-page summary of your education, experience (including volunteer work), and qualifications. In listing your job history, the job title isn't enough. You must describe your specific responsibilities and the skills required. Mention significant achievements.

RETURNING TO SCHOOL

For many women, the return to work must be postponed in order to obtain further education. They need special skills or advanced degrees to compete effectively in the job market. A high school diploma is critical. If you didn't graduate, adult classes are an available remedy. If you already have good academic skills, you may wish to bypass the classes and take the G.E.D. exam to gain your diploma.

Those who are already close to a college degree should consider postponing the job search until finishing the classes that remain. Be sure that your degree is useful in seeking employment. As a general rule, liberal arts majors don't do well in the job market. It's better to pursue a degree that qualifies you for specific jobs. Generally, business degrees are the most useful.

Many colleges now have special degree programs for women returning to the work force. "Weekend College" at Chicago's Mundelein College has designed special career programs for older women. Some of these programs require as few as fifteen courses for a certificate. Colorado College for Women, in Denver, offers a range of curricula tailored to the individual needs of women reentering the job market.

Schools are increasingly sensitive to the fact that older students must work as well as attend classes. It isn't necessary to face the hard choice: work or school. You can now do both. At Trinity College in Burlington, Vermont, students attend class every other weekend. Triton Junior College in River Grove, Illinois, offers a three-year associate degree, even though students only attend two days a week. Goddard College in Plainfield, Vermont, was the first of the "universities without walls" to give students credit for experience outside the classroom. Now there are dozens of schools that cut short formal academic requirements with "external degree" programs. Volunteer work, job experience, and special field trips or research projects can earn many units toward graduation.

Business, secretarial, computer programming, and other special schools provide another educational option. They can often be of greater immediate assistance than an academic college or university. Correspondence schools may also be worth trying, as long as you're careful to check out the school before signing on the bottom line. Not all of them are reputable.

CHILDREN AND WORKING

Some employers fear that children will distract single parents from their work. They worry about absenteeism when the kids are sick or a sitter doesn't come. Assure an employer that you have contingency plans for normal childhood illnesses or a childcare snafu. Agree that it's possible you might miss a few days if a child were *severely* ill, but stress that in your experience this would be a rare occurrence.

There are some jobs where you may be forced to define your priorities: career or children? You can't be on the road one week out of every month and be a happy, full-time parent. You can't work till eight or nine every night and cook balanced family dinners. What kind of life style do you want for you and your children? Seek a job that reflects your priorities.

Child care can be a serious financial problem. After paying for a sitter or daycare center, you may not have much money left over from your job. One answer is to work four days a week and spend the fifth volunteering at a daycare co-op. Your child care will be next to free. A second possibility is to job-share with another single parent. Many employers are willing to give a full-time job to two half-time workers. They know that half-time employees work harder and are absent less. Find a single parent with similar job skills and begin applying together for the same positions. When you aren't working, you can baby-sit each other's kids.

You may fear that as a working parent you can't do as good a job raising your children as a full-time parent could. There is no one formula for raising children correctly, because each child is an individual with differing needs. When children have a good daycare environment, there is every reason to believe that they are acquiring valuable skills by socializing and experiencing the world away from mommy or daddy. There are some experiences that they must have on their own. As long as you give your children guidance, love, and attention when you are with them, they will thrive.

POSTDIVORCE DISCRIMINATION ON LOANS AND CREDIT

Women in particular have had trouble securing loans and credit after a divorce. Many women have no independent credit rating and are denied cards in their own name. When applying for a major loan, they are often required to find a cosigner (many an ex-husband has cosigned an ex-wife's car loan) or put up a disproportionate amount of collateral.

The first thing you should know is that the Equal Credit Opportunity Act does provide you some protection. Credit departments, loan offices, banks, and credit card companies by law may not discriminate against you because you are single or a woman. If credit is refused, they must explain why. If two people have the same income and assets, a bank or loan company cannot require a cosigner for one (because she happens to be a woman) and not for the other (because he's a man). While this law can be circumvented, the mere threat of legal action against a credit institution may produce desirable results.

Establishing your own credit, independent of an ex-spouse, is often done in gradual stages. Step one is to get an easy-to-acquire credit card (usually from an oil company or a local department store). This will help you establish a credit track record when applying for more versatile cards like VISA and Mastercharge. These major cards are important symbols of your financial stability and ability to pay. They indicate that you're a good risk should you later apply for a loan to purchase a car, pay a child's college tuition, and so on.

HELP FROM PUBLIC AGENCIES

There are many free or low-cost services available from government agencies and nonprofit organizations. These include medical care (in the form of Medicaid, free clinics, emergency services at public hospitals), education, special training, legal assistance, child care in some areas, food, housing, and psychotherapy.

Sometimes it takes Ph.D. level research skills to find these agencies and services. But they are there. The phone book can be a major resource. Call agencies that have promising names (for example, Legal Aid Society or Free Medical Clinic) and tell them what you need. Ask for referrals if they don't provide the particular service you need or you require additional services. Keep calling and keep asking questions until you've tracked down what you need.

If you're severely short of funds, you may be eligible for food stamps or Aid For Dependent Children (AFDC). This help is available so that you can have time to get back on your feet, and there is no shame in making use of a resource that can protect you and your children as you struggle with the economic impact of your divorce. Two suggestions when going to the welfare office: (1) find out in advance what documents you will need and bring them with you (birth certificates, rent receipts, income tax return, bank book, utility and medical bills, and so on); (2) ask for your welfare worker's name and establish a positive rapport with this person. He or she is your link to the system and can make things harder or easier for you.

LIVING ARRANGEMENTS

Housing for the Noncustodial Parent

The noncustodial parent is usually the one who has to move out. This means a sudden change in your environment and life style. The most common choice of postseparation housing is a studio or one-bedroom apartment. An apartment's advantage over shared living arrangements is the privacy it provides. The disadvantages are high cost and an increased danger of loneliness.

One way to avoid loneliness and pay a reasonable rent is to move to a singles apartment complex. Everett recalls the tough time he had adjusting to a one-bedroom apartment after moving out of his spacious home. But he loved the swimming pool at his complex and discovered that he enjoyed the many opportunities his new environment gave him to socialize with other singles. Now, during surges of loneliness, he takes comfort in the awareness that friends are only a few doors away.

Sharing an apartment or house with a roommate saves money and can provide important emotional support. Roommates often become friends who comfort you in those days when you ride the postdivorce rollercoaster. Roommates can be found through a number of methods:

1. Spread the word to friends, relatives, and fellow workers that you seek a roommate.
2. Read the share-rentals section of the classified ads in your local newspaper.

3. Look at bulletin boards in supermarkets, laundromats, college campuses, church halls, and so on.
4. Go to a roommates bureau.

Another housing alternative is to live in a communal setting. After her divorce, Betty went out apartment hunting. She heard about an old mansion that had twenty rooms, a hot tub, antique furniture, and spacious grounds. The only catch was that she would have to share the mansion with eight others. She didn't know whether she could get along with so many unrelated people, but decided to take a chance. She found that she liked communal living and now regards her roommates as "almost like family."

Most people experience some rough weeks when they move to a new apartment or home. Things feel all wrong. The walls squeeze in on them. The clock ticks, traffic drones monotonously outside the window. The familiar comforts of home and family seem forever lost, part of a closed chapter. Expect these feelings. Give them time to pass. But if your sense of displacement doesn't diminish within several months, consider the possibility that you have chosen the wrong environment. If you are living alone, you may need to live with people. If your window gives on a busy thoroughfare, you may need to move across from a park. If the walls are bare and you have three straightbacked chairs for a living room ensemble, you should consider redecorating. "It took me awhile to realize that I didn't have to settle for some backwater dump and call it home just because my marriage ended. I didn't have to live in a building where I could hear all the toilets flush. I could find an environment that made me feel good, then customize it so it reflected who I am." *(58-year-old longshoreman)*

Finding Housing With Children

Looking for a place to live with your children may be a bit more difficult because your desire to provide them with as much stability as possible is likely to make you less able to experiment. Nonetheless, communal living may still be an excellent option. It's nice to know that someone will probably be home when your child comes home even if you can't be there. The presence of other responsible adults can take a great deal of the burden of single parenting off your shoulders.

If you are looking for a place for just you and your children, you will undoubtedly run into landlords who do not like to rent to families. Children mean noise and damage to many apartment owners. As a single parent looking for housing you should do two things. (1) Get lots of references (from employers, previous landlords, a note from your babysitter stipulating that yours are the sweetest kids she's ever known, and so on). Make up the references if you have to. (2) Bring your children to the interview with the landlord. Make sure they're scrubbed, polished, and well behaved. Some landlords will let themselves be charmed by your kids and therefore be more willing to rent to you despite their prejudices.

Laws against discrimination are probably your last resort. Many states have such statutes. Learn the law and be ready to quote it when landlords turn you down with the old "somebody saw it last night and decided to take it" lie.

HEALTH

The initial shock of divorce can make you a high risk for various stress-related diseases (ulcers, colitis, high blood pressure, and so on). During the first months of adjustment, special care should be taken to protect your body from the effects of rapid change and strong emotions. Exercise is an excellent "stress protector," as are stress-formula vitamins, a good diet, visits with friends, and "asking for help" from people who care for you.

Studies show that divorced people don't live as long as those who are married. It turns out, however, that longevity isn't a factor of marital status, but rather of the propensity of divorced people to become isolated. You can be healthy as a divorced person as long as you keep close contact with signficant others. The risk of premature death is two to three times higher for isolated people than it is for those who have close friends.

Poor nutrition is also often a result of isolation. Shared meals are a time of family closeness, and without that closeness cooking and eating often become lonely tasks to be hurried through as quickly as possible. Meals become starker, and nutritional balance goes by the board. Newly divorced men in particular have a problem with their diets because they frequently don't know how to cook. The "Swanson set" diet of processed food or restaurant food they rely on usually has many fewer vitamins and nutrients than freshly cooked foods.

If you do find yourself sitting down to night after night of TV dinners, consider changing not only *what* but also *how* you are eating. Find a way to include others in your mealtimes, whether by issuing or accepting invitations or by taking the larger step of adding a roommate to your living arrangements. If you feel shy about your cooking abilities, widen them by finding someone who'll be willing to show you how to prepare a new dish as a trade for your purchase of its raw materials. A well-balanced meal includes more than the ingredients nutritionists specify. It also includes the balance of intimacy that the people who share it provide.

SURVIVING EMOTIONALLY AS A SINGLE

Becoming single requires far more than adjusting to a new budget and a new job. As a separated or divorced person you're aware of the emotional toll that this transition takes. The rollercoaster shoots you from anger to hurt to sadness to moments of giddy relief. One of the most painful and difficult parts of the adjustment is learning to cope with loneliness.

How To Beat Loneliness

Loneliness is an inevitable part of being newly single. So much of the old life is suddenly gone: the sense of partnership, the company of another adult, the shared tasks, even the fights. It's hard to do things alone that you once did together. Eating out or going to a movie may be a strange, unsettling experience if done alone. Even the strongest, most independent people have moments when time drags and life suddenly seems empty.

Some people react to loneliness by becoming frightened. It's painful and they want the pain to stop. They fear that the loneliness has no end, that they're helpless to overcome the isolation. Other people react by succumbing to depression. As one man put it, "I feel kind of tired all the time, weighed down. I call my ex-wife, but she doesn't want to talk to me. I call my daughter, but she's busy chasing boys. I can't seem to get out of it, I can't seem to get interested in anything."

It's not necessary for you to endure unremitting anxiety or depression as a result of being alone. There are effective techniques to help you fight the loneliness.

1. Accept it. Part of the pain of loneliness comes from fearing or resisting it. Tell yourself that what you're going through is similar to what millions of other divorced people experience. They got through it and so will you. Notice how your loneliness waxes and wanes. At times you feel relatively content, while at others the emptiness gnaws at you. The next time that the loneliness is acute, remember that there are moments when you feel perfectly all right. As the recovery process continues, the periods of comfort will increase as those of loneliness dwindle.

2. Find interests. Frenetic activity is not the answer to loneliness, but interests that are genuinely enjoyable will give you something to look forward to. Think of a sport that you once played or would like to learn now. Are there classes you want to take? Have you always wanted to learn French cooking, but never had the time? Is there a candidate or political cause that means something to you? It's not necessary to be busy every waking hour. It is healthy, however, to have points of activity spread at intervals throughout the week.

3. Build a support network. This is a time to rekindle neglected relationships with relatives and friends. Take the opportunity to meet other parents in your child's co-op nursery, P.T.A., or scout troop. Reach out to the people you like at work. There are also numerous support groups throughout the country for the newly separated and divorced. These groups have members who will share your experience and can appreciate the difficulties of your return to single life. Some people prefer to rely on a single intimate friend who has also undergone the trauma of divorce. This friend is more likely to be sympathetic and available during lonely periods.

4. Avoid the triggers of loneliness. In general, it is advisable to avoid places where you shared happy times with your ex. Don't plan to garden all day Saturday if gardening feels depressing and lonely these days. Stay away from couples that make you feel like a third wheel and underscore your sense of isolation.

5. Get out of the house. Develop a list of places where you can go by yourself: comedy nightclubs, theaters, discos, lecture halls, museums, and art galleries. Experiment to see if you can enjoy jogging, bike riding, or even a leisurely stroll. When you know that there are places to go and things you enjoy doing, staying home becomes a choice. You aren't trapped in the house without alternatives.

Beyond Survival

There may be times, during the transition from separation to independence, when just coping with your emotions will be the best that you can do. Other moments may find you gritting your teeth, dulling yourself to whatever you're feeling, and trudging forward with whatever it is you have to do—come up with an extra few dollars because the daycare center has raised its rate, put up with a strident office manager for one more day, or come home to a sink full of dirty dishes and your next-door neighbor's blasting stereo.

These times are survival times. Often they seem like useless frustration—that there's no lesson in them to be learned, that just getting through is all that can be done.

But the fact that you can get through them *on your own* is a valuable lesson. Beyond survival is a you that wasn't there before. A person with self-confidence in your ability to take care of yourself. And with a new sense of what "taking care" might mean: a freedom to explore your own interests and to give yourself the things you need to feel alive as well as stay alive.

For many men and women, divorce is the first time in their lives that they have ever been on their own. "I come from a large family, and living in the dorms at college felt like having a lot of sisters my own age. Then I married Bob. When I look back now, I think I was really a child all those years. It was like a shell I had to crack. And it was hard. But you know how little kids will say, 'I wonder what I'll be when I grow up?' I feel like I am grown-up now." *(38-year-old lab technician)*

You may learn to relish your independence, or you may learn from it that you are most alive when you are sharing a close relationship with another. In either case, a key gift of being single can be the realization that you needn't give up who you are in order to be close. The sense of yourself that you earn will be a major part of the person you are when you go on to establish future relationships.

19

Making Contact

Meeting people is often a matter of luck. Sometimes you meet attractive people totally unexpectedly. But most of the time it takes work and a sense of commitment to maximize your chances of encountering interesting people. You have to sacrifice the comfort of your home and go out and mingle with strangers, often in unfamiliar surroundings. It takes time, energy, money, and a willingness to take the chance of being rejected.

As a recently divorced person, there are special reasons why meeting people can be difficult. The emotional wounds may still be too fresh for you to risk genuine openness with members of the opposite sex. You may still be angry and hurt, uncertain of who to trust. For some people, the prospect of an intimate relationship conjures up a fear of being trapped in the same kind of marriage they've just escaped. Others, who felt betrayed by an ex-spouse, see the spectre of another rejection. As one woman said, "I keep asking myself do I really want to go through all this again? Do I want to be out on the same emotional limb?" Uncertainty about personal attractiveness and the fear of rebuff keeps many newly divorced people at home. "Who wants a balding film editor with a paunch, a '68 Volkswagen, and a fetish for collecting antique silverware?"

Divorced people often have less time for socializing than singles who were never married have. The responsibilities of children and a home may make inordinate demands on their time. Single parents are also extremely cautious about bringing someone new into their children's lives. "It's hard to find a decent man. I have to look not only for someone I like and feel attracted to but also for someone I think would be good for my children." *(36-year-old grocery clerk)* "I can't have men trooping in and out of my bedroom. I think that's harmful for the children. But most men seem first and foremost to want sex." *(30-year-old journeyman printer)*

There are very good reasons for the recently divorced to be cautious about new attachments. The scars of an old relationship and the commitment to one's children mean that divorced singles socialize with special wariness and constraints. There are, however, certain classic excuses that keep many divorced people from reaching out.

Only losers are out there. At the root of this view is the conviction that winners get married and stay married. Anyone who has never been married or anyone who has divorced is likely to be a loser. The truth is that marital status has nothing to do with psychological health or personal effectiveness. In fact, the decision to divorce may indicate that you are healthier or stronger than the countless unhappily married people who choose to remain so. There are 64 million singles aged 21 to 65 in this country. Like any large group, they represent a continuum from the miserable to the very happy, the ne'er-do-wells to the successful, the angry and bitter to the open and loving.

I'm no longer young. There's no denying that ours is a youth-oriented culture. The media has made a cult of youth worship, but there's a difference between billboards and real life. People do grow older, and their tastes and interests change with the passing years. Contrary to popular myth, few 50-year-old men want a sustained romantic relationship with a 25-year-old woman. There's too big a gap in life experience, needs, and tastes. Most people realize how lonely it would be to share their life with someone too young and too immature to be a peer.

Being older doesn't mean that you have lost your attractiveness to people in your own age group. The people who were twenty when you were twenty are fifty now that you are fifty. They've gotten older and wiser right along with you. Many of them are single, like you, and looking for someone to share their lives with.

What's true about being older is that many people find it hard to start over again. The innocence and enthusiasm of youth are less in evidence. There's a feeling of having done it all and felt it all before. Many newly divorced singles describe a great weariness overtaking them when they fantasize about reaching out to someone new. These feelings are natural; they are part of the healing process following a divorce. Don't mislabel the exhaustion produced by the hurt and trauma of divorce as proof that you're "too old." As you continue to heal, your interests will gradually turn to the possibility of new relationships.

I'm unattractive. Many divorcing people see themselves as unattractive, both physically and psychologically. But your actual attractiveness has almost nothing to do with success or failure in social interactions. It's how attractive you *think* you are that really counts. If you see yourself as flawed and uninteresting, you will be diffident and shy. Your psychological position will be that anyone who spends time with you is doing it out of kindness or because they themselves are worthy of nothing better. If you basically accept yourself as an OK person, this attitude will be communicated to the people you meet. Your comfort with yourself will make others comfortable, and your belief in your worth will help others see your value. Attractiveness is much more a matter of the spirit than the arrangements of flesh and bone.

One of the most attractive qualities a person can have is self-acceptance. If you accept your own failures and flaws, others are likely to do the same with you. Becoming self-accepting is, of course, easier said than done. But it can be achieved if you see that acceptance must be your highest priority. You can't make yourself over at this point in life, but you can come to see how your struggle to survive, to love, and to grow has shaped you. You have endured pain. You have tried to do your best to protect yourself and the people you love. The result is a unique person: you. There are people who want to know about your struggle, your dreams, the things you believe in. There are people who *will* find you attractive. Believing that they are there is the first step to finding them.

Some recently divorced singles find that one major obstacle stands in the way of self-acceptance. Often it is a specific physical flaw, or the fear of being a poor conversationalist.

(1) *Physical flaws*. One of the most common is a concern about weight. Everyone has a "natural weight" that his or her body is genetically programmed to hold. The trouble is that your natural weight is very often not the ideal weight on insurance charts, nor does it resemble the half-starved performers you see on TV. Diets rarely succeed in keeping pounds off because your body keeps wanting to return to its natural weight. Exercise and the elimination of certain foods like ice cream can lower your natural weight somewhat, but trying to stay significantly below your body's natural size is a constant struggle. In fact, according to the latest research, dieting has a paradoxical tendency to *increase* your weight. Your body interprets weight loss as a danger signal and hastens to re-establish your own weight *plus a little more* when you go off your diet.

If diets can't bring permanent weight loss, what should you do? If all you need is a temporary weight loss to boost your self-esteem, you should by all means diet. But if you want to take a long-range approach to your weight, you might consider rethinking your goals. A body that is toned, healthy, and vigorous is an attractive body. It doesn't have to be Hollywood thin. People who exercise and stay flexible and strong very often feel good about themselves, regardless of their weight.

Some people reject themselves because of other physical traits: a small bust, a big nose, thin legs, thick thighs, baldness, or crooked teeth. Many of these traits can be changed surgically, cosmetically, or through exercise. If you can't or you don't want to change, the best course is to start noticing people with the same trait. Would it stop you from liking them, spending time with them, sleeping with them? Read the chapter on Sexuality for further discussion.

If it *is* possible to change a trait you don't like, come to a decision. Do you want to go to the trouble, expense, and risk of making yourself look different? If the answer is yes, do it. Delaying will only postpone the time when you can feel really good about yourself.

(2) *Conversation.* Some people are convinced that they are bores. They find conversation awkward and have great difficulty initiating contact. Said one man, "I'm just no good at small talk. My mind goes blank and I let these silences fall." The father of an 8-year-old put it this way: "I can talk about my boy, I can talk about cabinetmaking, I can talk about baseball. Anything beyond that is very hard work for me."

It's true that the art of conversation in particular and communication skills in general will increase your chances of developing a satisfying relationship. On the other hand, millions of shy and quiet people still manage to reach out to others. Talking gets easier as two people establish trust.

As with physical flaws, you have the choice to either accept or change your communication style. You may just be a person of few but sincere words, and your quietness may be part of your charm. If you feel committed to changing yourself, read the art of conversation section in this chapter. Conversation is a skill, and you can acquire it with practice.

But the kids need me. This belief makes it hard to take any time for yourself. Your children do need you, but not every hour, every night. Parents need time off to socialize with other adults so that they may get emotional and sexual needs met. Failure to take this needed time for yourself results in symptoms of chronic emotional malnutrition: irritability, depression, feelings of being over-burdened and fatigued. As one woman explained, "If I'm with my kids five nights in a row, I turn into a shrew. They seem like bottomless pits where I keep pouring my energy. Their voices get shrill and grate on me. I spend two evenings out each week, and I feel like I do it *for* my kids. I take care of myself so I can take care of them."

Many parents feel that they should sacrifice themselves for their children. It's true that many times you have to put the needs of the children first, but it's also true that you will wither emotionally on a constant diet of sacrifice. Your needs, therefore, must be an important priority.

Taking time for yourself usually means finding a sitter. Sitters aren't cheap and it isn't always easy to locate one. Nevertheless, it is possible to cultivate reliable sitters who know your children and know how to deal with emergencies. Here are some of your baby-sitting options:

1. Ask your parents, relatives, neighbors, friends, or ex-spouse to baby-sit for you.
2. Hire a teenager. They work more cheaply. You can locate one by calling friends or fellow workers who have a teenager at home.

3. Join or form a baby-sitting cooperative where two or more single parents take turns caring for each other's children.
4. Have your children take care of themselves. Some children are simply too young to take care of themselves, but many are mature enough to spend a few hours without supervision.

I'm too busy. Single people tend to be very busy because having nothing to do often leads to loneliness and depression. Activity provides a temporary relief from the mourning process that follows separation. The busier you are, the less contact you have with your feelings.

Unfortunately, while the flight into activity helps at times to mute your pain, it may also serve to isolate you. You may have no time to socialize or make new contacts. The answer is to leave room in your schedule for socializing, and to make that time a priority. You may have to stop taking work home, renege on some commitments, or drop a class you're taking to make room. Whatever it requires to make time for meeting people—do it.

I don't know where to look. During your years of marriage it's likely that you developed a few special interests and activities. When you continue these interests as a single, you may discover that they have one drawback: you don't find other single people there. Since divorce is a time of change, this might be an opportunity to expand the things you do and the places you go. Here are some suggested new activities that can be fun as well as good ways to meet people:

- *Dancing.* Whether you like rock music or the big band sound, there are numerous dances and classes you can attend to meet singles. Modern dance classes or even jazzercise classes provide an excellent opportunity for making contact. International folk dancing, square dancing, and ballroom dancing classes are also a good way to meet people.
- *Parties.* Let your friends, relatives, and co-workers know that you're socially available again. Ask them to add your name to their party list. Of course, it helps if you occasionally throw a party yourself. Don't use the excuse that your home is too small, because the more crowded the party is, the more successful people will consider it to be.
- *Sports.* Volleyball, golf, tennis, and softball are the major coed sports. These activities are particularly ideal for single women, since they are usually a minority on coed teams. Call up your local recreation department and ask for a list of sports teams, leagues, and activities. Other areas of sports activity for singles are the racquet ball clubs, health spas, and coed gyms which are now springing up everywhere. Many of these establishments specifically cater to single people and have juice bars and lounges where it's easy to mix.
- *Special interest groups.* Whether you like chess, bridge, poetry, international affairs, or great books, there's a group of like-minded people

you can join. Volunteer groups, charities, and political action groups are places where you can lend your energy to a good cause and socialize at the same time.

- *Classes.* Call up your local community college or high school to find out about the adult education classes available on almost every subject under the sun. Many cities have private nonprofit groups that publish catalogs of classes offered by qualified teachers in their homes. Cooking classes are perhaps the best place to meet other singles. If you're interested in classes for the social opportunities they afford, take the ones with a high proportion of the opposite sex. For example, men do well in jewelry-making classes and women in tax and accounting classes.
- *Awareness groups.* Sometimes called encounter or gestalt groups, they are all part of the human potential movement. A large percentage of the people who attend these groups are single, and the atmosphere of openness is conducive to making real contact with others.
- *Special events.* Look through event listings in your local newspaper. Art openings, museum exhibits, lectures, and sporting events are only a few examples.

There are also organizations and places specifically designed to introduce singles to one another. Their main function is to create an atmosphere or structure where strangers can make contact with one another.

- Singles groups. These are the most obvious places to meet singles. There are thousands of nonprofit organizations across the country that specialize in activities for single people. Call up your local church—you'll find that they either sponsor a singles group or can refer you to a church that does. Be ecumenical. You usually don't have to belong to a particular church to attend its activities for singles. The calendar and events sections of your local newspaper will also list a wide variety of activities sponsored by singles groups.
- Professional dating services. For a fee the dating service will enable you to meet other singles. Some are inexpensive ($5 to $35) while others can cost a thousand dollars or more. Look in the "Introductions" or "Personals" section of the classified ads and you may find listings for the following types of dating services:
  - Telephone dating (you are given phone numbers to call)
  - Computer dating (the computer matches you with your date)
  - Photodating (you get to see the person's photo and a sheet of information about him or her before you go out on a date)
  - Videodating (you also get to see a videotape of the person before going out)
  - Matchmaking (the matchmaker chooses your romantic partner for you on the basis of a personal interview with you)
  - Luxury social clubs (you meet people in luxurious homes, on yachts, or at country clubs)

- Personal ads. In Europe it is quite common and socially acceptable to meet your mate through an ad in the newspaper. This method is rapidly becoming more popular in the United States as well. If you are a woman *under* 40 or a man *over* 40 you will probably be swamped with replies. Other age groups are not as successful, but personal ads can still work for them. This is an inexpensive way of choosing from a potentially large pool of singles.
- Singles bars. Just about everybody decries singles bars, but even though few people admit to going to them, most seem to be jammed night after night. Many who go to these bars are not really single, but that's true elsewhere as well. Some of the "swingers" who patronize the bars regularly will seem obnoxious or pathetic, but no environment has a monopoly on bad taste. The fact is that singles bars are full of attractive single people. One of them might be the person you're looking for.

It takes time for the newly divorced single to feel comfortable again socially. As one woman put it, "For the first month I went to Unitarian Singles, it was just a sea of faces. I was surrounded by strangers. I had moments where I felt awkward and anxious, almost to the point of nausea. After a while I started recognizing people, saying hello, and using some kind of icebreaker from the lecture to start a conversation. Believe me, it was a long, slow process."

You can find other singles; there are lots of places to meet them. What may pose more of a problem is the actual process of making contact with a stranger.

THE FIRST MOVE

The first key is to let people know that you want to meet them. You can do this through positive body language. At parties and social gatherings, stand or sit close to others. Avoid hiding out in the corners of a room. Make eye contact with as many people as possible and don't be afraid to touch people.

Ideally, everyone you found attractive would respond to your positive body language by making contact with you. Unfortunately, only a small percentage will do this. The vast majority will be indifferent or remain your secret admirers. If you wish to meet these people, it will be up to you to take the initiative. You will have to do the reaching out.

Some people (particularly women) are reluctant to make the first move for fear that they will be mislabeled as too aggressive or too forward sexually. It's true that certain people will feel threatened or misinterpret your motives. But it's also true that by not initiating contact you run the risk of missing out on many satisfying friendships. Many men and women appreciate someone who is willing to take a chance and say hello.

Of course, not everyone is going to find you attractive. Rejection is inevitable. How do you handle it?

Some people can shrug off rejection. Their trick is that they don't take it personally. And why should it be so disturbing when others aren't attracted to you? You are probably romantically attracted to relatively few of the people you meet. Unfortunately, if you're like most people, you do take rejection personally. Yet the discomfort of rejection is the price you must pay to maximize your chances of connecting with someone special.

One consolation is that the more times you're rejected, the easier it becomes. The first time can be devastating, but after a few bad experiences you become less susceptible to being hurt. It's like learning karate: after enough practice you eventually develop the scar tissue on the side of your hand to the point that you can break a brick and not feel pain. The same holds true for the pain of rejection. Practice getting rejected and your discomfort will diminish.

What if you've recently become single and are too scared to get your feet wet? How do you reduce your fear? One way is to focus on physically relaxing your body. Taking long, deep breaths will reduce the tension in your body and relax your mind as well. Scan your body for tension. Check for tightness in your legs, buttocks, back, stomach, arms, shoulders, neck, jaw, and forehead. Relax any area that feels tense.

The next step is to visualize yourself initiating contact. What do you fear will happen? Run a rejection fantasy through your mind. How does the person reject you? How does rejection make you feel? Visualize the person accepting you and thanking you for coming over. How does that feel? The greatest fear is of the unknown. If you fantasize about the many different reactions a person may have to your approach, you will be less fearful.

A few common sense precautions can minimize the chance of rejection. People who avert their eyes each time you look their way will probably not welcome your approach. Initiate contact with the person next to them who smiles when you make eye contact. During a conversation, people sometimes give cues that they find you unattractive. For example, they may look away frequently while you're talking, let the conversation drag, or excuse themselves to get another drink or to talk to someone else. When people react this way, take the hint and move on to someone else. Don't spend half an hour with a person who gives cues of disinterest.

Avoid making too great an investment in the outcome of any interaction. If you expect a sexual spark or "meaningful relationship" with each person you meet, you're setting yourself up for failure. Develop the attitude that you're just out to meet people (male and female) and to make friends. Some of these people won't like you; some you won't like. Many will remain casual acquaintances. A few may become friends. One of them may be just right for a great relationship.

Opening Lines

"What do I say to break the ice?" is a common question. "I don't want to use some phony, manufactured line." Most opening lines do sound a bit artificial. But why is that a problem? The important thing is that people meet each other and have a chance to converse. The vehicle is far less important than the end result.

A conversation has to start somewhere. "Is it hot enough for you?" may sound inane, but it does start the conversation off on a topic that anyone can discuss. "Haven't I seen you somewhere before?" may be corny, but it's often effective. The important thing to remember about opening lines is that you don't have to be clever. There is no right way or wrong way to start a conversation. A spontaneous line that pops into your head will probably work as well as one that's carefully rehearsed. If you need to rehearse, do so. Otherwise, you can rely on the ad lib.

The readiest source of opening lines is noticing what's going on and commenting on the situation. Ask yourself the following questions:

1. What is the person wearing? Some examples of opening lines:

   "That's an awfully warm coat."
   "That blazer must have cost you an arm and a leg."
   "I wish I looked as good in red as you do."

2. How does the person feel?

   "You sure look comfortable."
   "How come you're so sad?"
   "Do you always enjoy comedians so much?"

3. What is the person doing?

   "I see you smoke my brand."
   "You seem to really be into the music."
   "Do you always drink pina coladas?"

Sometimes the best opening lines have to do with your environment. For example:

   "This room is too cold."
   "People sure seem to be enjoying themselves tonight."
   "Not too many people here this afternoon."

Compliments are a great way to make contact.

   "I like your dress."
   "Your eyes are beautiful."
   "You look so calm and secure."
   "Your smile is so warm."

You can always start a conversation with a question.

"What's the score of the game?"
"Do they serve food here?"
"Isn't there supposed to be a lifeguard on this beach?"
"What time does this place close?"
"What do you think of the music?"

What do you say if you can't think of a good opening line? Consider Roger's solution.

> I spotted a breathtaking woman sitting in a restaurant. I'm not kidding, I was in love! But she was sitting with her girlfriend, and I feel shy interrupting a conversation. I was also nervous because I worry that really attractive women won't have much interest in me. I practiced different openers in my head: "Hi, I'm Roger" or "Would I be intruding if I joined you?" I must have gone through a dozen lines, but nothing felt right. I finally decided to say the first thing that came into my head. When I got up to their table, I froze for a second. I knew for sure she'd reject me. Then the line hit me: "How can I meet you?" She smiled and said, "You just did."

Doris had a similar problem.

> I saw this rather sweet-looking guy at the pool and smiled a few times at him. Sometimes that's all it takes. He smiled back, but didn't make a move. After five minutes I realized that I'd have to approach him. I came up with a million reasons why I shouldn't go over to him: he's probably married or has a girlfriend; he's turned off to aggressive women; I even considered the possibility that he was gay. I finally mustered the courage and said, "Would I be too forward if I said hello?" You've got to admit that's lame. But it worked!

THE ART OF CONVERSATION

There are only three things you have to do in order to be a good conversationalist. You have to know how to ask questions, how to listen, and how to disclose a little about yourself. An interesting conversation is usually a weaving of these three elements. Dull conversations have too much of one, not enough of the others. It's boring to converse with someone who talks nonstop about themselves. But the same person might be a lot of fun if he or she asked you some questions and paraphrased your answers so that you felt listened to.

Questions

Questions are the best way to get information and find the elements you share in common with another person. *Ritual questions* like "How are you?" or "How's life?" help things get started. These can be followed up with *informational questions* like "How do you like your new car?" "Are you getting anything out of this seminar?" "Has your sister finished her chiropractic training?" The key to asking questions is to follow your curiosity. What do you want to know about this person? What's unusual about him? How does she feel? What does she want? What does he believe? Don't be afraid to pry. Most people love to talk about themselves and are flattered when anyone takes an interest. People are their own favorite topics of conversation.

Whenever you ask an informational question, you'll find that you usually learn a little more than you asked for. This is called *free information*. If you ask someone if she drives or takes the bus to work, and she says, "The bus," you've gotten no free information. But she might tell you that she lives in the suburbs and drives, since the schools are a lot better out there for her nine-year-old boy. This is free information. You know where she lives, that she has a child, and that she makes sacrifices for his education. Now you can follow your curiosity and ask questions about any of these areas. And you'll get more free information—you may learn her marital status, taste in movies, where she went last year on vacation.

Active Listening

The second element of good conversation is the ability to listen. Sometimes this means that you keep your mouth shut, even though you're bursting to say "That reminds me of the time . . ." But active listening is more than keeping silent. It is the process of repeating back (or *paraphrasing*), in your own words, what the other person just said. Active listening is the highest flattery because it reassures the speaker that he or she is really getting your attention, and that you've taken the trouble to understand what was said. Here are some examples of active listening:

> "So the hang-gliding accident kept you almost housebound for three months. I can understand how you got depressed."

> "The divorce cost you $6,000 in fees, and the custody battle is still going on. I imagine you're damn angry."

> "So the adjustment took a good eighteen months before you really felt in control of your life again."

> "It was a consuming love, you couldn't do without him. But he often seemed distant and unapproachable. He'd only let you come so close."

The inability to listen is the most common cause of failed interactions. Many people have difficulty listening because they are too busy preparing their next remark, too focused on trying to win a point, or overwhelmed with fears of embarrassment. Real listening, however, means you are focused on the other person, rather than on yourself. You are attending to what is said, remembering it, and preparing to feed it back.

Self-Disclosure

Disclosure is a source of all real intimacy. It's what makes closeness possible. If you have difficulty talking about yourself, try the following exercise. Take some time to recall important incidents in your life that helped shape your character and personality. Write a four- or five-page autobiography that includes some of this basic information, things you'd be willing to share with anybody. Include:

- Important formative events in your childhood
- What school was like for you
- Your favorite teacher
- A few of your more interesting jobs
- The people you've loved and cared for
- Your biggest loss
- Your most wonderful moment
- Your greatest achievement
- Your hobbies
- Your best vacation
- The funniest thing that ever happened to you

Now add whatever else seems important and appropriate. Read over your autobiography whenever you expect to be in a social situation. It will help remind you of a lot of good stories and anecdotes.

Putting It All Together

Conversation is the art of blending informational questions, paraphrasing, and self-disclosure in such a way that people have a good time and want to keep talking. Temper your probing questions with self-disclosure so that others feel they are learning about you while you are learning about them. Two examples: "I often think of quitting this company, do you think about that too?" "I've always wanted to write short stories. Do you have to spend long hours alone, or can you work with your family around?" Another important skill is learning to combine informational questions with active listening. "You've often been hurt when you trusted someone, do you find it hard to be that vulnerable now?" "You've been an oncology nurse for years and helped a lot of people through their last days. Do you have to harden yourself to their pain?"

Informational questions function as a conversational lubricant. They keep things going and help you find new topics and areas of common interest. Paraphrasing helps deepen contact because it communicates that you understand, or perhaps even empathize with what's been said. Self-disclosure makes you a real person—someone who has a history of funny, painful, poignant, triumphant, lovely moments. And also someone who has opinions and beliefs, who has a unique view of the world. Make a conscious effort to use each of the three elements of conversation when you socialize. The contact will be livelier, more exciting, and potentially more intimate.

How You Look and Sound

Keep good eye contact. People lose interest in what you're saying if you don't look at them. It's quite common to lose your train of thought and feel uneasy when trying to maintain direct eye contact. If this is true for you, focus your eyes somewhere else on the person's face—the nose, mouth, or forehead. As long as your focus is within eight inches of the nose, no one will be able to tell the difference.

Smile as much as you comfortably can. It gives the message that you're open and interested in contact. Let your responses show. Nod, frown, look surprised. This tells the other person that you're involved and reacting.

Speak as clearly as possible. Talking softly or mumbling can turn people off. Tape-record a conversation with a friend and listen to yourself. If you have difficulty hearing or understanding what you're saying, practice speaking more loudly or clearly over the tape recorder. When listening to the tape, also pay attention to the rate at which you speak. If you speak too slowly or too fast, record yourself practicing at the opposite speed.

ESTABLISHING INTIMACY

The key to intimacy is asking for and sharing personal information. This creates an atmosphere of excitement and risk.

Asking for personal information can be scary. Be sensitive about the other person's boundaries. Be aware of often subtle cues that you're going too far or too fast. If you inadvertently strike a raw nerve, back off and apologize. On the other hand, if you ask only safe, impersonal questions, you are unlikely to really get to know someone. Your relationship will never go beyond a casual friendship.

Obviously, you don't want to put people on the spot thirty seconds after meeting them. Give them a chance to feel comfortable and safe with you. Gradually escalate the depth of your questions. Don't be afraid to ask, "Am I getting too personal?" or "May I ask you a personal question?" Let people know that you aren't asking out of inquisitiveness, but because you seek real contact.

Here are five extremely common conversational pitfalls that tend to retard the growth of intimacy:

1. Talking about others rather than yourself. People enjoy hearing interesting stories about your co-workers, friends, and relatives, but most of all they want to learn about *you.*

2. Talking about others rather than the person you are with. The problem with talking behind people's backs is that it is a poor substitute for real intimacy. There's a certain pleasure in arguing that so-and-so's a jerk, but you could become much closer if you forgot the backbiting and talked about each other.

3. Always talking about your ex. Newly divorced people have a tendency to focus conversations on their ex-spouses. This is a natural form of self-disclosure, but it sometimes serves as a way of avoiding closeness. Becoming a broken record about your ex also tends to be a bore. No one else really shares your obsession.

4. Talking in second or third person instead of first person. For example: "*You* get very lonely when a relationship ends" *(second person)* instead of "*I* got very lonely when the relationship ended" *(first person)* or "*People* are afraid to share *their* feelings" *(third person)* instead of "*I* am afraid to share *my* feelings" *(first person).*

5. Talking about the past instead of the present. For example, "I *felt* jealous when you bought that woman a drink" instead of "I *feel* jealous that you bought that woman a drink" or "I *felt* depressed about losing my job" instead of "I *feel* depressed about losing my job."

Healthy Honesty in Relationships

No matter how tactful you are, there are times when honesty is going to hurt or offend people. People often have difficulty accepting unpleasant truths about themselves. They may be easily offended and tend to be attracted to people who tell them what they want to hear, rather than the truth. If you make a habit of being honest, the price can be very high. You may run into a good deal of hostility, or just plain avoidance. Consider, however, the consequences of dishonesty:

1. The feeling of guilt. A sense that inauthenticity is wrong.
2. The feeling that no one knows or understands the real you.
3. The inability to get things "off your chest."
4. The loss of intimacy. To the extent that you conceal your true thoughts and feelings, you will be unable to get close to people.
5. The risk that someone will be attracted to an inaccurate image of you, an image that you will never be able to maintain. Sooner or later the real you emerges, often with explosive effects on the relationship.

Being honest may be risky, but it pays off. Any person who rejects you for being honest probably isn't much of a prospect for a healthy relationship.

One way to quickly establish intimacy is to express something negative. This is a risky technique, and it may be safer to wait until the relationship is really rolling before sharing your anger, sadness, or hurt.

Unfortunately, it's very difficult to break a habit of hiding negative feelings. Sharing them from the very beginning creates a healthy openness, while forcing yourself to express only the good feelings limits how close you can get. When you finally get around to expressing your hurt or anger, it's likely to come out with explosive force. You've waited so long and held back so much that it emerges with real destructive energy. The process of gunnysacking and holding back negative feelings is also hard on your friends and lovers. They feel betrayed by your Jekyll and Hyde personality—in the beginning you were sweet and accommodating, but now you are angry and dissatisfied.

Whenever you express negative feelings, it's important to make "I" statements, rather than "you" statements. "I" statements don't accuse—they just say what you feel.

Instead of saying:	Say:
"You never kiss me goodbye."	"I feel hurt when you leave without kissing me."
"You're always late."	"I feel terribly uncomfortable waiting for you."
"You never remember my birthday."	"I feel disappointed when you don't remember my birthday."
"You're irresponsible when you leave the cap off the toothpaste."	"I feel irritated when I find the cap off the toothpaste."

Try to say positive things along with the negative. Make it clear that despite your frustration or anger, you still care for the other person.

Instead of saying:	Say:
"I'm sick and tired of hearing the same stale stories."	"That's a really funny story, but I've heard it before."
"I'll never forgive you for cutting your hair."	"Your hair still looks nice, but I like it a lot better when it's longer."
"I'm getting sick of your drinking."	"Normally you're a moderate drinker, but tonight I feel uncomfortable with the amount of drinks you've had."
"You're always so selfish and irresponsible."	"I feel disappointed that you didn't call me to say you were going to be so late."

Please note that these are only suggestions. You need to say things that feel honest and comfortable to *you*.

Sometimes people take things to an extreme and start playing honesty games. One example is "Hot Seat." This game was popularized during the Sixties in encounter groups. The person on the hot seat was criticized and insulted in a no-holds-barred session. This game supposedly enabled people to honestly face themselves. However, the most common result was that people got hurt and resentful. Avoid dumping on people in the name of honesty. It's difficult to be both diplomatic and honest, but it can be done. Don't use honesty as an excuse for sadism.

Sometimes people put themselves on the hot seat by playing a game called "Confession." You play this game by reciting a long litany of problems, failures, and faults immediately upon meeting people. There are several common motives for this.

1. To gain attention, sympathy, or pity
2. To chase people away and thereby avoid the danger of getting close to them
3. To impress people with your honesty

It's foolish to divulge all of your negative qualities to strangers. Give people time to see your strong points as well as your weaknesses. Learn to reveal yourself gradually.

The key to healthy honesty is a measure of self-acceptance. You know that you're not perfect, but you accept your failures and limitations. It's a sense that you are basically OK the way you are.

It's important to realize that you are not (and never will be) your ideal person. There's nothing wrong with striving to be better, but failing to accept the you who exists right now makes it harder to be close to people. You are more vulnerable to criticism and hurt. You may obsessively put yourself down in the hope that no one else will. You may have to brag, or hide and lie about your feelings to keep yourself from being hurt. You may have to stifle all anger and negativity, or, on the other hand, preemptively explode at the first sign of criticism. Without a measure of self-acceptance, the job of protecting and defending yourself becomes the highest priority. This will inevitably interfere with your quest for intimacy.

A REFRESHER COURSE ON DATING

If you're recently divorced and haven't had a "date" for twenty years, you may feel insecure about resuming dating. You may feel a sense of awkwardness, like you're sixteen all over again.

Very often the first concern is how to ask for a date. The best way for most people is to ask in person. If you have developed good rapport with someone new, it's foolish to wait a few days and then ask for a date over the telephone. Your fear of rejection may get the better of you and prevent you from ever making that call. You are also less likely to be rejected if you ask in person. Calling several days later (or sometimes even the next day) increases the risk that the person has forgotten your name or what they found attractive about you.

A first date with someone new can often be stressful. People worry about whether they will be witty or fun enough. They also worry about the possibility of having sex (or the possibility that they *won't* have sex). Many women wonder whether the man will respect them or "take no for an answer." There are natural concerns about embarrassed, awkward conversations, long silences, how or how much to touch, and so on.

Try to make the first date a low-stress one. One way to do this is to suggest a cup of coffee, rather than a drink. Many people fear that if they have a few drinks their partner will become amorous. Coffee conveys a feeling that the first date is casual, with no expectations.

Another key to increasing comfort during a date is patience. Don't push for physical intimacy too soon. Get to know each other, enjoy the conversation, let things develop in a natural way.

Keep your first date low cost or go Dutch treat. Many women in particular feel pressured if a man takes them to an expensive French restaurant. A first date at a coffee shop will enable her to feel confident that she won't be expected to show her gratitude by sleeping with the man.

There are numerous types of first dates which can be fun and safe: an afternoon playing tennis or ice-skating; going to the zoo or a museum or art gallery; an evening at the symphony, opera, or ballet; attending a new play, musical, live comedy show, or a movie; a picnic or even a stroll down the beach or in the park. The possibilities are endless.

Who should pay for the date? This depends on a variety of factors such as local custom, who earns the larger income, what feels comfortable to the man or the woman, and who initiated the date. In conservative areas, it may be unusual for a woman to pick up the tab. In more liberal areas, the man frequently expects his date to pay her own way. Increasingly, women are insisting on paying their share. This creates a sense of independence and equality. There are no hidden obligations, no demands for reciprocity.

Do men feel comfortable with a woman paying? Many men feel insulted or threatened if the woman pays for all or part of the check. Many others, however, admire a woman who "pulls her own weight" and shares the financial responsibility of dating. It might be wise for a woman to openly discuss this issue before picking up the check.

Sometimes the ideal compromise is for the man to pay for dinner at a restaurant on the first date and for the woman to reciprocate by cooking a meal at home the next time (or vice versa if the man is unemployed and the woman earns a good salary). Another method is for one person to pay for dinner, the other for the show. There are no right or wrong answers to the question of who pays. Develop a policy that feels comfortable to you and be prepared to alter this policy as needed to please your partner.

It isn't really necessary to go somewhere special and spend money on a date. What's wrong with staying home? If you choose to invite someone attractive to your home for coffee, conversation, a drink, or a meal, bear in mind that the appearance of your home is important. Neatness and cleanliness help to welcome your guest. Don't allow what might have become a wonderful romance to end quickly because your guest is turned off by a sloppy environment.

What about alcohol? While wine or liquor is a traditional accompaniment to romantic situations, it may not be romantic to a date who doesn't drink or does so only moderately. If you don't have a nonalcoholic alternative available, your guest may not feel at home. If you don't drink, but don't object to others drinking in your presence, be sure to have alcohol on hand. Don't let your personal preferences dictate those of others unless you do have strong religious, moral, or other objections.

Are romantic touches such as flowers or candy outdated? They are not. Don't be afraid of being "corny." Your thoughtfulness will be greatly appreciated. Feel free to bring flowers or a bottle of wine. After a pleasant date there's nothing wrong with dropping a card in the mail thanking your friend for a wonderful time.

20

Sexuality

One of the most important issues divorced people face is how to deal with their sexual needs. Marriage provides a social decree that it's all right to have sex. What do you do if you're divorced?

Traditional sexual norms have been derived from religious guidelines. But the pill, the sexual "revolution" of the 60s, and a general relaxing of religious beliefs has produced a society where there are no sexual norms. Initiating a sexual relationship on the first date is quite acceptable for some people, while remaining celibate till marriage or remarriage is appropriate for others. Each individual must find his or her own comfort zone and hope to connect with a partner who has similar attitudes.

The point at which a newly separated person becomes available to resume a sexual life varies greatly. According to one study, 75 percent of singles reenter the dating world the first year and probably 90 percent by the end of the second year after separation. For some, divorce leads to a period of experimenting with a variety of sexual partners. A divorced mother of two found being single the most exciting time of her life. "I was a virgin when I married Ted at age nineteen and had only dated two previous guys. After the separation, I was out every night I could get a sitter. After awhile I got tired of the singles scene and became more selective, but it was important to learn that I was attractive and interesting to men."

People who felt sexually deprived during their marriage have a tendency to go through a period of experimentation after a divorce. It builds confidence in their sexual abilities, and after a year or more they often settle with one partner. Don't assume that because you are unready now to settle on one person that this is the way you'll always be. This is all part of the healing process. Often people who have just ended an intense relationship are not ready for another one, yet they want human warmth, reassurance, and maybe distraction. A series of uncommitted relationships may help meet some of these needs.

Although finding a new partner to share physical and emotional closeness might be one prescription for relief from loneliness, you may be fearful and hesitant. Some fear is natural and serves an important function. It allows you to slow down enough to give yourself time to recover from the emotional rollercoaster. You need that time to reestablish your identity and to recover from anger, guilt, or diappointment after your marriage. Jim, a biochemist, was married for ten years. When he divorced he took to camping out in his lab, where he did research for six months. "I didn't want to start another relationship. I needed to regain my perspective on life. I have that now. When I meet a good woman again I won't have to apologize for myself. I'll be a whole person."

Some want emotional involvement without the encumbrances of sex. Kate had loved her husband deeply and was still recovering from their divorce. "I tried having sex with a couple of good friends I thought I could develop romantic relationships with. But once we were in bed, I'd remember being close to Steven and just start crying inside. I can do without until I am really in love again."

The guiding principle is *what is right for you*. Well-meaning friends may try to pressure you into resuming your sex life. Thank them for their concern and let them know that you are taking care of your needs in a manner best for you. Be firm, especially with friends who may not be able to understand your resistance to what they consider a wonderful opportunity. Beth started feeling that there was something wrong with her: her friends would advise her to check out men that they found attractive, but she just wasn't interested. She felt out of touch with the times, isolated, and unhappy. But once she accepted what she called the "creative anachronism" of her own way of being, she became much calmer and happier.

If you feel abnormal, consider the two poles that have just been described. Between these positions are an infinite range of possibilities. There are men and women who attempt to fill the emotional/sexual void as soon as possible, falling in love before they ever really experience separation. Others enter into a couple of low-intensity relationships and tentatively check out their new freedom. Whatever your personal choice may be, choose it because it feels right for you, not because your friends or family pressure you or because you want to be "normal."

YOUR COMFORT ZONE

Distinguishing what you want your sexual life to be like from what your friends and family want it to be like may be simple for you, or it may be a battle. But in either case it will be a relatively straightforward task, once you have accepted that it is your right—and your responsibility—to identify your own needs and to take appropriate steps to meet them.

A much more complex task lies ahead: that of matching the reality of the new relationships you initiate with your changing and growing sense of what you want. You feel the excitement of touching and holding a new person, and that excitement is a part of what you want: a sense of life renewing itself, of new possibilities. Mixed in are a rush of other feelings: a longing to be held and a fear of rejection, a longing to bond and a fear of commitment, a longing to take control of your life and a fear of being controlled. Longing and fear. And who is this new person? What does he or she want?

You'll find it easier to deal with these issues if you take some time to explore several factors that may be inhibiting your ability to express yourself sexually. When you feel in touch with your body and clear about what makes you feel excited and comfortable, you'll also feel less anxious about a new partner and a new experience.

An equally important part of identifying your sexual comfort zone is being able to communicate your needs to your partner. You may have beliefs and fears that make you hesitate to talk openly about your sex life. Yet complete openness needn't come all at once, and you are free to go as slowly as you need to go, sharing limits as well as other parts of yourself.

About Your Body

How do you feel about your body? Most people have a long list of complaints. They are too thin, too fat, too tall, too hairy. Everyone has mental pictures of the ideal way to look. Movies, commercials, and billboards imply that you can buy that perfect image along with the perfect car. The reality for most of us is that we are a combination of good and bad features. We like and sometimes loathe parts of our appearance.

Feeling good about your body generally adds to the enjoyment of sex; it makes you feel more confident, more open, more able to experience sensation, more able to use your body lovingly and creatively.

Learning to really accept and appreciate your body takes positive effort. First, you need to forgive your imperfections. It would be great to lose ten pounds (or 50 pounds), get rid of a paunch, stop smoking, jog, or get a face lift. You might even do these things some day. But right now, you can begin to accept your flaws.

Think of some of the people you have been attracted to in the past. Did you hold it against them because their hair was receding, they wore glasses, they had big breasts, or a beer belly? Realize that everyone worries about some imperfection, real or imagined. When you are attracted to others, usually it is not because they are perfect, but that there is some combination of physical attributes, personality, energy, openness, mystery, that appeals to you. It could be the tone of their voice, a scent, their walk, or a mannerism. It could be their authority, tenderness, vulnerability, or strength.

You might have a preference for a physical type. You might prefer a man who is tall and muscular or a woman who is blond and slim. But these preferences don't usually keep you from being attracted to people without these features.

Now, here comes the leap of faith. Can you imagine that other people are like you in that they might find you attractive even though you are less than perfect? If you can believe that, you can begin to feel good about your body.

Be good to your body. Treating your body well is an important part of accepting and appreciating it. Buy your body good food, soothing lotions, or delicious soaps. Give your body a shower and shave, sauna or hot tub, or even a massage. Not later, after you lose weight, but now. Buy yourself a new haircut or new dress. Wear something that makes you feel and look good, a color that turns you on, a well-cut suit or a soft sweater that feels good to wear.

Don't let the flaws keep you from doing what you want to do in your life. "I have always wanted to swim, but I have always been self-conscious about how I looked in a bathing suit. I promised myself I would start swimming lessons once I lost thirty pounds. Well, I lost those thirty pounds a dozen times in my lifetime. And then I would gain them back again. One day I realized that my life would be over and I wouldn't have learned to swim because I was waiting for something that might never happen. I might never look great in a bathing suit, but I was determined to swim." *(31-year-old artist)*

Listen to your body. It has its limits. Don't expect it to function sexually if you are not aroused, or if you are feeling anxious. Don't expect it to function well all morning without food (four cups of coffee and a donut don't count). Don't pollute your body with drugs or alcohol. Give your body fresh air and long walks after sitting all day at a desk in a stuffy office. Give yourself a reasonable amount of time to eat in a relaxed environment. All these things will pay off and you will be rewarded with health, aliveness, and confidence.

Finding Your Ideal Conditions

Get in touch with the conditions in which you feel most likely to be turned on and sexy. What kind of person are you with? What environment makes you feel more relaxed, more comfortable, confident, and sexual? These will be the conditions in which you'll be able to function best, feel turned on, and enjoy the experience. These conditions are unique to each individual person, and are based on conditioning and past experiences. If you feel most comfortable when you are with someone you know, someone with whom you share interests and nonsexual activities, in an environment that is familiar and safe, then try to meet these conditions before you engage in sex. This is not to say that you will be able to find the fantasy man or woman in the perfect setting, but if you are aware of what is ideal for you, you can avoid finding yourself in an uncomfortable anxiety-provoking situation.

Tom remembers the wonderful experience he had when he went away with his girlfriend for a four-day vacation. Just the two of them—long hours of talking, reading, showering, and eating together. Their sexual contact felt natural and intense, and Tom felt confident and accepted and didn't worry about getting turned on or keeping an erection. Although he can enjoy sex in other circumstances, he realized that these were some of the ingredients of his ideal condition:

1. Knowing the woman well
2. Spending time together sharing nonsexual activities
3. Privacy
4. Being together for an extended period of time
5. Being with a woman who was sexually responsive, but not demanding

Mara had a satisfying relationship for two years with a man she met right after her divorce. They enjoyed meeting for dinner and drinks and intense conversation about their prospective projects. He was a writer, and she was a sculptor. He admired her work and she enjoyed feeling his approval. The relationship was nonmonogamous and nonrestrictive because Mara was just getting adjusted to single life and wanted a measure of independence. These were some of the items on her list of conditions for an ideal sexual relationship:

1. Someone whom she cared for and respected
2. Someone who was intelligent—someone who would understand her work and appreciate its importance to her
3. Nonrestrictive—no expectations
4. Playfulness and creativity in the way he made love
5. Someone who made her feel attractive

Try this exercise using memory or fantasy. Close your eyes. Take a minute to relax and empty your mind. Now try getting in touch with the kind of relationship or circumstances that make you feel really good about having sex, turned on, accepted, welcomed and appreciated. Imagine the kind of person you're with, his or her physical characteristics, the environment, the mood. This will give you an idea of what you can aim for and what situations to avoid.

Getting To Know Your Partner

So you've met someone you're attracted to, or think you are. Give yourself time to find out who that person is, how it feels to be with him or her.

When you first meet someone, social ritual and social anxiety cloud your ability to make a clear judgment. You might be straining to look relaxed, but your mind is whirling, trying to create clever conversation. You are trying to express your interest while simultaneously assessing how interested the other person seems. You might be shouting over the blare of music, or dancing. Alcohol only adds to the fog. All you can initially hope for is to determine whether this person is interesting or attractive to you, and whether you want to get to know him or her better. You need to check it out.

This is the time to slow down. Leave the noise of the party or bar. Go for a walk or go out for a cup of coffee. You might agree to meet the next day for a bite or a drink. Keep it a short date, an hour or so, just to chat. You need to see if you are as excited about him or her the next day. Draw this person out, ask real questions, and really listen to the answers. Do you want to know more? Are you really interested? Share something about yourself. How do you feel near him or her, how does it feel to hold hands, to sit close? Ask yourself, "Do I like this person? Is the chemistry right? Am I sexually attracted?" What do you think he or she expects from you? What are your expectations? Do they fit? (Is he looking for the mother of his children, while you are looking for a casual movie date?)

Give him or her honest feedback about how you are feeling. "I've really liked talking and getting to know you. Let's get together soon. How about dinner on Friday?" If you have discovered during your short date that this man or woman of your dreams turns out to be more of a nightmare, you can end it there—without any big disappointment or accusations of being led on or of being a sexual tease. With no need to feel obligated: you have taken an hour of each other's time to check out your first impulse. "I've enjoyed finding out more about you (your job, boat, family). Goodbye."

On rare occasions you might meet someone with whom you feel an immediate and intense connection. You are strongly attracted to each other, and you are able to open up to that person immediately. Some people find the excitement of having sex with a relative stranger intoxicating. What starts out as lust or love at first sight might develop into a deeper and more enduring relationship. But this is the exception to the rule. The best chance of finding a lasting and caring relationship is to get to know each other first.

Sex and Communication

New friends don't know all the details of your personal sexual history, anatomy, or preferences. The best and most successful way to communicate about sex is verbally. Nonverbal communcation has its limitations, especially between new lovers. It often forces people to guess and mind-read. Trust your partner enough to let him or her know what would please you. Respect your partner enough to recognize his or her limits. The important thing is sharing and providing mutual pleasure, not to qualify for the sexual olympics. After you know each other better, feelings of trust and intimacy will allow both of you to enjoy freer and less inhibited sexual activity.

Communicating about sex doesn't have to entail a long speech or lengthy interview. Simple words will suffice. "Do you want to try this?" "Are you comfortable?" "What would feel better?" "Slow down." People are afraid to seem selfish by asking for specific kinds of pleasure. They also worry about appearing critical when asking that something be done differently. If you can overcome your inhibitions about verbally expressing your sexual desires, the effort will be worth it. Your partner won't be forced to guess, and you won't have to do without having your needs met. There's an additional dividend: talking together about sex facilitates intense intimacy.

Having fun. Don't forget kissing, snuggling, playfulness, conversation, sensuality, exploration, fantasy, and laughter. Try not to get locked into the race from foreplay to intercourse to orgasm. You might miss out on a lot of potential pleasure and excitement. You will feel less anxiety and more confidence in an atmosphere of warm acceptance, relaxed good fun, and mutual discovery.

Positive feedback. Tell your partner what you enjoy, what is especially appreciated. He or she wants to be successful in pleasing you. Don't just say, "You were great," but be specific about what felt good. It will help your partner learn more about you.

Saying no. Having the freedom to say no to sex is essential for comfort in the dating world. It is also an important part of establishing intimacy: revealing yourself to someone new means communicating your personal limits as well as your other feelings and attitudes. Having sex when you feel uncomfortable or unwilling is as dishonest to your partner as it is untrue to your own sense of what is right for you.

Rejection is never easy to give or receive, and you may be fearful of your partner's reaction. What if you say no, and your partner misinterprets your motives or reacts by breaking off the relationship? A partner who is interested in knowing you, and building a relationship based on that knowledge, will usually take the time to hear you out and understand your position.

Many men and women engage in sex when all they really want is the warmth of touching, a hug and kiss or a massage. Karen is an example. "Sometimes I'd end up sleeping with a guy in order to get my cuddling needs met. I can't seem to just get a hug." The key is again to communicate what you want as straightforwardly as you can: "I just want you to hold me." "I'm enjoying kissing, but I don't want to go to bed."

Time limits. Be clear about any time limits you have. Are you inviting your partner to spend the whole night or a few hours? Do you have to wake up early for work or to care for small children? Or do you expect to spend a leisurely morning in bed? Respect your partner's time limits as well.

The unexpected. When something that is unexpected or upsetting happens, let your partner know. If you become upset because your ex-spouse just called you, if a sick child has to be returned from the baby-sitter's house, if you can't sleep, keep the communication open. Don't try to hide your feelings or brush them off, Your partner will know that something is wrong and may end up feeling responsible for it. Be honest. Don't withdraw or try to "gut it out." If you talk it over, maybe the two of you can come up with a workable solution.

SEXUAL ISSUES

During your marriage, you and your spouse developed shared responses to a number of sexual issues. Some of the choices you made were satisfying to both of you. You may have quarreled about other issues or agreed to be silent about mutual frustrations. The point is that the responses you developed grew out of the context of the two people you were and the relationship you had.

Beginning with a new partner will mean rethinking many of your old responses. In particular, a number of issues that you took for granted during your marriage are likely to look very different from the perspective of a newly single person.

The discussion here touches on areas that may have become blind-spots for you and suggests some of the ways your orientation toward them is likely to have changed. It's essential not to get stuck in stereotypical responses: "A man's inadequate if he can't always maintain an erection." "Birth control is a woman's responsibility." Open communication is the primary remedy, a remedy that can be aided by the one un-challenged benefit of the sexual "revolution": today's widespread availability of information on sexual matters.

Sexual schedules. Men and women tend to operate on different "sexual schedules." Most men become aroused more quickly than women, and most also climax more quickly and more readily through intercourse. In contrast, data from *The Hite Report* suggests that as few as 30 percent of women achieve orgasm regularly throught intercourse. Problems result when a couple locks themselves into a schedule that ignores these differences.

Expectations formed during your marriage of what sex should or should not be like may not be helpful. If you felt deprived or frustrated in your previous relationship, you may carry a burden of unresolved sexual anger into your new relationship. Conversely, grief or guilt for your marriage may lead you to feel that you don't "deserve" to be pleased, setting in place a pattern of frustrating self-sacrifice. Fear of rejection or fear of dependence can further entangle and confuse your expression of your sexual needs.

What will help is a sensitivity to your partner's needs and a willingness to communicate your own. Look for differences, and remember that *you* can be different. Here are some suggestions for rescheduling.

1. Talk to each other. What types of sexual activities are pleasurable to each of you? Can your partner help with the responsibility of his or her pleasure?
2. Be creative. Don't overlook the pleasures of leisurely, affectionate love making. Realize that there are other erogenous zones than the genitals. Don't assume that you and your partner are equally aroused by stimulation of the same areas. Try to prolong foreplay until both partners are fully aroused. Try massage, playfulness, stroking, exploration of each other's bodies. Switch passive and active roles.
3. Discard the rule that a woman must climax due to intercourse. For most women, it's easier to experience orgasm through manual or oral stimulation. Is climax always necessary? For both sexes, arousal itself can be intensely pleasurable.

Both sexes should also be aware that the stress of separation and singlehood can have adverse effects on sexual performance. Don't generalize from the awkwardness of an initial experience or seize it as "proof" of personal inadequacy. Give yourself and your partner time to understand each other.

Masturbation. There is nothing wrong with masturbating when you feel the need for sexual release. It is far lonelier to be alone with someone than alone with yourself. Respect your sexual self. It is a part of you that can provide a great deal of pleasure, if you permit yourself the freedom to accept it.

Masturbation also plays an essential developmental role, as it serves as a way for both sexes to learn about their sexual responses. For women especially, masturbation can be an important step toward achieving greater satisfaction with a partner. Lonnie Barbach's book, *For Yourself,* is an excellent resource for women who want to learn more about pleasuring themselves.

Male sexual problems. Many newly single men do experience sexual difficulties. Divorce is a time of high emotional stress, and your ability to perform sexually is intimately connected with your psychological state.

An experience of impotence, failure to ejaculate, or premature ejaculation can commonly result from one or more of these divorce-linked factors:

1. Anxiety or fear of sexual failure with a new partner. You evolved a familiar style of love making with your former spouse, and engaging in sex with someone new can be a difficult adjustment.
2. Guilt. Intimacy can also bring up painful memories. You may be subconsciously punishing yourself for the breakup or maintaining fidelity to your ex-spouse.
3. Lowered vitality. Disruptive changes in life style often result in poor health and nutrition. If joined with immediate factors such as fatigue or heavy doses of alcohol or drugs, sexual problems may result.

It's important to recognize that almost all men experience some form of failure in sexual performance at some time in their lives. Your best course is to refrain from attacking yourself psychologically and to accept the fact that there will be times when you are too tired, uncomfortable, or anxious to perform sexually.

If a problem with impotence or ejaculation becomes an ongoing concern, rule out any medical problems by seeing your physician. Then seek out a qualified sex therapist trained to help you solve problems such as these.

Birth control. Married couples, after much discussion, trial, and sometimes error, usually agree on and practice one or more methods of contraception. It is often mutually understood that these practices will become a ritual part of sex, and this can make it possible for discussion of the subject to be banished from the bedroom for years. But those who are taking steps into a new intimacy need to again come to an arrangement with their present partner acceptable to both. Unfortunately, even though many couples may be intimate in every other way, they find the prospect of this conversation embarrassing, and too often it is avoided until too late.

A general confusion over who bears the responsibility for an unwanted pregnancy often causes this hazardous delay. The development of the pill helped to perpetuate the outdated concept that birth control, along with cooking and sewing, was an integral part of a woman's domain. Everybody hailed the tablet that would eliminate fumbling with foam, condoms, and diaphragms. It seemed so simple.

Over the following years, women became increasingly dissatisfied with the pill for a variety of reasons ranging from ill health to menstrual pain and emotional confusion. Betty, a 37-year-old paramedic, put it this way:

> I was on the pill for over four years and that still makes me angry. From the beginning, they affected me badly. Every month when my period started, I'd vomit and I had an excruciating pain. And I'd cry constantly without knowing why. It took me a year to figure out that all this was because of the pill. But instead of using something else, I just changed pills. I think I took about four different types. Some had different side effects, but they were all equally hideous. I'm so angry that I endured all that for all those years. I'll never let myself suffer like that again.

Intimacy is impossible without responsibility. Whether you and your partner have agreed to a casual affair or are trying to establish a long-term relationship, you have made a commitment to care for each other's health and well-being *now,* for the time that you are together. Caring for each other means that neither should be expected to make unspoken sacrifices. Caring should also be something that both partners feel free to express and to ask for, without embarrassment. Louise, a 25-year-old graduate student, described how sharing birth control responsibilities had been part of her relationship.

> I tried the pill for awhile, but I didn't like it. It was like my sex drive diminished. Before that, I used foam and a diaphragm, and Stan would put it in me while we were being sexy with each other. It didn't really interrupt anything, and I liked the feeling of knowing that Stan was taking a part, that he wanted to take care of me. And after all, it's that feeling of someone caring that really turns me on.

Making birth control a shared responsibility may mean that you need the input of new sources of information. Check with your family doctor, Planned Parenthood, or family planning clinics in your area.

Venereal disease. For the newly divorced person, the problem of contracting or transmitting venereal disease may be an issue which in the past required little or no thought. As the realm of one's sexual world expands to include partners who are less familiar, the safety once taken for granted may be replaced by an all-too-often justified anxiety.

Ideally, every person who contracts syphillis, gonorrhea, herpes, or any of the other sexually transmitted diseases would correctly identify the infection, seek immediate treatment, and avoid any sexual contact until the cure is known to be complete. However, the nature of these disorders often makes identification difficult. Some have long incubation periods, and some exhibit a variety of symptoms which can seem to have a nonvenereal cause. Most produce symptoms which disappear after a time without treatment, thus leading the unwary to believe that the disease has "cured itself." Add to these confusing characteristics the social stigma still attached to V.D.—which often discourages those who have contracted it from informing recent sexual contacts of the possible danger—and the reason for venereal "epidemics" becomes clear.

There are no sure practices that will prevent the contraction of V.D. But there are various measures which can help reduce the possibility of infection.

1. Use of specific contraceptive or noncontraceptive foams, creams, jellies, and antiseptics
2. Use of a condom—if put on before foreplay begins
3. Washing genitals before and after intercourse
4. Urinating immediately after intercourse

Perhaps the wisest precaution that the sexually active can take is to seek out information on the subject. If genital sores or other symptoms linked to V.D. do appear, it is essential to consult a physician immediately, avoid all sexual contact until cured, and warn any recent partners about potential infection.

WHAT ABOUT THE KIDS

The first time you go out on a date after your separation or divorce is of course a big event in your life. It is probably a big event in the life of your children as well. This is an area in which you might not feel very confident, and you may dread your children's censure or scrutiny. Their reactions can run the gamut from ambivalence to resentment, from excitement to disinterest. They need to be able to express their feelings and know that you will help them through this adjustment.

Children will experience what is happening as it relates to themselves. These may be some of their concerns.

1. If your children were rooting for reconciliation, your beginning to date again may be a disappointment to them. They may have denied the permanence of a breakup until this point.

2. Children don't like to have to compete for attention. Single parent families are often very close and child oriented. If your children are used to all of your attention at dinner and having you home every night, they may consider your date an intruder.

3. Children may compete with you for your date's attention. They want to be seen and appreciated for their own worth, not just for being "Flo's kid."

4. They may be protective of the other parent. They might disapprove because they fear that your ex-spouse will be jealous or hurt. They may be protective of you, fearing that you will be hurt or disappointed.

5. Teenagers may feel embarrassed by your behavior if it varies much from the "old you." That new hairdo, clothes, and social life you are experimenting with may be uncomfortably similar to their own concerns. They might remind you to "act your age."

6. Children might be fearful that your style of parenting will change under the influence of a new friend. This is especially true if they feel that your new friend is stricter or more demanding than you are.

Parents have fears too. During legal wrangling over custody, some parents fear that if they resume dating they will be seen as an unfit parent or the children will seem to be neglected. Parents also are afraid that their children will become attached to their new friend. If the new relationship doesn't last, the children will suffer losing another important person in their lives.

Parents are frequently unsure how open to be with their children about their social or sexual lives. Some parents will never bring a date to their home while the children are there. Some feel free to have dates stay overnight, and share a family breakfast in the morning.

What is right? First you have to consider what *feels* right to you and what your children are used to. Young children are usually accepting of new people who are open and affectionate. Generally, if children feel cared for by you, if they know that you take their feelings into account, they will adjust. Go slow, especially with older children. Some parents complain that their children have become their chaperones, making them feel uncomfortable, defensive, or embarrassed with a date. Remember, it's all new to them too, and it pays to go slow. Here are some suggestions to help you get started on the right foot.

1. Give kids an opportunity to express their worries about the new situation. One of the hardest things in the world to do is to let your child express his or her fears about something you are fearful about, and *not* get defensive. This doesn't mean that if they object to your going out, you stay home. But letting them express their feelings has two big benefits. First, they get the message that you care about how they are feeling. Second, you can determine if there is anything you can do to make it easier or to reassure them. You may be surprised to find out that what is really upsetting them is not what you think. Maybe there may be some way you can work things out so they will be happier.

2. Be honest about how you are feeling. Let them know that bringing in a new person is new and hard for you also. "I was trying so hard to impress him at dinner that I could hardly remember what we ate. If you hadn't remembered that pie in the oven, it would surely have burned."

3. Don't forget to thank them for the efforts that they are making. If you appreciated their helping with dinner, telling entertaining stories, being patient, sharing toys, or going to bed on time, then tell them.

4. Reassure them that your love and concern for them is the priority in your life. The presence of a new man or woman in your life won't change your commitment to them.

5. Hold on to meaningful rituals. If storytelling and warm milk before bedtime is your child's favorite way to end the day, try not to miss that event. One parent of a four-year-old would go through the story-telling and warm milk routine at six o'clock at night even though his child did not go to bed for several hours. The spirit of the event is what counts, and children are often pretty flexible about the details.

6. Put some effort into getting a sitter that your children really like. Try to make it fun for them as well. Some children really enjoy sleeping at a cousin's house or a friend's house overnight. You can plan a special dinner they can share with their sitter such as pizza, popcorn, or homemade sundaes for dessert. You can make that Saturday night date something you all can look forward to.

21

Remarriage

Bob Steiner is a 48-year-old C.P.A./magician/writer/lecturer. For many years after his divorce, he was frequently asked if he would ever remarry. For the first few years he answered, "Yes, I'm sure I'll remarry." Later he started answering, "No, I'm sure I'll never remarry." Then he realized the absurdity of the question. "You don't decide to get married and then accept applicants for the position. If I find a woman I can't live without and she feels the same about me, I'll reevaluate my marital status. Until such a woman comes along there is no decision to be made and nothing to think about."

It's common for newly divorced people to look at remarriage as the solution to their problems. It isn't. The divorce rate is higher for second and third marriages than for the first. Divorced people who remarry quickly often find that experience hasn't improved their judgment.

George, a 53-year-old engineer, is an example. "I was single for three long years before I remarried. I'd never lived alone before, and I didn't like it. Looking back, I think I would have married one of the witches from Macbeth if she'd asked me. Sally, my second wife, wasn't really a witch, but she turned out to be insanely jealous—I was a virtual prisoner in my home on nights and weekends. The marriage was a nightmare, and I started thinking fondly of those years alone. I've been single again for almost four years now. It's conceivable I could take another chance, but I've gotten awfully wary."

Overall, more than 75 percent of men and 70 percent of women end up remarrying. The average age of previously divorced brides is 30, 33 for previously divorced grooms. Surveys show that about three-quarters of remarried people report feeling "happy or very happy" in the marriage.* They also report a tendency to choose a second spouse whose interests, values, and needs are closer to their own.

Three additional factors are mentioned that make a second marriage work:

1. Learning occurred in the first marriage. The first relationship is often seen as a sort of apprenticeship where mistakes were made and things tried for the first time. "I won't do that again" is a common response to painful experiences and patterns with a first spouse.
2. Changes occur with age and maturity. As people get older, they usually become more comfortable with their sexuality, have more realistic expectations, are more accepting of themselves and their limits. A demanding twenty-year-old may learn by forty that not all needs and yearnings can be fulfilled.
3. There is a strong motivation not to fail again. Remarried couples are prepared for the honeymoon phase to end. They know from painful experience the kind of work it takes to keep a relationship alive. And they want *this one* to work.

THE REBOUND

There's nothing wrong with getting married on the rebound if you are truly ready for a new relationship. The problem is that most rebound relationships are conceived in need rather than genuine attraction. The fear of loneliness can make you so emotionally hungry that you become guilty of what Dr. George Bach calls "collusion." When you collude, you ignore all the flaws in your new mate because to say anything would be to endanger your relationship. You're so fearful of being abandoned that you overlook basic realities about who the other person is and how you feel when you're together. Colluders are willing to stick with a painful relationship indefinitely for fear of hearing the final goodbye.

A second danger of the rebound relationship is that it may happen before you've had a chance to establish an independent identity. You haven't had an opportunity to learn who you are as a single person. You haven't yet learned to cope with the loneliness, the loss, and new responsibilities following divorce. "Three weeks after my separation, I jumped headfirst into a new relationship. I was so freaked out by the empty apartment that I grabbed the first man who showed an interest. I didn't know what I wanted. I had no idea how I could survive by myself. It took me six months to get out of that relationship, and by then I realized I had to decide what I was looking for." *(33-year-old dental hygienist)*

Give yourself time—time to know and enjoy yourself as a single person while waiting for your future mate.

*W. Leslie. *The Family in Social Context*. 3rd ed. New York: Oxford, 1976.

A CAREFUL CHOICE

Most people are more careful about choosing a second husband or wife than they were in selecting their first mate. In his book, *The Second Time Around,* Leslie Westoff confirmed that remarried couples are far more "serious and deliberate" in choosing a second partner. The first marriage was often the result of an intense infatuation that focused more on physical appearance and idealized fantasy. By contrast, remarried couples reported having a very specific "shopping list" as they looked for a second mate. They sought qualities like companionship, warmth, the capacity for intimacy and commitment, and the ability to be a good stepparent.

One divorced father described his shopping list in this way: "My first wife was very focused on getting through graduate school. It seemed her whole life was spent in front of the typewriter. There was a coldness between us, a lack of joy. If I ever marry again, I'll be with someone who focuses more on me, who has our relationship as her first priority. I want someone who doesn't pursue ambition at the cost of intimacy. I want someone who can negotiate and work through problems rather than retreat from them. I want someone who can open her heart to my daughter when she's with me. Above all, I want someone who is generous, whose natural inclination is to give rather than barter."

The Opposite Pole

One of the great dangers of remarriage is deciding to seek a personality that is the exact opposite of your first mate. A woman whose first husband was "too dependent" was looking for a more self-reliant man. "I got just what I wanted. He was a tower of strength, had independent interests, kept up ties with his own friends, and was completely fearless about saying no to me. But I rarely spent any time with him except Sunday mornings." A 40-year-old English teacher described his disillusionment: "The first time around there was lots of communication and no sex. So I wanted someone warm and sexually open. I found it, but it's like my second wife and I are from different planets. We're strangers, there's no communication whatsoever."

Looking for the opposite is a simplistic way to solve the problem of a failed relationship. It creates a kind of tunnel vision that keeps you from seeing important danger signals. Karen divorced her first husband because "Charlie was a homebody. It was beer and television every night. He was easy to live with, but our lives seemed empty, stupid in a way. It was just us and the TV. Now my second husband was into partying. Unfortunately, he liked to drink. He liked it a lot. When he drank he could be abusive. In the beginning he seemed like the funny, fun, attractive man I'd dreamed about, but he turned out to have a real viciousness."

It's important that your haste to compensate for qualities that were missing in your first marriage doesn't lead you to forget the good qualities you took for granted. Instead of just trying to plug emotional holes, seeking things you always yearned for but never had, look for a mate who offers basic compatibility. Look for someone who really fits you.

Reality Versus Fantasy Love

A person who has gone through courtship, marriage, disillusionment, and divorce is likely to have a different attitude toward romantic love than a never-married single. The old cliche that love is blind takes on a new meaning. Passionate love is an emotion that can grow as easily from something false as something true, that can bloom identically from knowledge or delusion. Over a lifetime, it's possible to fall in love with many different people, few of whom may be appropriate as mates. Feelings of love and passion can attach to the most unlikely, dangerous, or incompatible people.

The thing that makes it possible to love inappropriate people is the fantasy nature of many romantic attachments. An alcoholic is transformed into the noble victim of his habit. A remote and taciturn man is seen as a secretly vulnerable "sweetie" waiting to have his heart unlocked. The passive, bland, and unassertive woman becomes the shy embodiment of sensitivity and concern.

While divorced singles are less susceptible to the fictions of love, it's always a struggle to keep love based on reality rather than fantasy. As one woman put it, "When I meet a man, I have a tendency to fill in the blanks with my own projections. With the slightest bit of help from him, I can quickly sculpt a beautiful person from the few things I know. I fight that temptation all the time, and I do it by asking questions. Lots of questions. I pay attention to how he reacts to things, I listen to his stories, I ask him who his heroes are." *(41-year-old florist)*

Love can be a dangerous emotion. Caught up in the sway of their feelings, two people can let the unexamined "magic" of their bond carry them into commitments they may not be ready for. To be safe in a second marriage, love must be thought through. Critical and careful questions should be asked. Take time to know your new partner's values, beliefs, and ambitions. Find out how he pursues his needs, learn how she resolves conflict, see how he expresses anger. This important information will help you determine whether the person you love is a good marriage risk.

Liking and Loving

Loving and liking are equally essential components of a successful marriage. Romantic love and sexual attraction provide a very basic glue that holds relationships together. While physical attractiveness is largely skin deep, it is still usually the first step in romantic bonding. Liking somebody has much less to do with physical attractiveness. Liking means taking genuine pleasure and delight in someone, appreciating his or her unique view of the world, his or her humor and charm. If you like *and* are attracted to somebody, and these feelings endure over time, marriage may be a very good choice.

Compatibility Rather Than Contrast

"When I was young, I was looking for someone exotic, different from anyone I'd known. I wanted a man who wouldn't remind me of my family. He had to be special, maybe even a little weird. The second time around I want someone more like me, someone I can live with. I've had the excitement and passion of being with a man who would always be foreign and untouchable. Now I want someone I'll recognize and fit with." *(48-year-old graphic artist)*

While the first marriage may have grown out of exotic contrasts, or needs and deficiencies that could only be met by a very different person, divorced singles tend to focus on similiarities when looking for a second mate. Common interests as well as similar energy levels and styles of relating make it easier to live with somebody. Similar values, beliefs, and world view are also important. While contrast adds spice to relationships, the second marriage has a greater chance of success when finding areas of compatibility is the highest priority.

Changing People

Don't fall for the commonly held myth that any two people can get along if they really work at it. People can only stretch so far before they snap like rubber bands. Many people delude themselves into believing that they can change their lovers after marriage. Changing a person is a low-percentage operation. Most of the time, the person feels resentful of your pressure to change and refuses to do so. The result is nagging, arguments, bitterness, and possibly the dissolution of the marriage.

Sometimes it's possible to take someone who is basically attractive and compatible with you and make a few minor changes around the rough edges. For example, Gloria married Ron despite the fact that he had a few qualities she couldn't stand. "Ron was what I call a 'fixer-upper.' He was a good-looking, intelligent, affectionate person. The only problem was that he was completely unpresentable. His clothes were strictly bargain basement, usually unpressed, and you could tell he was color-blind by the way the things he wore clashed. His hair was always a mess. I like to go to fancy parties and nice restaurants, so it was often embarrassing for me to be seen with Ron. I married him because I figured that all he needed was a woman's touch. I was right. Ron will never make the list of the ten best-dressed men, but at least he looks decent now at social functions."

Ralph, an English professor, married Shelly, who didn't even have a high school diploma. His friends were shocked at the match, but Ralph realized that Shelly was a diamond in the rough. Despite her poor vocabulary and grammar, she was highly intelligent. All she needed was someone who could make it possible for her to learn and grow. Shelly eventually went on to become a school teacher.

Knowing Yourself

The right choice of a marital partner depends very much on how well you know yourself. Your needs, weaknesses, dreams, and fears will have a major impact on your relationship. Parts of yourself that you ignore in the marital equation may have a surprisingly strong effect on you and your spouse. Helen's need for security seemed to be met by John's strength and forcefulness. But John was a policeman, and every time he was fifteen minutes late, she was terrified that something had happened to him. Her efforts to have him transfer to a desk job created distance in the marriage. Arthur, who was quite shy, needed a woman who would take the initiative sexually. Instead, he married Jean, who was very insecure about her attractiveness and expected Arthur always to make the sexual overtures.

Knowing yourself includes knowing how you've changed. Your divorce has altered you. You've learned to survive on your own and gained strength, independence, and maturity. The people who were attractive to you ten or twenty years ago might be very wrong for you after your metamorphosis. As you begin looking for a second mate, be sure you seek a partner who fits the grown-up you. As a young woman, Allison had what her therapist described as "low self-esteem." She married an alcoholic because "I was afraid I'd be discarded if a man didn't need me to take care of him." Ten years later, she felt much clearer about her worth. "I still have a weakness for the sad and needy types. My first impulse is to help, but I won't let myself. I want a man who's doing OK, who isn't in pain. I want him to stay with me out of something other than need."

Your Shopping List

One of the truest and saddest aphorisms is that people get what they want. Whatever your highest priority in a marriage is, you will probably find it. So it's important to identify a set of priorities, a shopping list that reflects your real needs. Your list should include qualities that were missing in your first marriage, as well as traits that were present that you felt good about. List the qualities that are important to you in the following areas:

1. Physical attractiveness
2. Religious/ethical values

3. Parenting styles and values
4. Interests
5. Sexuality
6. Work / career / economic status
7. Style of relating / amount of closeness
8. Problem-solving styles
9. Housekeeping / home maintenance styles
10. Personality and emotional makeup
11. Energy level
12. Artistic / creative / cultural pursuits

These categories are not exhaustive. Use them and any others that may occur to you to generate your particular shopping list. Rank the items on your list in order of importance. You may not get everything you want, but hopefully you'll get the ones that are most crucial to you.

OBSTACLES TO REMARRIAGE

Children. Your children (or those of your fiancé) can sabotage the marriage. Children from a divorced household are often stunned by the news that their parent intends to remarry. They may fear that their new stepparent will try to replace their natural parent. They also may cling to the hope that their divorced parents will get back together again. Furthermore, disciplining the children can be a serious problem for the stepparent-to-be.

There are several precautions you can take to ensure that children do not become the rock upon which your marital plans founder:

- Don't announce the engagement suddenly. Gradually let your children know that you are very fond of the person you are dating.
- Listen to your children as they express their feelings about the remarriage. Try to reassure them that your ex won't be frozen out because of the remarriage. Answer any questions they may have about it.
- Be firm with your children. Let them know that you aren't going to change your mind. Your happiness is important, and your children have no right to deprive you of the love and company of another adult.

Love phobia. Love phobics are still frightened because of their previous relationships. They fear any sort of commitment because they have no confidence that a second marriage won't end in the same nightmare as their first. "My marriage was a dead relationship. I used to hum taps while I got undressed at night. But seriously, it was a very depressed, very distant relationship. There's no way I'm going to do that again. The first sign of deadness and I'm gone." *(51-year-old broker)*

Love phobics are always looking for signs that old patterns are about to repeat. They have an early warning system that would make NORAD jealous. "I run at the first sign of anger. My first husband was a rageaholic. I mean you could hear him for blocks. Now if conflict develops, I do a fast fade. I'm horribly anxious at the thought of having to live that life again." *(38-year-old mother)*

The problem with early warning systems is that they often make "false positive" mistakes. The sirens and lights go off, but the new person isn't really anything like your first mate. The resemblance is only fleeting or superficial, but the love phobic can't take any chances.

Here are two suggestions if your early warning system is keeping you from deepening relationships. (1) Don't leave at the first alarm. Test to see if the pattern you fear is really happening, or is just a temporary phenomenon. Share your concerns and see if the pattern changes. (2) Inwardly prepare yourself to say no. If you can say no, a commitment isn't such a big risk. You can protect yourself from unwanted demands; you can leave if you need to. The inability to say no *creates* the feeling of being trapped. And the result very often is the "butterfly syndrome" of flitting lightly from person to person.

REMARRIAGE WITH BLENDED FAMILIES

Stepchildren are an important consideration when you decide to remarry. Don't kid yourself that the transition will be easy. Blended families take time to jell and often have special problems. One woman described her struggle in the first month after her wedding. "Al moved in, and my son started acting strangely. He'd been supportive up to that point, but now he began staying out very late at night, and he'd explode when I tried to set limits. He moved a spare TV into his room and isolated himself. He was coldly polite to Al. He wouldn't initiate a conversation. He was a clam, and Al was very hurt by it." *(40-year-old travel agent)*

In their book, *Stepfamilies*, Emily and John Visher suggest the following guidelines for dealing with a blended family.

1. Schedule time alone. A new couple needs time away from children so that the relationship can grow. If all of your waking hours are spent reacting to the demands of kids, the marital relationship will grow malnourished from lack of attention.

2. Encourage new relationships in the stepfamily through activities involving different subgroups. For example, stepfather and stepchildren might undertake a special project without mom around.

3. Be certain not to undermine the children's loyalties toward the original parent. Being a stepparent is *not* the same as being a biological parent. A child needs the emotional room to cherish his attachment to the biological parent, no matter how involved the stepparent may be.

4. Give the relationships time to develop. It may take six months or a year. Resistance and fear are common reactions in the early days of a stepparenting relationship. There is no such thing as instant affection. The children will be wary, and you may be awkward.

5. Accept that the transition will be rocky. The kids will be dealing with feelings of insecurity and loss. Often they will act on these feelings in angry and hurtful ways. Stepfamilies simply don't feel the same or function the same as the original nuclear family. Facing that it will be different and perhaps more difficult helps to decrease the high expectations that lead to burnout and bitterness.

6. Keep open lines of communication with the biological parents. As much as possible, involve them in major decisions. Refrain from back-biting.

7. Have periodic family meetings to air problems and promote an atmosphere of openness. Encourage the children to express gripes with the stepparent. Reinforce honesty.

8. Create a stepparent role that does not compete with the natural parents. If your stepson and his dad go to little league games together, you would probably do well to stay away. Be particularly careful about disciplining the kids. Ease into it. Stay away from corporal punishment. Leave major discipline problems to the natural parents, unless invited to be involved.

KEEPING LOVE ALIVE

Regardless of whether you choose to remarry or continue in a noncommitted relationship, the challenge is how to keep love alive. Here are some suggestions for creating a healthy and vital relationship.

1. *Add variety.* Get away from it all frequently. Vacations enable you to experience each other in new situations and rekindle some of the romantic fires. Even a day in the country can be renewing. Try a new restaurant or nightspot, take a dance class, start a project together. One couple began writing children's books, another took up teaching rock-climbing classes. Stay on the lookout for new people to enrich both your lives. Be open to the unexpected invitation, the chance encounter.

2. *Get rid of the television.* Prior to the TV age, families communicated with each other every night. Now everyone sits around the television set and sinks into a stupor. If television is something that you can't give up, at least take a periodic vacation from it. Several nights a week, turn the TV off and spend the evening chatting or sharing an activity together.

3. *Add romantic touches to your relationship.* Remember all the little things you did while you were first dating one another and falling in love. Redo them, even if they seem a little corny. Give flowers, candy, and other gifts; write love notes; call home or the office occasionally just to say "I love you."

4. *Take risks.* Nothing brings people closer together than sharing danger. It's similar to the bond between soldiers, who often form the closest friendships of their lives during wartime. For example, Gina and Rob occasionally play *Secret:* each has to reveal an embarrassing secret to the other. One time they put on a song and dance routine for their friends. Neither of them had ever performed in front of an audience before, and both were petrified. They went through with it anyway, and now they have an important shared experience to look back on.

5. *Help each other do a job whenever possible.* For example, George sometimes comes down to Joanne's store after work and cleans up so that Joanne can go home early; Joanne often types George's letters when his secretary is snowed under with work. Patrick picks up Bernice's children at the daycare center whenever Bernice has to work overtime; Bernice pumps gas at Patrick's service station on holidays.

6. *Spend time with each other.* Sometimes couples who live together spend less time with each other than they did when they lived apart. It's easy to get involved in work and outside activities to the exclusion of each other. If you have trouble finding time to spend together, keep a diary of your daily activities for a week. After the week is up, sit down with your mate and compare schedules. See if there is any way of sharing in more of each other's activities.

Bibliography

Children and Divorce

Bienfeld, Florence. *My Mom and Dad Are Getting a Divorce.* St. Paul, MN: EMC, 1980.

Gardner, Richard. *Children's Book About Divorce.* New York: Jason Aronson, 1970.

Grollman, Earl A. *Talking About Divorce and Separation.* Boston: Beacon, 1975.

Ramos, Suzanne. *The Complete Book of Child Custody.* New York: Putnam, 1980.

Wallerstein, Judith S., and Kelly, Joan B. *Surviving the Break-up.* New York: Basic Books, 1980.

Coparenting

Folberg, H. Jay, and Graham, Marva. "Joint Custody of Children Following Divorce." *U.C.D. Law Review* 12: 523–581.

Galper, Miriam. *Co-Parenting: A Source Book for the Separated or Divorced Family.* Philadelphia: Running Press, 1978.

Grote, Douglas, and Weinstein, Jeffrey P. "Joint Custody: A Viable and Ideal Alternative." *Journal of Divorce* (Fall 1979): 43–53.

Ricci, Isolina. *Mom's House, Dad's House: Making Shared Custody Work.* New York: Macmillan, 1980.

Ware, Ciji. *Sharing Parenthood After Divorce.* New York: Viking, 1979.

Woolley, Persia. *The Custody Handbook.* New York: Summit, 1979.

Emotional Adjustment to Divorce

Alvarez, A. *Life After Marriage: Love in an Age of Divorce.* New York: Simon & Schuster, 1979.

Freese, Arthur. *Help for Your Grief.* New York: Schocken, 1978.

Gardner, Richard A. *The Parent's Book About Divorce*. Garden City, NY: Doubleday, 1977.

Helmlinger, Trudy. *After You've Said Goodbye: How To Recover After Ending a Relationship*. Cambridge, MA: Schenkman, 1980.

Tanner, Ira J. *The Gift of Grief: Healing the Pain of Everyday Losses*. New York: Hawthorn, 1978.

Visher, Emily B., and Visher, John S. *Stepfamilies: A Guide to Working With Stepfamilies and Stepchildren*. New York: Brunner/Mazel, 1979.

Legal Issues

Bohannan, Paul, ed. *Divorce and After*. New York: Doubleday, 1970.

Cassidy, Robert. *What Every Man Should Know About Divorce*. Washington, DC: New Republic Books, 1977.

How To Do Your Own Divorce in California. 10th ed. Berkeley, CA: Nolo Press, 1983.

Hunt, Morton, and Hunt, Bernice. *The Divorce Experience*. New York: McGraw-Hill, 1977.

Mediation

Coogler, O. J. *Structured Mediation in Divorce Settlement*. Lexington, MA: Lexington Books, 1978.

Haynes, John M. *Divorce Mediation: A Practical Guide for Therapists and Counselors*. New York: Springer Publishing, 1981.

Silberman, Linda J. "Professional Responsibility: Problems of Divorce Mediation." *Family Law Reporter* 7 (February 1981).

Winks, Patricia L. "Divorce Mediation: A Nonadversary Procedure for the No-Fault Divorce." *Journal of Family Law* 19: 615–654.

Sexuality

Barbach, Lonnie. *For Yourself: The Fulfillment of Female Sexuality*. New York: Doubleday, 1975.

_____, and Levine, Linda. *Shared Intimacies: Women's Sexual Experiences*. New York: Bantam, 1981.

Coleman, Emily, and Edwards, Betty. *Brief Encounters*. Garden City, NY: Anchor/Doubleday, 1980.

Hite, S. *The Hite Report: A Nationwide Study of Female Sexuality*. New York: Dell, 1976.

_____. *The Hite Report on Male Sexuality*. New York: Alfred A. Knopf, 1981.

Zilbergeld, Bernie. *Male Sexuality*. New York: Bantam, 1978.

Single Parenting

Collins, Emily. *The Whole Single Person's Catalogue*. New York: Peebles, 1979.

Edwards, Marie, and Hoover, Eleanor. *The Challenge of Being Single*. New York: New American Library, 1975.

Forman, L. *The Divorced Mother's Guide*. Berkeley, CA: Berkeley Publishing, 1974.

Gatley, R., and Koulack, D. *Single Father's Handbook*. New York: Anchor/Doubleday, 1979.

Klein, Carol. *The Single Parent Experience*. New York: Avon, 1976.

Knight, Bryan. *Enjoying Single Parenthood*. New York: Van Nostrand Reinhold, 1980.

Levine, James A. *Who Will Raise the Children? New Options for Fathers (and Mothers)*. New York: Bantam, 1977.

Women in Transition: A Feminist Handbook on Separation and Divorce. New York: Scribner, 1975.

Woolley, Persia. *Creative Survival for Single Mothers*. Millbrae, CA: Celestial Arts, 1975.

Survival as a Single Person

Ahern, Deedee, and Bliss, Betsy. *The Economics of Being a Woman*. New York: Macmillan, 1976.

Bach, G. R., and Deutsch, R. M. *Pairing*. New York: Avon, 1970.

Berson, Barbara, and Bova, Ben. *Survival Guide for the Suddenly Single*. New York: St. Martin, 1980.

Branden, N. *The Psychology of Romantic Love*. New York: Bantam, 1981.

Gettleman, S., and Markowitz, J. *The Courage To Divorce*. New York: Simon & Schuster, 1974.

Hanson, D. *How To Pick Up a Man*. New York: Putnam, 1982.

Johnson, S. M. *First Person Singular: Living the Good Life Alone*. New York: New American Library, 1978.

Krantzler, Mel. *Creative Divorce*. New York: M. Evans, 1973.

Singleton, Mary Ann. *Life After Marriage: Divorce as a New Beginning*. New York: Stein & Day, 1979.

Wanderer, Zev, and Cabot, Tracey. *Letting Go*. New York: Putnam, 1978.

Wassmer, Arthur C. *Making Contact*. New York: Dial, 1978.

Weber, E. *How To Pick Up Girls*. New York: Symphony, 1970.

Appendix

Referral Sources for Divorce Mediation

Academy of Family Mediators
111 4th Ave., Suite IV
New York, NY 10003
(212) 674-7508
Provides referrals, training, and certification of training programs and practicing mediators.

The American Arbitration Association
140 S. 51st St.
New York, NY 10020
(212) 484-3235
The Family Dispute Services division provides referrals to qualified mediators as well as training in mediation and arbitration.

American Association for Mediated Divorce (AAMD)
5435 Balboa Blvd., Suite 208
Encino, CA 91316
(213) 986-6953
Provides referrals and training; publishes a monthly newsletter.

American Bar Association
Special Committee on Alternative Means of Dispute Resolution
1800 M St. NW
Washington, DC 20036
(202) 331-2258
Clearing house on mediation and arbitration activity; publishes a national directory and a bibliography of alternative dispute resolution programs and publications; publishes a quarterly bulletin and sponsors workshops.

The Association of Family Conciliation Courts
Nova University Law Center
3100 SW 9th Ave.
Ft. Lauderdale, FL 33315
(305) 522-2300
International association of court administrators, judges, lawyers, and mental health professionals; publishes the *Conciliation Courts Review* and the *Joint Custody Handbook;* sponsors research and conferences on mediation and family violence; refers to court-connected counseling and mediation services.

Family Mediation Association
9308 Bulls Run Pkwy.
Bethesda, MD 20034
(301) 530-1220
Founded by O. J. Coogler; provides training and referrals; publishes a quarterly newsletter; initiated a national certification program for family mediators.

Society of Professionals in Dispute Resolution (SPIDR)
American Arbitration Association
1730 Rhode Island Ave. NW
Washington, DC 20036
(202) 296-8510
Provides referrals to qualified mediators; publishes a newsletter.

Other New Harbinger Self-Help Titles

Older & Wiser: A Workbook for Coping With Aging, $12.95
Prisoners of Belief: Exposing & Changing Beliefs that Control Your Life, $10.95
Be Sick Well: A Healthy Approach to Chronic Illness, $11.95
Men & Grief: A Guide for Men Surviving the Death of a Loved One, $11.95
When the Bough Breaks: A Helping Guide for Parents of Sexually Abused Childern, $11.95
Love Addiction: A Guide to Emotional Independence, $11.95
When Once Is Not Enough: Help for Obsessive Compulsives, $11.95
The New Three Minute Meditator, $9.95
Getting to Sleep, $10.95
The Relaxation & Stress Reduction Workbook, 3rd Edition, $13.95
Leader's Guide to the Relaxation & Stress Reduction Workbook, $19.95
Beyond Grief: A Guide for Recovering from the Death of a Loved One, $10.95
Thoughts & Feelings: The Art of Cognitive Stress Intervention, $13.95
Messages: The Communication Skills Book, $12.95
The Divorce Book, $11.95
Hypnosis for Change: A Manual of Proven Techniques, 2nd Edition, $12.95
The Deadly Diet: Recovering from Anorexia & Bulimia, $11.95
Self-Esteem, $12.95
Acquiring Courage: An Audio Cassette for the Rapid Treatment of Phobias, $14.95
The Better Way to Drink, $11.95
Chronic Pain Control Workbook, $13.95
Rekindling Desire: Bringing Your Sexual Relationship Back to Life, $12.95
Life Without Fear: Anxiety and Its Cure, $10.95
Visualization for Change, $12.95
Guideposts to Meaning: Discovering What Really Matters, $11.95
Controlling Stagefright, $11.95
Videotape: Clinical Hypnosis for Stress & Anxiety Reduction, $24.95
Starting Out Right: Essential Parenting Skills for Your Child's First Years, $12.95
Big Kids: A Parent's Guide to Weight Control for Children, $11.95
Personal Peace: Transcending Your Interpersonal Limits, $11.95
My Parent's Keeper: Adult Children of the Emotionally Disturbed, $11.95
When Anger Hurts, $12.95
Free of the Shadows: Recovering from Sexual Violence, $12.95
Resolving Conflict With Others and Within Yourself, $12.95
Liftime Weight Control, $11.95
The Anxiety & Phobia Workbook, $13.95
Love and Renewal: A Couple's Guide to Commitment, $12.95
The Habit Control Workbook, $12.95

Send a check for the titles you want, plus $2.00 for shipping and handling, to:

New Harbinger Publications, Inc.
5674 Shattuck Avenue
Oakland, CA 94609

Or write for a free catalog of all our quality self-help publications. For orders over $20 call 1-800-748-6273. Have your Visa or Mastercard number ready.